PRAISE F(
MILITARY T}

"Once again, Steven Zeeland has pulled off the masterful and the unpredictable. *Military Trade* is a document of scholarly importance—to historians, to sociologists, to students of gender and masculinity and the mores of modern military life—and it is a smoldering, seductive passage into the labyrinths of man-sex that disturbs, intrigues, and arouses as you sit up all night trying to put it down."

—Frank Browning, Author,
The Culture of Desire* and *Queer Geography

"Remarkable, and remarkably illuminating."
—Leo Bersani, University of California at Berkeley

"An important contribution to social science while being as readable as a steamy novel."

—*Libido*

"Like all of Steven Zeeland's books, *Military Trade* is a fascinating study of soldier sexuality."

—*In Touch*

"Zeeland is an intelligent observer, and his books are well worth reading for their insights into how men relate to one another in a military culture that disdains homosexuality but can never stop men from having sex with one another."

—Ian Young, *Torso*

"They may say, 'Don't ask, don't tell.' But a better way to describe what goes on in the military is the motto hanging over Steven Zeeland's guest bed. 'They will tell you no,' it reads, '. . . and you will tell them yes.'"

—Richard Goldstein, *The Village Voice*

PRAISE FOR STEVEN ZEELAND'S MILITARY INTERVIEW TRILOGY

THE MASCULINE MARINE

"A fascinating and candid look at the intimate lives and passions of a group of men played out against the homoerotic landscape that is the U.S. Marine Corps."

—Susan Faludi, Author,
Stiffed: The Betrayal of the American Man

"Sexy, witty, smart, and shocking. . . . Key reading for anyone interested in gay writing, gays in the military, queer theory, and the construction of gender."

—Judith Butler, University of California at Berkeley

"Provides startling insights into the amount of homoeroticism—usually implicit, but often surprisingly explicit—common among macho Marines."

—*Choice*

"Offers powerful and penetrating insights."

—*Journal of Homosexuality*

"Comes thrillingly close to fulfilling the deepest promises of pornography to fuse pleasure with forbidden knowledge. . . . As *The Masculine Marine* fiercely attests, Zeeland knows plenty about danger and desire."

Don Belton, *Transition*

"Eavesdropping on Zeeland's conversations with military boys about uniforms, tattoos, initiation rituals, and hot clandestine sex in the woods, the showers, or the fan room of a ship, readers get inside the messy, contradictory elements of sex and gender more completely than they could get in any cultural studies course."

—*The Stranger* (Seattle)

SAILORS AND SEXUAL IDENTITY

"A remarkable achievement . . . the first piece of solid research to provide a coherent description of the sexually charged atmosphere aboard ships of the U.S. Navy. . . . Zeeland's sailors learned early in their careers that the aphorism 'It's only queer when you're tied to the pier' is more than a casual stab at nautical humor."

—B. R. Burg, PhD, Author,
An American Seafarer in the Age of Sail

"Feels completely, deeply real. What's so fascinating about the book is its interest in the complexity of issues. In fact, Zeeland makes the point that lifting the gay ban will probably mean less open homoeroticism and less actual sexual contact between men. . . . You'll want to read this book. And you'll be looking forward to the next installment in the series."

—Lambda Book Report

BARRACK BUDDIES AND SOLDIER LOVERS

"Unique among the writings on gays in the military . . . A valuable album of self-portraits—with both individual and group shots—that capture the complexity of relationships among a group of men while they are coming to terms with their own and each other's homosexuality."

—Allan Bérubé (From the Foreword), Author,
Coming Out Under Fire

"Captures the many ironies of military life. Despite its long-standing ban on gay men, it was the military that first allowed many of these men to discover their erotic preferences."

—Canadian Journal of Law and Society

"When the army proffers its invitation to potential recruits to 'be all you can be,' it may be taking on more than it bargained for."

—Newsweek

Military Trade

HAWORTH Gay & Lesbian Studies
John P. De Cecco, PhD
Editor in Chief

Military Trade

Steven Zeeland

Harrington Park Press
An Imprint of The Haworth Press, Inc.
New York • London

Published by

Harrington Park Press, an imprint of The Haworth Press, Inc., 10 Alice Street, Binghamton, NY
13904-1580

"Wormy: Hell Bent for Leathernecks" first appeared in *The Stranger.*

Cover photo by David Lloyd. Used by permission.

Cover design by Marylouise E. Doyle and Steven Zeeland.

The Library of Congress has cataloged the hardcover edition of this book as:

Zeeland, Steven
    Military trade / Steven Zeeland.
        p.   cm.
    Includes bibliographical references.
    ISBN 0-7890-0402-X (alk. paper).
    1. United States.—Armed Forces—Gays. 2. United States.—Navy—Gays. 3. United States.—
Marine Corps—Gays. 4. Marines—United States—Sexual behavior. 5. Soldiers—United States—
Sexual behavior. 6. Sailors—United States—Sexual behavior. I. Title.
UB418.G38Z46 1999
306.76′62′088355—dc21   98-31595
                                                                                                                    CIP

ISBN 1-56023-924-7 (pbk.)

For M,
born on the Fourth of July

ABOUT THE AUTHOR

Steven Zeeland is the author of *The Masculine Marine: Homo-eroticism in the U.S. Marine Corps* (Haworth, 1996); *Sailors and Sexual Identity: Crossing the Line Between "Straight" and "Gay" in the U.S. Navy* (Haworth, 1995); and *Barrack Buddies and Soldier Lovers* (Haworth, 1993). He is a Research Associate at the Center for Research and Education in Sexuality (CERES) at San Francisco State University. His writing has appeared in *The Face, The Stranger,* the Irish *Sunday Independent,* and *The Times* of London.

CONTENTS

Foreword:
The Field of Mars

To be the fastest runner, the strongest wrestler, the best at throwing the javelin—this was virtue when Horace in his dreams ran after Ligurinus across the Field of Mars, and Ligurinus didn't lose his virtue by being caught.

Tom Stoppard, *The Invention of Love*

Since this is a book of confessions, I had better start by making one of my own.

I'm not a military chaser. Oh, yes, I'm a military *admirer*. What man obsessed with masculinity—and that means most of us—isn't? Boys (and tomgirls) realise very early on that sport and killing are the two principle masculine virtues and those who don't play with the girls and their dolls play with balls and guns. The endless, impossible, occasionally ugly but entirely beautiful pursuit of the masculine ideal begins very early in life but never comes near consummation. And while some may make that hopeless pursuit a personalised, "perverse" one rather than an internalised, "normal" one, all men, not just the military chaser, pursue Ligurinus across the Field of Mars in their dreams.

Even as the West demilitarises and demobs, and masculinity is pathologised and problematised, many young men—and some women—look much more "military" these days than they ever did during the draft. Buzz-cut hair, combat trousers, tattoos, dog tags, and big boots are no longer worn only by those civilian men who used to play with girls and their dolls but now make gay porn videos with names such as *Army Manouevres.*

And why not? The military man is an archetype that is almost timeless; it deserves respect, rather than simply shooing out of the living-room like an old flatulent dog just because it is politically inconvenient and might offend the vicar. Moreover, in an atomised world of rampant individualism and market absolutism the concepts of "service," "duty," and "honour" have a well-deserved, feudal, almost courtly romance attached to them. As well as a very definite *ancient* one.

According to the *Concise Oxford Dictionary* the word "ephebe" derives from the Greek for a young man of eighteen to twenty undergoing military training. This was also the fleeting age at which Greek youths were considered most desirable by older men; contrary to popular, somewhat convenient belief, the "beautiful boy" the ancient Greeks adored was really a young *man*. Much of Greek art was devoted to the celebration of the ephebe's beardless beauty *and* virility—unlike, say, the Persian model in which some boys were singled out to be raised as eunuchs and used as sexual playthings that didn't get pregnant or get premenstrual syndrome. The system of same-sex erotics in place in ancient Greece and later in Rome generally honoured the loved object, rather than debasing it (as is the modern fashion), and encouraged and applauded virility in a young man rather than mocking it (as is also the modern fashion). Ephebes who had been chased would eventually become chas*ers* and the economy of desire was brought full, poetic circle.

More prosaically, there may also be something in the very "ephemeral" nature of military service itself that makes military boys such powerful symbols of desire across cultures and epochs. When asked to explain the appeal of sailors Christopher Isherwood put it succinctly: "They go away."

So, a military admirer I may be. But a military chaser I'm not. I'm too lazy, too selfish, and too vain. I simply don't have the passionate dedication, sainted patience, severe single-mindedness, and almost *artistic* altruism/masochism that—as this extraordinary, compelling, appalling, touching, hilarious book shows—is native to the species. *Let* them go away, I say. I'm far too interested in *me* and the details of my needs to efface myself by running after an Ideal (okay, with the exception of one blond, Scottish Royal Marine, but that's another, appalling-hilarious story—see *The Queen Is Dead* by Mark Simpson and Steve Zeeland).

I have, however, been military *chased*. Back in 1990, bumming around Southern California for a year, I happened to be having my hair cut in the military YMCA in San Diego (they did a mean flattop and I was still in my post-rockabilly Elvis-joins-the-Army phase). I was accosted by a small, very confident, slightly ovoid, thirty-something Puerto Rican who introduced himself as "Stan" and said he was a captain in the U.S. Navy. He had mistaken me for USMC issue. Disappointed, he grasped at straws: "Are you Australian?"

Not having been in Southern California very long, and being only twenty-five years old, I hadn't yet grasped the basically rhetorical nature of such questions and I uncharitably disabused him of that idea too.

But Stan generously decided that he liked me anyway and even more generously introduced me to his harem of military boys, which comprised several sailors and Marines—but mostly, for some reason, Marines—none older than twenty; none less attractive than, say, a young Sean Penn; and none less friendly than an abandoned collie pup. (Stan, in typical military chaser modus operandi had found these young men on his nightly sweeps of the streets, Navy bars, and dirty bookstores of San Diego: lonely young men who often joined the military to find the dad they never had—only to meet Stan instead.)

And none of them gay. This was admittedly the greatest attraction to me. Having spent three of the longest, loudest months of my life in West Hollywood, I was glad to meet young men who didn't carry pagers that beeped alternately with messages from their agents offering them work as an extra and their reflexology clients enquiring if they offered extras. But then, these boys weren't exactly what I'd call *straight* either. Most if not all of them were having sex with Stan, and I mean full-on, five-alarm, full monty sex—not just indulgently allowing him to blow them through a Budweiser haze while girly porn played on the VCR. Stan's fat mulatto dick was ploughing these Midwestern boys' peachy white asses on a regular basis. Anticipating my scepticism, he would proudly show me his photograph album, like a Jewish mother recalling her son's bar mitzvah: shiny Polaroids of young jarheads lying butt-naked on his bed, aforementioned butts raised in the air, their nail-bitten fingers pulling their blank ass cheeks, reddened in the camera flash, apart, heads cricked round—"Look toward the camera!"—revealing a grin part farm-boy, part slutty coquette. (Stan's erotic impulse, when it came to his attitude towards the loved object, was more modern than ancient.)

I had discovered a world that wasn't supposed to exist except in fantasy—the sort of illegal, unhealthy fantasy that pinched-faced gayist columnists denounce from their paper pulpits. A world where good-natured, handsome boys with easy smiles were available for companionship and sex. Boys much like the ones back home in the North of England I'd grown up with, playing war games in the back garden, building secret summer dens in hay fields, wrestling indoors and getting carpet burns, playing dares in apple orchards posted with signs saying "PRIVATE—GUARD DOGS ON PATROL!", dreaming a long, hazy dream of manhood. It was a return to innocence, albeit of a filthy kind. I was, to all intents and purposes, living in a Tom of Finland drawing (pre-1970s), where *guys just had sex with guys,* in that corny, laughable, absurd phrase, and didn't have to issue press releases the following morning. Needless to say, I had the time of my life.

Naturally, this was highly irresponsible behavior attributable to my "quasi-fascist internalised homophobia." And really, I should have fled there and then to the nearest gay bookshop, bought every copy of *Outing Yourself* that I could lay my trembling hands on, and formed a gay reading group with these young men where I would explain that their friendliness towards me was either the result of their essential gayness, in which case they needed to leave the homophobic military and open a tanning salon on Santa Monica Boulevard; or else it was an unnatural rebellion against their essential straightness, in which case they should feel very guilty and confused and find a nice girl with child-bearing hips to marry right away. But, you know—and this is something that I have to live with for the rest of my life—somehow I never got round to it.

What's more, all these "straight" boys fell in love with Stan (and one or two may even have fallen for me). At which point he would unceremoniously dump them. As Steve Zeeland (or, as I like to call him, "Oprah Whitman") points out, military chasers are often drawn to the camaraderie and self-sacrifice of military life, and often display near-suicidal self-sacrifice themselves in regard to the objects of their affections—but they can also be sociopathic in their exploitation of these naïve, lonely boys. Stan managed to be the perfect example of both extremes.

Not that his recklessness and ruthlessness wasn't sometimes admirable in its own mad, bad way. One especially bizarre night on Camp Pendleton I shall never forget. I found myself with Stan in one of those cute, *Full Metal Jacket* elliptical tin-roofed barrack huts. He was, naturally, handing out cards with his telephone number and address to young Marines chilling out in their white boxer shorts or just damp towels wrapped around their waists. "Anytime you're in San Diego, guys, you just come and look me up," he boomed. "Bring your buddies. The more the merrier!" *And they took them.* I smiled sheepishly, gritting my teeth in an agony of embarrassment, failing to carry off even 10 percent of Stan's nonchalant attitude that this was a perfectly normal thing to do and that we had every right to be there.

Driving back to the main gate we got lost (Pendleton is about the size of Wales and it was dark and pouring rain) and a couple of sentries in ponchos with torches and guns stopped us. It suddenly dawned on me how dangerous this situation was. I mean, I was a foreigner on an American military base on a war footing—Iraq was being bombed at that moment—with a man who claimed to be a captain in the U.S. Navy but about whom the only thing I knew for certain was that he wasn't.

To this day, I don't know how he bullshitted them, but he did. I realise now that he was a drag queen of sorts—his lies really were truer than the actual humdrum truth the rest of us have to deal with. In a sense, he was the real inspiration for *Male Impersonators,* being the most prolific and gifted example of this phenomenon I have ever met. He literally became the man that you wanted him to be, like one of those *Star Trek* aliens that feed off your brain waves and inhabit your memories. Stan the poor, uneducated Puerto Rican had grasped at an early age that all men are impostors and had decided to put on the best show in town.

To a Marine fascinated by Hollywood, Stan was a close friend of Steven Spielberg. To a Jewish businessman, he was an agent for Mossad. To me, someone who wanted to be a fighter pilot as a kid but was thwarted by incipient pacifism, he was an F-14 Tomcat jock. Preposterous? Yes, of course. But Stan was a great performer and even greater psychologist. People believed Stan because they wanted to. He deployed their worst enemy against them—themselves. Even though I knew Stan was tapdancing, I played along. When the morning of my much-promised flight in an F-14 with him finally arrived and he called to tell me that it had been called off for "operational reasons," I was hardly surprised, but still somehow disappointed. The fact that this grifter was a military chaser was sort of appropriate—the pursuit of the Ideal has, in many ways, nothing to do with the individual and his accidents (in the Aristotelian sense) who happens to wear the uniform (the sign of the Ideal); so the military chaser/shape-shifter becomes whatever he needs to become to continue his pursuit of the Ideal—which may be forever receding but is always unchanging. As one of Steve's respondents puts it: "an unending supply promises a promiscuous monogamy." After all, the military boy is by definition, and probably by nature, a boaster, a teller of tall stories that sometimes, just sometimes, he comes close to living up to.

However, I doubt that the Pentagon would have taken any of this into consideration when prosecuting Stan for impersonating a Navy officer on one of their bases during the Gulf War, no matter how entertaining he was. I think they would have thrown away the key in his case and the nonimmigrant visa in mine. And in this particular case, on this particular dark, rainy night on Camp Pendleton, I don't think that the sentries believed him or were even impressed, they just didn't want to have to listen to him fuck with their heads anymore and waved us on. I suspect that sixty seconds after we drove off they had forgotten all about us. Sometimes I was convinced Stan had those kinds of powers.

Depriving people of their illusions is not only a thankless and churlish task; it's almost impossible. When I tried to suggest to Stan's boys that he might be anything other than 100 percent truthful or reliable they made it clear they didn't want to hear this kind of thing and I didn't raise the matter again. Probably most of them are out of the military now and married, several times over. But I suspect that most of them recall their time with Stan with more fondness than embarrassment; after all, he did make them all feel (and I include myself in this), for a little while, very special. Even so, I can't help wondering if one of them did finally get around to murdering him.

Back in Britain now for several years, despite a yearning to recapture that time in San Diego, made stronger by my collection of Stan's Polaroids which he insisted on continuing to send me long after I left (until the brown packages suddenly stopped coming and my letters to him were returned stamped "Forwarding address unknown"), I still haven't managed to become a military chaser. This is partly because the British military is only about the size of the NYPD (Dog Handlers Section), and partly because British squaddies are less approachable and more cliquey than the American variety, for entirely sensible reasons to do with class, terrorism, and the fact that their personal hygiene is not always as scrupulous as that of GIs. All in all the British military chaser is less likely to be faced with a "promiscuous monogamy" than a promiscuous celibacy.

But mostly my failure is due to the fact that I haven't met a British Stan—someone who turned military chasing into military *delivery*.

I miss him.

Mark Simpson

Mark Simpson is the author of *Male Impersonators: Men Performing Masculinity* and *It's a Queer World: Deviant Adventures in Pop Culture,* and is the editor of *Anti-Gay.*

Acknowledgments

Dear Steve,

I seriously considered joining the Marine Corps because of your book. Going through such an ordeal would make me much more of a man. Alas, it was not for this lifetime. I'm now 27. Had I read your book at 18, I may have done it, and I wish I had. The Marine image is very erotic to me, I admit, but it goes much deeper. The sense of honor and devotion for other men is something that is missing from the general gay community. I eagerly anticipate more on this subject from you.

M.

I have never been in the military. I am what some people would call a "military chaser," a civilian with a passion for servicemen. The term may not be terribly flattering, but it is coldly accurate, at least in my case. I've chased a soldier across the ocean, a sailor to a remote island outpost, and a Marine from one corner of the country to another. Along the way, I started writing books about military men and their admirers. I've tried to explore serious questions about desire, identity, and the contradictions of military life—questions that grew out of my unabashedly erotic interest in servicemen.

In the five years since the publication of *Barrack Buddies,* I've received more than 800 letters from readers. Roughly one-third of the people who have written me are active-duty service members or veterans, but the rest are civilians who feel an affinity for military men and military life. Their letters posed new questions. What exactly is it about servicemen that so enthralls gays? And what happens when an idealized sexual fantasy becomes a long-term real-life pursuit—or even a vocation? I undertook this book as a forum for military chasers to document our chapters in the long history of soldier and sailor lovers, and to see what we might have in common.

For twelve months, I solicited contributors through a page on my Web site, http://www.stevenzeeland.com, and through an advertisement in a newsletter devoted to sailor and Marine chasers. I also collected essays, interviews, and oral histories from men who approached me at readings, wrote to me in care of my publisher, or came to my attention through other chasers.

I explained to all potential contributors that I was not just looking for hot tales of conquest, but some earnest reflection on the origins, evolution, and personal meanings of their passion for military men. Of course, as in my previous books, I also collected hot tales of conquest. Some people have a problem with this. Asked one reviewer of *The Masculine Marine*: "Is this a fuck book masquerading as social science?"

No. It's social science masquerading as a fuck book.

Several reviewers have compared me to Boyd McDonald, the late editor of *Straight to Hell: The Manhattan Review of Unnatural Acts*, whose collections of "true homosexual experiences" (which I respect) were also anthologized under such titles as *Meat, Cum,* and *Raunch.* This puzzles me. As implausible or silly as it may seem to some, I really am much more interested in what sex stories reveal about how we *think* about sex. But I do take pride in the fact that my books are enjoyed by masturbators and academics.

In his introduction to *Flesh and the Word 4*, Michael Lowenthal points out that one obstacle to taking seriously the anonymous letters included in *Straight to Hell* is that their authenticity can be questioned. On the other hand, Lowenthal invokes Toni Morrison's distinction between "fact" and "truth."[1] Many of the men I interviewed for my previous three books were friends and acquaintances whose lives I followed closely for months or even years. I found that when they told lies, it was most often to underrepresent their sexual experiences, not exaggerate them. Particularly in *Sailors and Sexual Identity*, several of my Navy interviewees can be seen downplaying their exploits out of fear that they will be perceived not as conquering studs (horny straight men), but as trashy sluts (horny straight women). (Most of the lies I caught Marines telling were boasts about combat experience.) As my interaction with the contributors to *Military Trade* has in most cases not been as intimate, I cannot always verify the accuracy of their claims. But I hope that readers will share my own evaluation of most of the stories collected here: No one could make this up. But if they did, why would they want to, and what would that mean?

Of the reviewers who have misunderstood my intentions, so far none have been further off the mark than the guy who wrote: "No one is going to be convinced that Marines can ever tell us anything about genuine masculinity, but Zeeland, in capturing the sheer flamboyance of their manly drag, may win some converts to the military cult." Recruiting military chasers is the last thing I want to be responsible for. (And there are many viewpoints represented in this book with which I do not agree.) My purpose here is to further explore questions about desire, identity, and belonging, and to attempt to capture something of the *unruly passion* felt by civilian men for servicemen: The (often illegal) ways they have met. The (sometimes unreasonable) extremes to which they have gone. The (nowadays decidedly unfashionable) love they have sometimes found and continue to search for. These are for the most part stories that would not otherwise be chronicled. They are about more than "mere" fleeting thrills.

I am grateful to all of the men—and one woman—who wrote, e-mailed, and publicly accosted me with their military chaser stories, including Georg, J., Randy, Timo, "Tommy," and Phillip Torrente.

For helping me recruit contributors, I am indebted to Dan Devlin of The Naval Network, a club for admirers of sailors and Marines. Mike Leathers and Rolf Hardesty kindly provided comments on early versions of the manuscript. Jon-Paul Baumer not only made important introductions, but once again generously provided several fine photographs. Bill Palmer, Vice President of the Book Division of The Haworth Press, has helped me immensely, as have my publisher, Bill Cohen, and my senior editor, John P. DeCecco. Rebecca Miller-Baum, Trish Brown, Marylouise Doyle, Peg Marr, Paula Patton, Sandy Jones-Sickels, and Margaret Tatich at Haworth are also deserving of special thanks. Writer friends who helped me at least momentarily shore up my sanity, but who hold no responsibility for my offenses, are Aaron Belkin, Allan Bérubé, Leo Bersani, Frank Browning, Scott Heim, Scott O'Hara, Brian Pera, Matthew Stadler, and Matthew Bernstein Sycamore. Steve Kokker and Tom Waugh provided inspiration and encouragement in the final lap; D. Travers

Scott offered invaluable advice at the last minute. Without Heinz Kort, Bart Snowfleet, Hannelorre Schultes, and Brian Younker I could never have gotten started. For their special life-support services in Seattle, I am beholden to David Clemens and Eric Gould.

     Finally, I thank Samantha, Jeremy Buchman, and Mark Simpson.

S. Z.
Seattle

Introduction:
The Bitterest Envy

They recalled the fresh young image of the Handsome Sailor, that face never deformed by a sneer or subtler vile freak of the heart within.

Herman Melville, *Billy Budd*

Trade traditionally refers to men who accept the sexual advances of other men owing to financial need, sexual deprivation, alcoholic stupor, or other "situational" reasons, and not because of some "innate" gay desire.[1] According to historian George Chauncey, the sexual category became extinct in the gay urban world of the 1960s or 1970s.[2] In the late 1990s, high-profile gay sexual conservatives invoked the ghost of trade to reprimand young gays judged to have inherited "debasing, emotionally empty, self-loathing" attributes from preliberation homosexuals.[3] But outside of gay communities the sexual pursuit of straight servicemen by gay civilians lives on.[4] A closer look at civil-military sex challenges certain widely held assumptions about both chaser and chased—and poses questions about the wisdom of those who seek to divide the world into "straight" and "gay." The interviews and essays collected in this book suggest that, paradoxically, for many men, the advances of the gay rights movement have in some ways actually made it more difficult to form affectional bonds with other men. Gay sex has never been more openly advertised. But the military love of comrades is something that gay life can't offer.

Military chasers—men possessed of a more than casual romantic and erotic interest in soldiers, sailors, airmen, and Marines—will be dismissed by some these days as a gay cliché, leftovers from or throwbacks to the grim dark ages before Stonewall. In the current era, we are doubly perverse. Most of us are gay men who pursue sex with straight men. And often we do it in public.

1

But an appreciation for the youthful masculinity of fighting men
is nothing to have to get defensive about. After all, the history of
soldier lovers spans the globe, and predates the word "homosexual"
by several thousand years. And if a taste for uniformed trade is
politically unfashionable, it is not unpopular.

No theory of sexuality can adequately account for personal
quirks. But most military chasers can be said to have in common a
passion for an organic, embodied, archetypal, "authentic" masculinity; for immersion in *numbers* of servicemen; and for a "pure"
homosocial camaraderie or "buddy love"—but one that allows for
sex between men.

A Masculine Ideal

Zeeland: How important is it to you that the men you meet be conventionally masculine?
John: Out of all the things to consider about meeting a guy, that is the most
important. Looks come second.

What do military chasers want? John gives a blunt example of
the most common instant answer: "In most cases, you're guaranteed that if the guy's a soldier, he's gonna be a real man."

The men in this book make frequent references to a desire to
consume, worship, appropriate, or simply be surrounded by a "pri-
meval," "tribal," or "animalistic" warrior masculinity. Porn writer
Rick compares Marines to bulls and pit bulls (he likens gay civilians to pigs and black widow spiders). Hollywood executive John
says that he idolizes Marines because our culture is being feminized
(he quotes Jung). Entrepreneur Cory has relocated to a desert Marine town "because of the ambient testosterone that's in the air."
Heavy metal superstar Wormy voices his wish to be reincarnated as
a Marine "boot." Almost like members of Melanesian warrior
cults, military chasers draw strength from the very idea of the
semen of sword-bearers.[5] Asked why he has pursued military men,
a gay academic faxed me: "Among the reasons that immediately
come to mind are a certified masculinity; the association of masculinity with potency, with aggression, with being on top, with large
genitalia, with buckets of semen."

But military chasers are often the first to admit that masculinity is seldom as simple as that. After echoing Quentin Crisp's contention that chasers idealize "the fearless man of action,"[6] John concedes, "There's a certain amount of vulnerability to being in the military. Someone else has control over you." Adds the academic: "Conquering the conquerors has its own pack of thrills." Andrei, a Russian cadet chaser, reflects that although he is "more passive than active in terms of what I like sexually, in bed I tend to be more active than [the cadets] are, come to think of it." His compatriot, Denis, titters, "It's very interesting that you can pick up a straight soldier, and the role that they like in bed is passive! Incredible!" Through their intimate firsthand acquaintance with some of the stereotypically most conformist young men imaginable, military chasers are confronted with the nightmare protean unruliness of human sexuality in general, and with the wildly contradictory nuances of military masculinity in particular.

Inevitably, like military men themselves, chasers find it safest to fall back on defining an attraction to masculinity by what it is not. One explanation that has been repeated to me more times than I can count is: "If I wanted to have sex with a woman, I'd have sex with a woman." (I am not entirely convinced of the logic behind this declaration. If you want to be conventionally masculine, which still popularly means identifying as straight, but you are only aroused by *dick*, it seems to me you might reasonably seek out women with penises. Which, of course, a certain subset of the straight male population does.[7])

Some military chasers are blatantly misogynistic. Porn video maker Don says that he is attracted to Marines because "women want to control you," and adds: "I personally do not want to see a Marine all tied up being dominated by some bitch." A Navy reservist Marine chaser I interviewed practically screamed at me: *I piss standing up!*"[8] Almost all military chasers are unabashedly anxious to repudiate effeminacy in the men they desire. Ironically, the straight men being chased are often more at ease "playing with gender" than the gay-identified men doing the chasing. From Oceanside, California to St. Petersburg, Russia, there is a horror story told among military chasers so often that it's tempting to see it as universal. The chaser seduces a man who appears to meet the exacting strictures of his rigidly masculine straight-stud ideal, only to take him home and discover that he is wearing women's panties. (Here, only Howard relates that he was able to rise to the needs of a cross-dressing sailor with aplomb. Though his pickup from a Navy country and western bar wanted to dress in women's clothes, "because of his good looks and masculinity I found it kind of charming.")

A taste for uniformed trade is popularly linked with "fascist masculinity." It's true that at least one contributor to this book is reputed to have picked up Marines and dressed them in vintage SS regalia. A disproportionate number of international visitors to my Web site, "A Lover of Soldiers," come from countries with a history of authoritarian rule. John says that Marines should be blond and blue-eyed, and is disappointed when a blind date turns out to be Asian. One reason for Cory's preference of sailors over soldiers is that a high percentage of the latter come from inner cities. (Maynard, the one African American whose stories are included here, cites a preference for "white boy next door" types; he writes that he has found them easier to approach than black and Hispanic military men.) All of the photographs that contributors to this book suggested for inclusion as illustrations depict white men.

But military chasers come from left, right, and middle. A liberal Democrat State Department employee told me that he eroticized military men as an act of solidarity after he was outed at work during the 1993 gays-in-the-military controversy.[9] I eroticized Army boys as a pacifist, which I remain. Such friction can make for an especially powerful erotic charge, as in the famous case of Jean Genet reporting on the 1968 Democratic National Convention.[10] Wormy goes so far as to say he eroticizes Marines because they are the defenders of democracy. "Nobody ever got off on that," laughed a friend I repeated the quote to. But there are antecedents. Walt Whitman, perhaps.

And whether military chasers are significantly more misogynistic or racist than gay or straight men in general is unknown.

Getting swept up by an attraction that seems to run counter to everything one believes in may not be all that different from suspending disbelief at the movies. Coming to view masculinity as socially constructed, as I have, does not necessarily diminish the erotic charge of masculine archetypes. I still like to think of the men I am attracted to as exhibiting an *unstudied* masculinity. (Some boys are better at imitating their fathers than others. And the masculinity of Dad makes frequent appearances in this book, whether in the guise of gay daddies Lance and Wormy, or of the military dads Cory, John, and Martin remember from childhood—or even, in Andrei's case, of a butch lesbian mother who loved to wear army uniforms.) On the other hand, how can Marines who *learn* how to become masculine at boot camp be termed "unstudied"?

Ranking Desire

Among military chasers, not all service branches are created equal. There is surprisingly little overlap between military chasers and uniform fetishists. (Here, Martin is the only crossover. To most military chasers, uniforms are valued not as arousing in themselves, but as a mark of authenticity. "It's only at the beginning" of a seduction that military drag is of interest to Andrei, for whom uniforms are "like lighthouses to a ship, orienting me, showing me the way [to] 'macho' men, strong [and] handsome." Howard actually finds sailors sexier in jogging shorts. The only article of military clothing that has ever done anything for David is the Navy dress blues, and that's because he's found it the most practical uniform for sex in a car. "The thirteen buttons open a flap. Whoever designed that uniform must have had deadly intent. The suckee doesn't have to take down the pants, or even open the belt—the flap folds down and everything is immediately available.") But there is clearly a fetishized preference for Marines and sailors over soldiers and airmen.

Most chasers view Marines as the ultimate prize (though many add that, given the opportunity, they might actually prefer elite but scarce outfits such as Navy SEALS; Army Airborne Rangers or Special Forces; and, according to one interviewee, a subbranch of the Air Force the name of which he cannot remember). Cory, who prefers to play a sexually submissive role with Marine trade, explains:

> Marines are an assault force. Period. End of story. The bravery and aggression associated with the Marine Corps is one of the reasons why they're my favorite. Plus the fact that they have the most rigorous physical training of the five branches, which generally leaves them superior physical specimens to many of their colleagues in the other branches.

Yet, surprisingly, other factors can sometimes outweigh muscles and butchness per se. Cory is representative in finding sailors more enticing than soldiers. Though U.S. Army men are typically seen as tougher in both body and demeanor than men of the U.S. Navy, regular soldiers just can't compete with The Sailor as gay icon. This widespread erotic allegiance testifies to the enduring power of a centuries-old mystique.[11] Writing about British sailors, James Gardiner notes:

> The popularity of the Jolly Jack Tar in gay mythology stems from a double fantasy: first, that long periods at sea away from feminine company accustoms sailors to the idea of turning to their own sex for physical relief (all sailors are really homosexual); secondly, that enforced abstinence at sea makes them ready for anything, even a homosexual, once they get ashore (all sailors are "real men").[12]

And Allan Bérubé observes that in the World War II era, each chaser based his cruising techniques

> on his own sexual folklore about men in uniform. Generally they believed sailors to be the most available and Marines the least. Sailors acquired this reputation because they were out to sea without women for long stretches of time, they were younger than men in the other branches and their tight uniforms looked boyish, revealing, and sexy. Marines were a challenge because of their tough image.[13]

Nowadays, sexual folklore about men in uniform is as accessible as the corner adult video store (or maybe even the gay section of a big chain bookstore). Retail distillations of time-honored sexual stereotypes can provide off-the-rack inspiration for jaded gay civilians to prey on military boys.[14] In Russia, Denis—whose interviewer observes that he sees soldiers "as quaint sexual objects rendered more exciting by their uniform, an attitude slightly condescending and fraught with the need to feel superior"—cites as a reason for his interest in soldiers military-theme porn videos imported from Southern California.[15]

Unsurprisingly, there is an overwhelming preference among military chasers for enlisted men over officers. Long-standing notions about the greater virility of working class men play an obvious role. Recalls Quentin Crisp, "When any of my friends mentioned that he had met a 'divine' sailor he never meant an officer. Women seem to feel differently about these things. They prefer airmen, by which they always mean the higher ranks."[16] But there are exceptions. Some middle-class chasers voice a preference for the company of upwardly mobile young officers. Cory's hottest experience in recent years was with a Marine Corps lieutenant who, he points out with pride, has since become a lawyer. (David concludes his oral history of forty years of military chasing by boasting that he helped elevate a common sailor to successful civilian architect. It is my own perverse habit to adopt semiliterate enlisted men and transform them into civilian philosophy majors and Ikea shoppers. But this doesn't have to be as erotically self-defeating as it sounds. I seem to be typical of military chasers in finding ex-military men almost as powerfully attractive as active-duty. In fact, Rick and Maynard cite as their dream "settling down" with someone recently discharged from the service.)

Some readers may be skeptical about the strong emphasis that many of the contributors to this book place on the *character* traits they see servicemen as embodying, typically: honor, valor, gallantry, chivalry, selflessness, and integrity. But this is in fact an important distinguishing characteristic. As Rick observes:

> Those of us who find sex, affection, companionship, and maybe even love most desirable with military men are looking for more than a hard body in a uniform. We are drawn to what the military has made out of a man, and what he has used the opportunities found in the military to make out of himself. Deep down I suspect that we are looking for a hint of the heroic. That's an atavistic desire in our cynical age, but there is a beauty in still believing in honor and nobility of spirit.

Bill earnestly looks to Army Rangers for values that will inspire him to be a better person.

> For many years, I thought I lacked courage. I've noticed that personal courage in Army Rangers. I find that really admirable. If that could be taught to more of us as a general populace: honor, and dignity, respect for your fellow man, and willingness to lay down your life for one of your comrades. In a country where

everybody sues everybody and everybody fucks everybody over, that kind of camaraderie is just absolutely incredible.

And Cory enthuses:

> For me, the [military is] filled with men who are heroes. . . . These are people who often have old-fashioned values that I grew up associating with the best men. Men who believed in virtue. Who believed in honor. Who had a sense of personal integrity. Who had a commitment to something bigger than themselves, like the cause of freedom that they think our country represents. I'm awestruck by every new crop of Marines that comes into town. And how the tradition of service, and the sense of selflessness, sense of gallantry continues.

Of course, idealists often have to make some concession to pragmatism. Cory seeks to connect with the virtue of Marines by penning "Good $$$ for USMC BJ" on toilet walls.

But the homosexual prostitution of servicemen is another centuries-old tradition.[17]

The Hunter and the Hunted

> The trade was running as thick as salmon up those narrow cataracts in the Rockies. Head to tail, tail to head, crowding, swarming together, seemingly driven along by some immoderate instinct. It was not a question of catching; it was simply a question of deciding which ones to keep and which ones to throw back in the stream.
>
> Tennessee Williams, "Two on a Party"

Some chasers are searching for a husband. Others freely admit to being whores. Most of us incorporate elements of both. "A never-ending supply promises a promiscuous monogamy," my sailor-chasing academic correspondent observes. Even the quest for "Lance Corporal Right" acknowledges a certain interchangeability of servicemen, not only as we may first imagine them, but as how we cannot help but come to imagine them at that delicious moment when the roster of recruit-conquests reaches such a number that they begin to blur. In *Querelle,* Lieutenant Seblon pants:

> Whom to choose, from among these males? I could hardly let go of one before desiring another. The only reassuring thought: that there is only one sailor, *the* sailor. And each individual I see is merely the momentary representation—fragmentary as well; and diminished in scale—of The Sailor. He has all the characteristics: vigor, toughness, beauty, cruelty, etc.—all but one: multiplicity. Each sailor passing by may thus be compared to Him. Even if all sailors were to appear in front of me, alive and present, all of them—not one of them, separately, could be the sailor they jointly compose, who can only exist in my imagination, who can only live in me, and for me. This idea sets my mind at rest. I have Him, The Sailor.[18]

Unending ranks of uniformed young men—men that the military has already reduced to numbers—can offer the promise of finding a mate . . . of drowning in semen . . . perhaps even of the sustained dissolution of self.[19] "We both save them from death and are vicariously thrilled by its prospects in their lives."[20]

And sometimes death's prospects in our own lives. Central to the appeal of the baby-faced Marine is that he is trained to kill with his bare hands. The owner of a gay bar near a Washington, DC, barracks theorizes that some gay men attacked by Marines are masochists who willfully provoke a fantasy-fulfilling bashing.[21] Describing one of various military chasers he has harassed on the streets of Oceanside, California, a Marine named Jack has observed: "This man is so bold—it's incredible. I know that this man has been *shot.* I'm sure they've all been beaten up. And at risk to life and limb, they continue to do it."[22] David eavesdropped through a heating vent as two sailors discussed the disposition of his body. One of his Marine chaser buddies was found at the bottom of a swimming pool. A sailor pulled a knife on Maynard. A soldier pulled a knife on Doug. Howard was choked and beaten about the head by a sailor who, after coming home with him and enjoying a massage, was offended by his offer of a blow job. As Howard was carried to the ambulance, his assailant pointed his finger and screamed to the assembled neighbors: "He raped me!"

Those tempted to point their own fingers and lecture that these stories are a perfect example of why gay men need to pair off as domestic partners might pause to consider that domestic violence may be nearly as common, especially considering the numbers of sexual partners many lifelong military chasers rack up. David, for example, reports only one brush with trouble in over forty busy years in which he had sex with an estimated 4,000 sailors, most of them straight, many of them drunk.

Gays can be as sociopathic as anyone else. Among the historical records of sailors rolling queers, there are records of queers robbing sailors.[23] And I've heard as many stories of military homosexual rapists as I have of military gay-bashers. Bill concludes the tale of his murdered soldier-chasing buddy, a man who truly seems to have earned his unsavory sobriquet, "Vulture Dick":

> I just felt that he had really crossed over the line. When you drug and rape someone—that's your fantasy, that's not theirs. I was really sorry that he was dead, but I felt like he did it to himself.

Not all military chasers are nice people.

The *boyish* appeal of servicemen cannot be overemphasized. A former Navy officer, Lieutenant Tim, has emphasized the "youthful masculinity" of sailors. "No matter how old a group of sailors are, because of the retarded lifestyle of the Navy, they're a very boyish group. . . . There's just an incredible vulnerability about them. You realize how much these guys need to be taken care of."[24] Sadly, a concomitant realization is how easy it is to exploit these young men. Comments Rick:

> Of course it can't be ignored that military men tend to be young, in good physical shape, lonely, outside of their home communi-ty's social controls, low on cash, and often inexperienced enough to be sexually manipulated. . . . There may be a fine line between military chasers and military predators. Chasers want the military man's reality, while gay predators only want their image and the implied status of having "had" a military man. I've known queens who went into heat at the sight of a Marine or sailor in

uniform and tittered away about "getting" them. Like their Black Widow mothers, they wanted to suck the life juices out of a masculine man and toss the empty husk aside afterwards.

On the other hand, there can also be a fine line between "military predators" and "military prey." Many chasers date the origin of their preference for military boys to an early experience being seduced by one. Doug was picked up hitchhiking by a Marine sergeant. Maynard found that a sailor he was admiring "had been busy picking me up." Bill was innocently playing pinball (in an adult bookstore) when he was approached by an Army Ranger who asked him, "How does this place work?" And the socially aggressive but sexually timid Howard found that "In more cases than not, I was doing very little seducing. A lot of [the sailors] grew impatient and made the first move."

"Military trade" can involve far more complex exchanges than sex for money or "a mouth is a mouth." Notes Maynard: "It must be good to be temporarily treated like a prince. It means access to a private home, a stereo and videos of their choice, an oasis from overcrowded berths and barracks." Howard found that for many San Diego sailors, simply coming to his apartment "was paradise. Basically it almost seemed like just knowing any civilian would give you some kind of star quality." When I asked my ex-Marine ex, Alex, what I had in common with Versace assassin and sailor-chaser Andrew Cunanan—my rival for his affection—Alex replied: "Well, you both paid attention to me."[25] My nickname for Alex was "Baby Seal." But he sometimes enjoyed telling me that he dreamed, and daydreamed, of murdering me with an icepick.

There is simultaneously a vulnerability *and* menace about military men that derives from their apprenticeship in institutionalized violence, but also from the troubled backgrounds that propel so many of them toward the military. "Let's face it," military admirer Mark Simpson wrote me. "Military boys are fucked up. And that's another reason why we like them. . . . Being looked after by someone is always preferable to looking after someone because you can always find someone else to look after you. Attention is easy to find; giving it is easy to lose. Boys are like cats—who knows how many saucers of cream and stroking hands are waiting for them around the neighborhood?"[26]

Yesterday's Trade

Some of the men in this book will make easy prey for those insistent on denouncing "internalized homophobia." To be sure, some military chasers are transparently homophobic. But these days, *all* gay men who advertise their personal taste for conventionally masculine, straight-appearing men—to say nothing of those of us who chase straight-behaving men—are regularly and loudly excoriated for having internalized society's hateful disdain for the stereotypical unmanly homosexual. Thunders one gay ayatollah, "Would African-Americans . . . accept the usage of the term 'white-acting?'"[27]

But the comparison is sloppy. It is a peculiarly late-twentieth century idea to insist that men who like men must not be attracted to men generally, but must restrict themselves to a tiny population that embraces a stigma-driven sexual minority identity.

Still, it must be admitted that most military chasers are at least as eager as conservative gay activists to believe in the existence of true, oh-so-rigid *heterosexuals* whose same-sex experiences *don't really count*. Indeed, it is precisely this sense of difference that drives us on. Without it, there would be no space to chase.

Somehow, it's little comfort to know that before gay liberation, a larger percentage of the male population felt free to have sex with other men.

One of the most insightful and important analyses of a military sexual culture is an article by George Chauncey called "Christian Brotherhood or Sexual Perversion?" in which he analyzes court records from the U.S. Navy's investigation of homosexuality in 1919 in Newport, Rhode Island.[28] He paints a picture that at first glance may seem very familiar. The Newport Army and Navy YMCA was the epicenter of a rollicking community of drag parties, drug and alcohol consumption, and wildly promiscuous sex between men. As many as 5,753 sailors and soldiers passed through the YMCA on any given day,[29] joined by civilian men who "followed the fleet up from Norfolk."[30] Investigators learned that one cruiser fellated between fifteen and twenty recruits in a single night.[31]

Chauncey's most surprising observation is that "Relatively few of the men who engaged in homosexual activity, whether as casual participants in anonymous encounters or as partners in ongoing relationships, identified themselves or were labeled by others as sexually different from other men on that basis alone. The determining criterion in labeling a man as 'straight' (their term) or 'queer' was not the extent of his homosexual activity, but the gender role he assumed."[32] Not even the U.S. Navy thought there was anything queer about a man having sex with another man—as long as he played the "man's part." In fact, Navy investigators employed straight sailor "decoys"—hand-picked because they were young and handsome—to anally penetrate or be fellated by "perverts" in order to acquire evidence. No one batted an eye when the straight investigators typed up reports that included such confessions as "I decided to let him take it then. I worked up a hardon and he hopped to it. I gave him a load and he ate it nicely."[33] Or, "I consented, and after using the cold cream he rolled over on his belly and opened his legs like a woman and assisted me to enter by way of the rectum. We stalled along for about twenty minutes and then I went off. He kissed me when I left."[34] Ultimately, so many men were implicated that "The chief investigator later claimed that the chairman of the first court had ordered him to curtail the investigation because 'If your men [the decoys] do not knock off, they will hang the whole state of Rhode Island.'"[35]

Contrary to current popular assumptions, sex with "straight" men was not always limited to casual sex. Chauncey found that some "husbands," as the "queers" called them, "entered into steady, loving relationships with individual men known as queer."[36] Neither were the "straight" sailors exclusively prey. Chauncey found evidence of "sailors eagerly seeking the sexual services of fairies."[37] In 1927, a private investigator reported that "whenever the fleet comes into town, every sailor who wants his d--- licked comes to the Times Square Building. It seems to be common knowledge among the sailors that the Times Square Building is the place to go if they want to meet any fairies.'"[38]

Chauncey's closing point is of special importance. The "fairies," "cocksuckers," "pogues," and "husbands" of early twentieth-century Newport "all engaged in what we would define as homosexual behavior, but they and the people who observed them were more careful than we to draw distinctions between different modes of such behavior. To classify their behavior and character using the simple polarities of 'homosexual' and 'heterosexual' would be to misunderstand the complexity of their sexual system."[39]

The dubiousness of simple polarities is something that many contemporary gay men seem constitutionally unable to grasp.

In *The Rise and Fall of Gay Culture,* Daniel Harris scorns the idea of a "nongay homosexual"; the gay taste for "militaristic," "fascist masculinity"; and the notion that all men are potentially capable of behaving homosexually, the leitmotif of what he terms gay "super-hero pornography" novels of the 1970s:

> The propagandistic use of the conversion narrative to incrimi-nate the entire gender, to blacken with homosexual aspersions every quarterback and auto mechanic, may at first sight seem like a clever form of liberating sexual sabotage, but on closer scrutiny, it proves to be fundamentally self-loathing. . . . In this most macho of never-never lands, anti-subcultural characters in an exotic array of uniforms engage in an unending costume party, a game of dress-up, a masquerade ball in which the customary dramatis personae of the gay fantasy life participate in a bizarre and stately minuet, with the cowboy pairing off with the Iroquois tribal chieftain, the corporal with the captain, the deputy sheriff with the felon from the county jail. . . . Superhero sex . . . exists only on the page.[40]

Harris is certainly not wrong to observe that porn can be silly. But a wealth of research documents that "nongay homosexual" sex was not unknown to settlers of the U.S. West, is not exactly un-heard-of in prison, and has even been known to occur in the U.S. military. Though perhaps not "intrinsically" more erotic than gay piano bars, such imagery holds understandable appeal to men in-habiting liberated but incestuous gay ghettos, where seduction all too seldom deviates from scripts as predictable as the porn films Harris makes such amusing sport out of ridiculing.[41] As a "clos-eted" officer who teaches at one of the military service academies e-mailed me: "If I were, say hypothetically, alienated from openly gay culture, where there is no need to sublimate or suppress open expressions of desire and indeed there is every requirement for self-presentation in very conformist ways, then I might well be attracted to other forms of male bonding where the fruit is more forbidden precisely because the erotic energy is channeled in more diffuse and unpredictable directions, making it all the more seductive."[42] (Note to Daniel Harris: I do not mean to suggest that everyone should be actively bisexual. The irascible persistence of my own Saul-like conversion to liking *only* military trade is evidence enough that some people's sexuality can end up anything but fluid. But as one of my (bisexual) ex-lovers once pointedly suggested to me, perhaps adults are potentially bisexual in inverse proportion to their would-be child-star stubbornness.)

In *Life Outside*, his indictment of the gay "cult of masculinity," Michaelangelo Signorile makes the grossly chauvinistic claim: "As gay men, we . . . have the possibility of developing the kinds of close friendships straight men can't, precisely because of their fear of homoeroticism."[43] But straight men have the possibility of developing the kinds of close friendships gay men can't, precisely because of our expectation that any homoeroticism must inevitably lead to sex. As Steve Kokker observes in this book:

> Being gay ironically precludes a kind of closeness to other men every bit as important as a traditionally defined love relationship. Gays often dismiss male bonding as mere homoerotic game-playing, as if straight men repress actual sexual desire for each other and settle for second best. . . . Yet if male bonding, intimate camaraderie, and group belonging are what straight-chasers are really after, sex is by no means unwelcome—in fact, it's ironically what we most often have to settle for. And what a sweet consolation prize it appears! It makes it easier to believe that we're getting what we think we wanted. Of course, we're not, really—hence the "chaser" part of "straight-chaser."

The Bitterest Envy

When I peruse the conquer'd fame of heroes and the victories of
  mighty generals, I do not envy the generals,
Nor the President in his Presidency, nor the rich in his great
  house,

> But when I hear of the brotherhood of lovers, how it was with
> them,
> Then I am pensive—I hastily walk away fill'd with the bitterest
> envy.

> Walt Whitman, *Calamus*

Some military chasers may be opportunists who seek out straight servicemen because they can't compete in the gay scene. But others are eminently gay-marketable men who are looking for something that gay life cannot offer them.[44] Steve Kokker used to be a good, peace-loving gay Canadian. Then he went to Russia.

> What struck me hardest in St. Petersburg, even more than the individual military men I'd meet, were the group scenes: cadets horsing around, walking with arms draped across shoulders, marching in formation, or simply hanging out. I felt particularly touched by the easy way they shared laughter, space, and affection (complex maybe but never complicated), and by the aura of inclusion and cohesiveness which united them. Although I later saw how my ideals didn't always hold true in reality, this vision was endlessly more seductive to me than the image of social unity offered up in gay clubs. I knew that what I secretly desired was to be a part of such a group, to belong as they do, in a world (I imagined) of fraternal affection, bonding, and the odd dip into homoeroticism. In short, I wanted to be their buddy.

Doug says that his attraction to Marines is grounded in "Their masculinity. Most of 'em are in excellent shape." But he insists "the main thing is their behavior. Just the attitude of, 'I'm gonna look after my buddy.' That's it more than anything else. It's not just sex."

Howard was surprised to discover that sometimes not getting sex with sailors brought a special reward:

> There were some where I just felt a special charge, because they just got so close to me. And I had to do my best to hold back. But I loved just the intimacy and the camaraderie, and the fact that they would treat me as one of their counterparts, and call me "dude" and whatever, just like I was another one of the guys.

The conventional explanation is that these gay men were deprived of masculine camaraderie in their formative years, and eroticize/sentimentalize the buddy love they believe exists among military guys to make up for it. Rick asks:

> How much of a military chaser's erotic response to men in uniform is a way for them/us to feel what it might be like to belong to a tightly bonded brotherhood? Most chasers whom I've known are as much loners as I am. I never had a genetic brother, and I have consciously envied the closeness and interdependence that I have observed in herds of Marines. My personality would never have fit in the Corps—I would have fought to the death to maintain my personal sense of independence—but I have always paid for that in a deep sense of aloneness.

But not all military chasers necessarily have an outsider aloneness to compensate for. Doug says that as a six-foot, nine-inch-tall football player he has never been wanting for masculine camaraderie. Why should having known buddy love since his youth make him want it less now? Indeed, much of the 1993 national debate on gays in the military was dominated by aging straight male vets who spoke in weepy, reverential tones about the importance of preserving the "purity" of the military male bond as they had lived it: unconsciously homoerotic, maybe, but never "homosexual." Many military chasers are not without some sympathy for this viewpoint. Even if, of course, they're not actually prepared to go without sex.

Recently I spent a day in Washington, DC. I did some research at the National Archives. I bought some postcards at the Naval Memorial. Then, consulting my guidebook (which included mention of Whitman "making daily rounds to succor the ailing soldiers"[45]), I went to kill some time at the Smithsonian Museum of American History. Stunned, I suddenly found myself standing in front of an exhibit I acutely recollected viewing on my first visit to Washington, when I was ten years old. It was a World War II latrine consisting of a sink, two toilets with no partition or doors, and a piss trough.

Probably what most impressed me at ten was the fact that there was a toilet behind glass at a museum. But I remember studying the placard, which said something about barracks life breaking down class and ethnic barriers to help recruits bond.

My least favorite book on gays in the military is an obscure title published a few years back by a well-meaning liberal straight-identified psychologist. According to this author, there is no legitimate cause for anxiety about homosexuals serving in the military because there is no homoerotic charge to military life: all service members understand that naked bodies are embarrassing and, except for a few bad apples, not even gays get turned on by it. She calls this "the etiquette of disregard." Still, to reduce the anxiety that homoerotic tension might somehow arise, she advocates retrofitting latrines, showers, and barrack rooms with "modesty shields."

In this she imagines that she is doing men a favor.

But perhaps this is really what many gays want. The period in which I write has seen a dramatic crackdown on sexual encounters between men in just the sort of venues that form the backdrop to this book—semipublic sex spaces where many of the participants are likely to be "closeted" or nongay men. Televised pervert-in-the-park style arrests meet with enthusiastic approval from high-profile gay leaders who are anxious to make a pact with the mainstream: *Tolerate us, and we will confine our sexuality to our middle-class bedrooms—and we will police those bad gays who do not. For such men are criminals, and a public health menace. And many of them are not even really gay.*[46] In pushing their commandments for happy, healthy, and spiritually pure gay behavior, gay sexual conservatives aid and abet genuinely homophobic strategies to restrict potentials for homoerotic, homosocial, and homosexual interaction that have flourished in other times and places. It seems that everywhere you look these days, vanity partitions of one sort or another are going up to ensure that men who don't call themselves gay are protected from line-crossing potentials for same-sex desire.[47]

On the other hand, new barriers can sometimes present unforeseen opportunities. In this book, Bill recounts how his local health department used the AIDS epidemic as an excuse to shut down the adult bookstores where he used to cruise soldiers. The one video arcade that survived legal challenges was forced to install windows in the doors of video booths,

> Which is not necessarily all bad. I've found that people are pretty resourceful. When you throw an obstacle, they're pretty good about resolving that obstacle. And now actually the glass doors sort of attract a brand of people that are a little bit exhibitionistic and/or voyeuristic. And so it's a different clientele. The sad thing is that there's probably a lot of basically really shy straight Army boys that would come in and play if there was a bit more privacy.

And this is sad—and not only because it frustrates the desires of men such as Bill and me.

In part because it is slower to change than other areas of society, something of a communal spirit still survives in the military. But for how much longer?

The final chapter in this book is an interview with a former Marine who confided that the men in his unit had modesty concerns. If openly gay men were allowed to serve in the Marine Corps, they objected, Marines would no longer feel comfortable masturbating together.

If you only read one chapter of this book, skip to "Tom: The Brotherhood of Marines." Tom experienced the famously intense bonding and "brother love" of Marine Corps infantrymen. These men engaged in games of nude wrestling and testicle-licking, lay about the barracks floor with their heads in each other's laps, and competed to see who could give the best massage. Most paired off as "couples." When one Marine was killed in a car crash, his weeping buddy was hugged and consoled by Marines who treated him as a grieving widower. Says Tom, "I enjoyed my buddy relationships more than any boyfriend I've ever had."

But times were changing. Public discussion of gays in the military led to new anxieties about intimacy between military men. One day a lieutenant yelled at the cuddling Marines, "I'm getting really tired of seeing this. Quit laying all over each other. Clinton didn't lift the ban!" And Tom, dutifully obeying the gay fundamentalist commandment, "Everyone must come out of the closet. . . . Badger everyone you know,"[48] declared his homosexuality to seven of his closest buddies.

All of them voiced acceptance. But, he reports: "This massage thing —it stopped altogether."

Now, as a gay civilian, Tom is free to have all the gay sex he wants. But the handsome and muscular twenty-six-year-old haunts an Internet chat room for Marines, looking for the love between men he had back when he was "repressed."

Bill:
The Ballad of Vulture Dick

These days, most civil-military cruising takes place on-line. Bill, a spunky forty-nine-year-old construction company owner and bar-band rock and roller, meets his Army boys the old-fashioned way, in a Pacific Northwest adult video arcade so David Lynchian that the red lights that burn over the (glass) doors of occupied booths are shaped like pinecones. It was in this place that he used to consort with Dick, a military chaser murdered by a soldier whom he drugged and raped.

Bill: I was born in Montgomery, Alabama. I never really saw much of my father until I was about fifteen or sixteen. My father's a good man, but he's a very stern, strict man, and he has a very hard time showing any sort of affection to any of his male children. None of us have met his expectations. He and I actually had fistfights.

Growing up in school, I never had too much trouble dealing with my sexuality. I figured out when I was twelve or thirteen that I wanted boys. Gay roles were very stereotypical back then. And I didn't like that. Because to be gay in Montgomery in 1966 you had to be a screaming queen. If that's how somebody wants to be, that's fine, but that's just not who I am. I love to suck dick, I love to fuck, but I'm not a queen.

My view of military guys in the 1960s was probably that they were pretty much off-limits, and if you tried to make an approach that you would get your lights punched out. I was also pretty much against the Vietnam War. I never really gave much thought to the military guys at that point in my life. I liked the long-haired hippie look.

When I was eighteen years old, I moved to Birmingham. I met a gal there from Atlanta. The band I was in was playing in a battle of the bands contest. I got her pregnant and we got married. She died of peritonitis of the intestines when she was six months pregnant. I went on a drinking bender that lasted for about eighteen months. I started smoking a lot of pot, and I got caught. I spent two and half years in the penitentiary for posses-sion of marijuana in the state of Alabama.

There was a lot of institutional homosexuality in prison. Guys that normally wouldn't play on the outside—they come in and swear they'll never do it, and two months later they're seeking you out.

While I was in prison, I met another musician. We started the first rock band ever in the penal system in Alabama. We got to go out and play on Saturday nights. Of course the guards took all our money, but we were just so happy to get out that we didn't give a rat's ass. So anyway, Lee was from the Seattle area. When I got out I decided to come here, and ended up staying. I formed a rock band, got married, had a little girl. She's twenty-four now, so she's not little anymore.

I liked sex with women, but women wanted eternal commitment. If you say, "Honey, I really just want to be friends but I'm tired of your box," the bitch is gonna pick up a skillet and knock you in the head with it. That's just not something that plays out well with women. Guys, on the other hand, want fifteen minutes of a relationship, and then they want to move on. I want something in between.

Until the early 1980s my preference in men was still the long-haired musician type of look. I quit being in a band, though, because I wanted to be a stable provider with a strong financial background for my daughter. I formed a construction company. And one of my friends said, "Bill, there's this [adult bookstore] in Tacoma. You should check it out. There's just absolutely the hottest men you've ever seen." This was probably sixteen, seventeen years ago. I went down there and my eyes absolutely hurt the first time. I'd never seen so many gorgeous Army men in my life.

The bookstore is in an area that's sort of known for its nefarious activities. You've got a tittie bar at one end. You've got massage parlors. And then you've got a bunch of sleazy motels, where everybody goes for two-hour sex. At that time you had three adult bookstores; now there's only one.

The first time I did an awful lot of looking, but I just didn't get any-where. A couple of weeks later my curiosity and my penis got the better of me and I traveled back down there. I met this [other cruiser] named Dennis, and we were chatting. I turned around and three really gorgeous men walked in. He said, "Oh, they're Rangers." Because they had that high-and-tight haircut. And I said, "I don't care if they're Martians, they're gorgeous." He said, "You're new here. They came in here together. You'll never get anything." At this arcade there was a little game room where you played—oh, back then it was Pac Man. So one of these Army guys played a game next to me, and I was playing my game. He said, "How does this place work?" I said, "I don't really know what you mean. This is only my second time here." He said, "I heard it was a good place to get your dick sucked." I said, "Well, I've *heard* that you go back and watch a fuck flick, and if you want company you leave your door unlocked or slightly ajar." He gets up and disappears. I finish up my game, and decide, well, I'm going to venture back there and see what's going on in this snake pit.

I walked to the back. They had pictures of what was playing in the different booths. And this same guy comes right behind me. I could see off the reflection [from the display case] that he was looking at me. I was really nervous because I thought maybe he was going to beat me up or something. He goes in the booth and leaves the door wide open. I'm sitting here at this marquee just as long as I possibly can. And then I turn around and he's standing in the doorway. I decided it was my move, so I went in there and had just some extraordinary sex.

I came out of the booth, and Dennis—the guy that had said, "Oh, you'll never get anything"—is standing there. If looks could kill you would be talking to a corpse right now.

I thought: it just doesn't get any better than this. So I went back to play my video game, and about five minutes later one of his Ranger buddies comes up and tugs on my sleeve and inquires, "Do you want to do me now?" I ended up going back with him and the third one to the barracks.

In my fantasies driving back, I was thinking, well, I'm gonna be the slut that services all these Army boys. But apparently they sort of like used me as a vehicle to make it all okay to do whatever it was that they wanted to do among themselves.

I have to say, I'm forty-nine years old, and that stands out as the ultimate sexual experience I've ever had. Maybe that's what cemented my affinity for military guys. And with the exception of a few [periods when I've been in] relationships over the past fifteen years, I tend to make it down there every Saturday night.

For the longest time it was really pretty wide open. You could do whatever you wanted to do. Then the health department used the AIDS crisis as an excuse to try and shut this business down. They weren't successful in forcing them out of business, but they did make them take the solid doors off, and put on glass doors, so the police or health department or whoever can see in there. Which is not necessarily all bad. I've found that people are pretty resourceful. When you throw an obstacle, they're pretty good about resolving that obstacle. And now actually the glass doors sort of attract a brand of people that are a little bit exhibitionistic and/or voyeuristic. And so it's a different clientele. The sad thing is that there's probably a lot of basically really shy straight Army boys that would come in and play if there was a bit more privacy.

Zeeland: What can you do now with the glass doors?

B: Well, you're not supposed to do anything in the booth. But you can make eye contact. If I see somebody I like, I leave a note on their car: "You're hot as a two-dollar pistol. If you'd like to party. . . ." Sometimes the note's a little more graphic than that.

I've had several of the Army guys that have responded to my notes say that they felt that was very cool, because they didn't feel threatened. They said they would have probably rebuffed me if I had tried to strike up a dialogue with them in the bookstore, where they might be seen by some of their friends or something like that.

Z: But you don't actually have sex in the bookstore?

B: Sometimes you do. I can't say that I've never had it. It is exciting, but it would be so embarrassing to have a cop's flashlight shining on you when you've got a mouth full of somebody.

Z: They come through and shine flashlights?

B: Periodically, yeah. You can buy crack cocaine on any corner, children are being murdered, but they're going to protect us from people masturbating. I'm just so glad to live in this country. We're so well protected.

Z: How many Army guys are we talking about since 1980? And what percentage would they be out of your total sexual encounters?

B: Oh my Lord. [Laughs.] Well, probably 75 percent of my total. And I'd say ten or twelve a year. So sixteen years, about 160? 200? And I'm still HIV negative.

Z: Were a lot of these encounters anonymous, where you didn't talk at all?

B: Yeah, it is more of the anonymous, wham bam I'm gone. Fortunately, some of them, in second and third encounters, we do develop more dialogue.

Z: Do you usually meet up at the same place?

B: I typically get a motel room. Because I have no desire to see my name in the paper for lewd and lascivious behavior. And it's hard to have a dialogue in a peep show booth.

Z: Physically constraining, too.

B: Oh yeah. Good God, you kneel down and you stick to the floor. They get a shovel to pry you up. I don't think so!

From time to time they make the bookstore off limits to these guys. And so then they have to really risk a lot to venture there. But they're horny, so. . . .

[Opens up laptop computer.] I tend to be very organized. These are some of my encounters, and a couple that I would like to encounter. Let's see. [Scrolling through notes.] "Red Chevy, Washington plates now, met about one year ago, earring left ear"—I gave him a ten. "Oklahoma, Ranger, hung and hot. On a scale of 1 to 10 he is 20." This one comes in, and I just thought, oh, there's no way anybody will get this. So he goes back and he's watching a movie. I'm in the booth across from him. The next thing I knew I turn around and his pants are down and he's showing me his ass. And so I flopped out St. Peter and waved it at him. He looked and smiled, and he followed me out and we went back to my motel. I'm so disappointed that he hasn't looked me up.

Nathan, I had a relationship with him for about a year. "What a doll. I will sure miss him when he's gone." He's gone.

Zak from Tennessee. Zak was another funny one. The first time I left a note on his car, he yelled, "Fuck you, you fag motherfucker!" And then, two or three months later, he said to me, "You still wanna suck my dick, mister?" Go figure!

Buddy from North Carolina. I left him a note on his car a year and a half ago. It was a very naughty note. Something to the effect, "You're hot as a two-dollar pistol and I want you to come and fuck my face all night." I told him a place to meet me and he drove in there and just totally flipped out; I guess he thought the note was from a woman. So I just drove off. He didn't follow me or anything. And then about a year later I saw his car again. It's just this little evil streak in me. I left another note. And I'll be damned, he showed up at the motel room. He was ready to play. A couple months ago he said, "I really like this. You've made me gay." I said, "Well, Buddy, I don't really think that's right. Those feelings were there. Maybe I'm the catalyst that brought them to the surface. I wish I could accept credit. If I could make people gay, I would simply walk through Ft. Lewis, lay my hands on this one, lay my hands on that one." I'd have my harem, but it's not that easy. I think I've given him a little bit of a comfort level. He's married. See, a lot of these guys are married. Which is really strange to me. What's their excuse? It's not that they're not getting sex.

Z: Have you noted any preferences in what they want to do sexually?

B: More guys are bottoms. I don't know if it's a universal thing with men, but I would just guess that the strong homosexual fantasy entertained by men in general is to be fucked, and maybe feel what it's like to be a woman, or be dominated. It's somewhat of a disappointment to me, but I've learned to cope really well. I like a big butch man to just throw me down and have his way with me. But it doesn't break my heart if it goes the other way. And if you continue a sexual relationship with these people, usually you can turn the tables and get what you want to. You just have to play it out and talk.

[Back to scrolling.] I don't remember this one from South Carolina. Some of them I haven't actually scored yet, but they're just—if I see them in the area I sometimes make a note, and then if you see them again. . . .

This is another one. Paul from Montana. This one's funny! I met him, and he was really standoffish at first. And then—I've carried a concealed weapon for about six years, and he is actually the first person that's ever spotted it. He says, "You've got to leave your gun in your car." I thought, what the hell; he's a little guy, so I figured I could probably overpower him, unless he had a weapon. So we got in his station wagon. The first time I just gave him a blow job. And then two months later, he started coming back for a weekly fucking. He went to Korea. He came back about a month ago. I've only seen him once since he got back. But what a transition.

Let's see. Marty was a lot of fun. Cute little Army Ranger. "The libido of a rabbit. Could not get enough. Dropped out of sight. Probably got transferred."

B: I'm at a stage in my life now where I would really like to be in a relationship. I'm seeing a counselor every two weeks to try and figure out why I'm not in one. I really want to be in one. And I don't know if a relationship will work, because when you're used to this high-volume method of procuring, it may or may not be possible. I feel okay about what I'm doing now, but it's just not fulfilling all the emotional needs in my life. My counselor said that if I've got this thing for Army dudes, that I need to try and meet 'em in someplace other than a bookstore or a tittie bar. "See if you can't develop a dialogue and conversation, get to know them and have them get to know you. And see where it goes."

About five years ago, I was in a relationship with an Army Ranger that lasted a year and a half. I met Ray at this same bookstore. He was a big Polish kid. Blond, blue eyes, 200 pounds, just solid as a rock. The night he came into the bookstore all the queens were chasing him. And I was in one of those moods where I thought, "Oh, he's probably straight. I'll never get it." So I was just playing my videos and minding my game. And he struck up a conversation with me. We just started talking. Didn't do anything that night. We met a couple of weekends later, didn't do anything then either. And the third time he says, "Do you want to go have some fun?" So we did.

He was into kinky stuff. He sort of introduced me to my first sadomasochistic experience. When he was like fourteen or fifteen, his uncle and his cousin, who were seventeen and eighteen, had tied him up and basically raped him. So we acted out numerous variations of that scenario. I'd never, ever done that. I fantasized it, but I almost thought that maybe some things one [had] best keep in the fantasy mold. I didn't want to get so jaded that I'd have to go sit on a fire hydrant for my next rush. I just was afraid of S&M. And I'm still a little cautious about it. Having sex with somebody and paddling them and saying, "You're a naughty boy," that's one thing. But I don't know if I'm ready for the slings and the dungeons and all that. I might like it too much.

Z: Apart from good sex, what have Army Rangers come to represent for you?

B: Well, first, they keep themselves in such good physical shape. Rangers have sort of a cocky attitude. They like to be looked at. They are absolutely the best, and they know it. But there's also a camaraderie between them that is just unbreakable. One of Ray's friends was totally straight, and he walked in on us doing the big nasty. And he didn't say a thing. That kind of loyalty just really impressed me. So I think it's a combination. There's the physical stimulation, but mentally there's that strong sense of honor, and self-respect, and respect for your fellow soldier that I really envy and like. And I see . . . lacking, I guess, in civilian life.

Z: Has it been lacking in gay civilian life as you've experienced it?

B: Yeah, I think it's lacking in that, too. One of the quotes on your Web site—somebody said that Marines looked exactly the same as the clone that you would find in the gay bar, except for their integrity. Something to that extent. And I've found that to be quite true about Rangers.

I've been clean and sober for fourteen years. I only go out once a week. Because I do think that cruising can be every bit as addictive as any drug. Unfortunately, some of my friends are caught up in that. Night after night after night. I just don't want it to spin out of control. I enjoy certain aspects of the hunt, and the good sex that follows. But I feel kind of good that I've reached an emotional security within myself to want to pursue a relationship. I like myself better now than I ever have in my life. So therefore I think it would probably be easier for somebody else to like me. If you're selling a pile of shit, it's going to smell like a pile of shit. Queens can be really tacky to one another. Downright vicious. I once had a guy run into my car because we were both after the same trick.

I had a really unusual situation last year. A friend of mine named Dick unfortunately earned the name of "Vulture Dick." He was an older gentleman, very debonair. Well-dressed. And I don't like older guys per se, but I thought to myself: If I can look this good when I reach this guy's age. . . . He looked so distinguished. Almost like a stage actor, or royalty or something. And Dick would cut you off—if he saw something he wanted, he would mow you down. Dick had another bad habit which led to his demise. He liked methamphetamine. And that can push you over the edge, and really cloud your judgment. To make a long story short, Dick picked up a young Army boy who had just had a fight with his wife. He took him back to his house. He got the kid really drunk. While Jamie, the kid, was passed out, he tied him up and raped him. When Jamie regained consciousness, he struggled to break free, and ended up hitting Dick pretty hard, and killed him.

I had to go to the trial. I testified for Jamie's defense. And it was very hard for me, because Dick was my friend. I'd had coffee with him, and we ogled the same tricks. But I just felt that he had really crossed over the line. When you drug and rape someone—that's your fantasy, that's not theirs. I was really sorry that he was dead, but I felt like he did it to himself.

Jamie got acquitted. It was a very unsettling situation to have to go through, but I felt really good that I did it. I think that if we as gay people want to be respected, that we need to be willing to admit that sometimes people within our community do things that they shouldn't. And it's just best to deal with that head-on. There's a lot of resistance. I talked to a [gay newspaper publisher] friend of mine. I tried to get him to publish an article, asking for anyone with any input to come forward. And he didn't want to do it, because he didn't want to air gay people's dirty linen in public.

For many years I thought I lacked courage. My testifying at that trial was an example of standing up for what you believe in spite of whether or not it's popular. Living an openly gay life is something else I'm glad I did. And I've noticed that personal courage in Army Rangers. I find that really admirable. If that could be taught to more of us as a general populace: honor, and dignity, respect for your fellow man, and willingness to lay down your life for one of your comrades. In a country where everybody sues everybody and everybody fucks everybody over, that kind of camaraderie is just absolutely incredible.

The chief battle I've had to fight in my life is to just learn to like and believe in myself. To learn to leave substance abuse alone, and realize that I'm not the horrible person that my father told me I was. But I am happy with myself. I've changed the things that need to be changed, and I'm working on other changes. And I think that maybe that mind-set, that Rangers seem to have, to succeed at all costs no matter what the obstacles are is a good example to follow.

Ray, the Ranger that I had a relationship with—one time I took him to work at my construction company. We got to the job site, and I said, "Ray, I want you to go into that room and tear that wall down." Then someone called me. I was on this call for like ten or fifteen minutes. When I got off the phone, I thought, oh, I didn't tell the kid where the hammers were, or where the cats' paws were, or nothin'. So I go in this next room. He had torn that wall down by hand and foot!

He told me later that he thought it was a test. He said the Army did things like that to see what their problem-resolution ability was. I mean, he kicked the sheet rock out, he kicked the studs out with his feet. I fell in love with that man right there.

Rolf:
Hollywood Marines

Rolf Hardesty is the pen name of a man who has made several careers in writing, communication, and broadcasting. In this essay, he describes another of his occupations: pimping Marines to Hollywood stars. The author of an article in *Manshots* magazine, "Reviewing the Troops: A History of the Military Image in All-Male Erotica," Rolf was the first stranger to write to me after the publication of my first book.

Angelenoes who can afford it head for the mountains or the shore in August. And that's where my four housemates had gone on that muggy Friday evening in 1968. They'd left me in charge of our glorified commune: a three-story, seven-bedroom Edwardian mansion we were leasing—complete with furnishings, a pool, and a tennis court—from the widow of the founder of Hollywood's first studio.

As I walked across the front lawn heading for an evening stroll on nearby Hollywood Boulevard, an oversized Cadillac swerved into the circular driveway. A three-hundred-pounder sporting a greasy pompadour sat at the wheel, with at least eight closely cropped young men packed beside and behind him. The whole thing looked like a mobile fraternity stunt: How many Marines could you squeeze into a Fleetwood?

"Is this the party house?" the driver called to me in what sounded like falsetto. I stood mute, short-circuited by the capon voice and the sight of all those Marines sardined into the car. The driver piped his question again, and this time he named a famous set designer who was supposed to be hosting the party in question. In fact, I *knew* that designer, whose home lay a block to the west. But, wild with curiosity, I fast-talked the whole group into the house on the pretext of getting a street map and of serving a round of drinks to the thirsty crew.

Our hastily summoned houseboy, his white jacket buttoned wrong, wheeled a movable bar out to the verandah where the Marines chortled and jostled around him. Meanwhile, indoors, I cross-examined their driver who, I now realized, must be about my age: not quite thirty. He'd introduced himself as "Tussie," and he got right to the point (having seen through my butch façade): it seemed he made part of his living by recruiting young servicemen to serve as entertainment at weekend parties. He would pick up likely-looking hitchhikers near military bases, take them to his nearby trailer home, and "screen" them for their suitability.

I must have seemed mighty naïve to Tussie, because at first I couldn't square the notion of "obviously straight" young toughs—like those horse-playing on the porch—with the shocking business he had just described: homosexual prostitution! Sure, I'd heard about the local scene during World War II. And, yes, America was at war again, here in the late-sixties. But somehow, cocooned in Hollywood's gay cocktail culture, I'd failed to see that thousands of combat-destined servicemen were now retracing the route their fathers had traveled a generation earlier.

Looking Backward

I'd grown up in Southern California, in a household consisting of a bluestocking and her succession of husbands: a sea captain, a police chief, and a former wrangler turned war-industry foreman (three remote, ultra-masculine father figures and one charming but dithering mother). By high school, I'd grown into a gangly geek with few friends, no social life, and a lot of private uncertainty about my sexuality.

By dint of all-A's and a timely bequest from a grandmother, I managed to get into an uppity little college an hour east of Los Angeles—a school that claimed to be a "West Coast extension of the Ivy League" but that couldn't escape the influence of nearby Hollywood: Kris Kristofferson was my cadet commander in the school's ROTC unit, Richard Chamberlain set the student social tone, and the most exciting game on campus involved those of us who were busily launching a student FM station.

Throughout those college years, I remained technically celibate ("My only love is the station"), although I dated and petted and panty-raided when my fraternity demanded it. Instead of releasing my aggression through sex, I vented it indirectly. For, by the time I'd received my BA, I'd become one of the school's most poison-tongued intellectual snobs.

In 1960, with the draft ahead of me and with ominous news coming from Vietnam, I opted for a student deferment and ducked into grad school at UCLA, moonlighting for L.A.-based radio stations in order to pay for my tuition. Such radio work suited my poor self-image in which I remained the gangly geek. But on the radio I could create a strong, seductive persona through the alchemy of a practiced baritone. It's possible I'd have stayed celibate in that disembodied voice-world for the rest of my life . . . if a street-wise friend hadn't stepped in. Ours had been a purely intellectual friendship, in the course of which I'd failed to notice that my friend had any sex life at all. But in the summer of 1962—our twenty-fifth year, his and mine—he revealed his hidden private life, and he showed me all the secrets of grooming, weight-training, and sucking cock. (Buggery I would learn on my own.)

His help came at just the right *genetic* time. For, finally, I'd not only filled out but had also "grown into my features," with the result that, before the year had ended, I'd found an appreciative audience on TV *and* in the bars.[1]

Making Up for Lost Time

During the next five years, 1962 through 1967, I spent every spare moment exploring all the sexual byways. Well, not quite "all": I'd drawn the line at corpses, anyone seriously under the age of consent, and anyone over seventy-five. Those byways, of course, included the flocks of would-be young actors in Los Angeles. For, at this same time, I'd begun working in movie marketing, finding myself in line at studio canteens by day with some of the same actors I'd seen at the notorious Red Raven the night before.[2]

As a newly glamorous member of the entertainment industry, in 1966 I was admitted to gay Hollywood's exclusive cocktail circuit. That private circuit seemed a perfect alternative to the din, the defensiveness, and the tired rituals of the town's gay bars. In truth, over my previous four years of playing sexual catch-up, I'd grown unhappy with the bar scene. Or, to be more accurate, I'd grown unhappy with my behavior in that scene—disgusted to find myself turning into the sort of vain, fickle, back-biting barfly I despised; sick of hearing myself spinning the same deceitful line for each new quarry; and dismayed to realize that I'd been making it with a succession of men who were eerily *like* me not only in gender but in personality, background, and orientation. Where was the opposite pole? Where the positive to my negative? The whole routine had turned incestuous. And the sheer number of my conquests had left me with an inescapable fact: that, although I still hadn't figured out exactly what I was looking for, I knew with certainty that I hadn't found it. But "it" continued to elude me now, even among the gilded youth

of Hollywood's party circuit—until Tussie's fateful arrival in that borrowed
Fleetwood.

Debating the Cost

By December 1968, Tussie's hitchhiking servicemen had booted the actors
off my sexual duty roster. Three of my four fellow-lessees in the mansion
hated the change, finding the new, short-haired crew unsuitable for our blow-
dried parties. One of my housemates even warned we'd all be murdered in
our beds or, at best, burglarized. The only one who shared my new taste was
the financial wizard who'd packaged the lease deal in the first place. But even
he frowned when I told him I looked on paying for sex as "a form of
liberation." For that's exactly how I did view it: as a way to break free of the
cocktail circuit, with its gay-to-gay inbreeding. The wizard warned that paying for sex would corrupt any budding romance. Yet, to me, the money was
just an ice-breaker, a cover charge that gave me access to young men whose
temperaments, backgrounds, and lifestyles all stood far from my own—so far
that, *without* payment, I'd never get to know them on any level, let alone the
sexual. And (I predicted) the day would come when one of those young
men—call him Lance Corporal Right—would opt to stay on with no further
payment. (We'll see what became of that prediction.)

But how much money was actually involved? In Tussie's case, not much.
My trailer-dwelling pimp only borrowed the fancy cars of his johns, and then
only for recruiting on their behalf. For each intro, Tussie would receive $15.
And, typically, his Marines and sailors would pocket $50 each for the week-
end.[3] Even such modest fees proved enough, however, for the bored, adven-
turesome young troops in whom Tussie specialized. And often the troops
would recruit others in their units, as had happened with the eight who
crowded into that storied Cadillac.

So the cost, at least at the outset, was manageable for someone earning
good money. And my new bedmates were returning dividends in the form of
a mellowed worldview: Soon, on my TV interview shows formerly devoted
to "serious" authors, I'd added rock stars, cartoonists, and other giants of the
Youthquake—all recommended to me in the course of weekend pillow talk.
And TV reviewers now began to note my new empathy for guests in place of
my old condescension, little guessing the source of this newfound common
touch.

My wizard friend sniffed at my new on-air populism, just as he'd frowned
at my paying for sex. Even so, early in 1969 he offered me the upstairs unit

of a mission-style duplex he'd just purchased in L.A.'s Hancock Park district. With eight rooms all to myself, I shifted into military overdrive: I began adding troops from three other pimps to those of Tussie. My fetish had become a raging compulsion.

Watching the Talent Scouts in Action

Much the priciest of those three was "Vin," a little baked apple of a man who spoke to his servicemen in a flat, Paul Lynde twang. For johns, however, he used the purest of pre-Stonewall camp, an argot in which the speaker became "your mother" when talking to any younger homosexual. Each of us johns had a favorite Vin anecdote. Mine involved another luxury car—a Lincoln Continental—leased by a john for Vin's regular use. Picture Vin behind the wheel, barely able to see over the dashboard, his head wreathed with a single strand of hair teased round and round to cover his bald spot. On the windshield I'd spotted an official-looking decal and had asked Vin its significance.

"That's an officer's sticker, honey. It gets me onto military bases."

"They let *you* on the bases, Vin?"

"Let me on the bases?! Honey, they *salute* your mother!"

Vin's sticker lent weight to his claims that he'd bribed key sergeants and chiefs at four of the local bases, that those insiders gave him access to shower-room peepholes, and that Vin's insiders conveyed his engraved "talent coordinator" cards afterward to the best of the shower-takers, explaining that "some civilian in a limo" had passed the card along. I found the peephole claim incredible. And yet Vin's stable of beauties did trump most of the talent available from any other source. So, it seemed possible that we military mavens did have friends and bribable allies "everywhere," as Vin claimed. (By the early 1970s, with the first open sale of all-male hardcore films and full-frontal magazines, Vin's guys would pop up in centerfolds and on the best of the 8 mm film loops. The "biggest" of Vin's stable was Gary throw-it-over-your-shoulder-and-burp-it Boyd. And a score of other traffic-stoppers would bear Vin's label, as well.)

Physically, he seemed the least likely of trainers for the ring of strapping, combat-ready young champs who loomed around him. But the little pimp exuded a strange but unmistakable authority. He did all the talking. And, because he guarded the pass between serious money and the primest of beef, his johns and his troops put up with a brand of high-handedness from Vin that no other pimp would have dared. For those of us near the bottom of the food chain, this high-handedness meant that Vin broke more engagements than he kept. And, often, when he and his beauties did show up, they'd stay only long enough to collect a handful of studio passes (which I could supply through my contacts). Then he'd whisk the beauties out of reach, with the vague promise that maybe they could fit me into their schedules "next weekend."

A total contrast to Vin in style, image, and dependability was "Abner," a stocky, grizzle-bearded West Virginian with the manner and grooming of an unmade bed. He went chiefly for quantity, and his fees were consequently modest. Abner did most of his prospecting on foot in and around "Cannibal Park" in San Diego's red-light zone (which has since become the chi-chi Gaslamp District). The off-duty troops he approached must have thought they were about to be panhandled. Abner's folksy spiel, including a string of the hoariest of jokes, put the troops at their ease. Over a coke or a beer at one of the area's cheap cafes, he would segue into his cover story: He'd "been asked to recruit a security force for weekend celebrity parties up north in Hollywood." Abner would then produce snapshots taken at some elegant, mixed-gender garden party with a fancy villa in the background. Later, over drinks at his modest pad, he'd explain that only the most "broad-minded" of security guards would do, because Hollywood stars often had a lot to hide.

"What if you were on duty at the home of _____," one of Abner's clients, a leading man with a studly image, "and the star himself took you aside and offered you an extra fifty bucks to let him *blow* you? What would you do?" As with an artichoke, Abner would peel off a leaf at a time until he'd reached the prospect's core. Then he'd insist on acting out the imaginary scene, right through to the climax. Afterward, he'd place a few phone calls to "the hosts of next weekend's parties" and would get the recruit to write down his on-base phone number. Only then would Abner hand over a list of selected client phone numbers—and only if he had no serious doubt about the recruit's state of mind.[4]

Visiting an Institution

I dealt with a third pimp, as well—one who worked through a venerable L.A. institution. Over time, I learned that this place had served as a kind of switchboard for Southern California's military trade ever since 1945: Bob Mizer's Athletic Model Guild [AMG]. In 1960, Mizer had published his *Thousand-Model Directory,* to celebrate AMG's fifteenth anniversary. The directory contained tiny near-nude photos, fifty to a page, of a staggering number of servicemen plus a few civilians. And Mizer would continue to lens new models at the rate of two or three a day every day until his health broke in 1992. His guild, located in the midst of decaying Victorian townhouses not far from L.A.'s city hall, came to resemble a fortress under siege: a double row of chain-link-and-razor-wire fencing surrounded his compound of five double-storeyed buildings. Those buildings housed a still-photo studio with flyaway backdrops and elaborate lighting, a mail-order office, a dormitory for itinerant models, a costume wardrobe worthy of a movie studio, and an archive of photo layouts. Atop one of the buildings he'd made a papier-mâché mountain range spiked with dried-up fir trees fished out of post-Christmas trash cans. Down below, Mizer's swimming pool served as a tropical lagoon, its sides draped with Astro-turf and ringed with fake palms. Elsewhere, dead motorcycles, rusted barbells, and overturned plaster columns crowded the corners of the yard. And the whole scene throbbed with *life:* guard dogs, wandering geese, a cage of bar-rattling gibbons, and usually a brace of sunbathing Marines.

Mizer himself rarely ventured outside his compound, so any would-be models had to find their way to him. And this they did, even though Bob never offered a finder's fee. But that wasn't a problem—because, typically, older men would bring their young tricks to the AMG so the boys could play big-time models. For that reason, Bob never refused to photograph any prospect, no matter how spindly or out of shape, going on the theory that he wouldn't embarrass a recruiter who just might show up next time with a winner.

In the mid-1960s, Mizer's small-format quarterly magazine, *Physique Pictorial,* began to include mysterious squiggles in the corner of each model's photo. When decoded, those little cryptograms told each model's measurements, hard; the range of his sexual repertory; the degree of his enthusiasm; and the price for his services. Bob's decoder sheet was carefully worded. For instance, the symbol labeled "Enjoys tongue-in-cheek humor" meant, in reality, that the model liked rimming. (A subsymbol indicated whether he preferred to be rimmer or rimmee.) Mizer offered all these data for use by prospective johns. But he himself accepted no fees from anyone for introductions, instead making his living solely from the sale of his magazine, his photo sets, and his studio's line of silent 8 mm films showing models wrestling in the near-nude or acting out silly little soft-core pantomimes.

At least one full-time pimp, however, did use the guild as his base of operations: a bizarre creature known behind his back as "the Magpie," because of his psychotic chatter and a voice shrill enough to crack enamel. Gaunt, hawk-faced, and much given to nervous twitching, this fifty-year-old was a sight to scare off any but the densest or the most desperate. Yet

somehow, working his beat in L.A.'s central Greyhound terminal, he managed to snare enough real talent to justify his tiny room at the guild and his
place at Mizer's communal table. For my purposes, the Magpie's preference
for civilian drifters and his scant success with servicemen meant that I rarely
drew anything from his talent pool. But, to give him credit, he did send me a
certain omnisexual Navy welterweight—a (literal) knockout, with curly Tus-
can locks, a super-sexy boxer's nose, olive skin as smooth as the finest glove
leather, and a contender's body with die-cut definition. After our first encounter, I offered him the post of "midweek regular" as soon as he got his
discharge. And for years thereafter, I pounded manners into his sassy ass
every Wednesday night. This remarkable sexual athlete, as versatile as a
Swiss Army knife, amassed a long list of paying admirers and graced the
covers of at least three skin magazines.

So, even the Magpie was entitled to the same respect I felt for all homosexual pimps—respect for their hard work, their paltry rewards, and paltrier
thanks—respect for their having shouldered a job at least as tough as the
Salvation Army's.

Taking the Bait

At the start of the long Labor Day weekend in 1969, I had my first
face-to-face meeting with Abner, at my new Hancock Park apartment. Early
in our meeting, he invited me to become his "representative" and to man the
northern end of his underground railway. This conduit would connect the
talent in San Diego and Oceanside with the johns in Los Angeles. Abner
needed a dependable L.A.-based freight forwarder who would be willing to
(1) collect the incoming talent at local train and bus stations, (2) "requalify"
some of those guys at his home, and (3) fine-tune their contact schedules so
that each john would receive only those guys whose range matched the john's
needs. And, as follow-up, the L.A. rep would also have to assure that Abner
got paid all his finder's fees.

Eager to have "the right of first refusal," I accepted. Only later would I
see the folly of my paying each young man to let me test his full range, then
paying Abner for the intro, on top of the hassle of running guys to and from
depots, coordinating with two dozen johns, and playing bill collector. But, in
1969, I still felt frantic to make up for all the years in which I'd been either
celibate or had chased the wrong quarry.

Then there was "the Mike factor." For Abner had baited his hook with a
morsel I couldn't resist: a rangy blond eighteen-year-old, standing six-two,
with shoulders the width of a doorway and a power-packed, Corps-built

body. A heroic chin, ice-blue eyes, and a perfect profile completed the picture. Over the weekend, would I consider showing Mike around?

By that point in my sex life, I'd tried almost every variation in the invert's manual of arms. I'd found I was best of all at topping, and Providence had equipped me for that role. During that weekend, I discovered my Marine guest's snug, insatiable rump and found it a perfect fit. (In later years, he'd return to Detroit and would marry the girl he'd knocked up prior to enlisting in the Corps. But, back in 1970, young Mike had just begun his five-year sabbatical from straight sex.) Although he and I were to make the same moves I'd been practicing with fellow queers since 1962, sex with Mike proved subtly new. It pulsed with a sense of discovery, a feeling of total honesty that I'd never found with any bone-deep homosexual. No matter Mike's sexual role at the moment, his responses were always *male* responses, unfeigned and unrestrained.

During that weekend I found Mike's personality just as big a turn-on as his physicality. True, he and I shared the same gender, northern European ancestry, and (near) height. But temperamentally we were complementary opposites: Mike had grown up in a bruising Detroit neighborhood, had done poorly in every school subject except athletics, and had gained all the swagger and bravado of the physically self-confident. While I loved to take social risks, Mike thrived on physical risks.

I'd never before had the chance to study a real blond so completely—the red-gold lashes, the blue veins on the near-transparent skin of his cock. And I loved the way his ears reddened whenever he felt embarrassed, or pleased, or miffed. As we shared our first postorgasmic cigarette, Mike asked me, shyly, what I'd really thought of him when I'd first sighted him—"and no bullshit, okay?" I've never been more eloquently honest. Then, tit for tat, I asked Mike what he'd thought of me. He paused, then thrust out his chin, as his ears grew red: "I thought, 'Thank God, a skinny one!' " Nobody before or since has handed me a nicer verbal bouquet.

In no time, Mike seemed completely at home, and the teenage hormones switched into warp speed. Indeed, his leaps over the sofa, his galumphing around the flat, and his intermittent whoops all nearly got me evicted by my wizard landlord downstairs, who had gone trickless that weekend. But, inevitably, Monday night came around and Mike had to return to base (with double what he'd been promised in his wallet). And not a moment too soon; I was totally drained. Now, I began to prepare myself emotionally for what Abner had warned would happen. "Never forget, Rolf, that these guys are

basically straight; they're doing it just for the money, and most likely they'll
be shipped out before you can see 'em again." That made sense, and Abner
spoke from years of experience. Further, Mike had told me his own unit was
due to ship out in the coming week.

So, think of the shock when, the next Friday evening, I opened my door to
find Mike, grinning bashfully with a duffel bag slung over one shoulder. He
announced that he'd decided to abandon the Corps (this, remember, in the
middle of a war) and to "move in" with me. Before I could speak, Mike
spotted a towel-clad SEAL emerging from the bathroom behind me, and then
a Marine in jockey shorts, bringing a Budweiser from the kitchen: two
brand-new arrivals from Abner's conduit.

Mike sulked around the apartment all that evening, and he got into a
shouting-and-shoving match with the other Marine, seemingly over a basketball telecast. When I returned from a run to the liquor store, Mike had
disappeared, taking his duffel bag with him. In the months to come, he'd
resurface for a few days, I'd schedule appointments for him with a good
lawyer, and we'd make more plans "to settle down together." But then I'd get
a phone call from the latest arrivals, I'd try to persuade Mike that I was "just
doing one more favor for Abner," and I'd watch him go off again in a huff.

Eventually, with the help of that lawyer, Mike wangled a "general" discharge after a minimum of brig time. For a while thereafter, toughened by his
experiences, he freelanced as one of L.A.'s pricier escorts; he posed for nude
layouts and appeared in a string of porn flicks, cast as a steel-rigger, West
Point cadet, and—most objectionable for a former Marine—an Army private.
Then it was back to Detroit. (To this day, twenty years since I last set eyes on
him, if I run into a john from that era, his first question will be, "Have you
heard from Mike?")

During the 1970s, I would sort through nearly 500 of Vin's and Abner's
guys. Out of that crowd, I would find a few who, like Mike, seemed worth
the effort of "trying for something permanent." But all those efforts would
collide with The Game and my addiction to it. Ironically, the only truly stable
relationship that did grow out of The Game involved one Fred, physically a
kind of fire-sale Mike, who became my live-in housekeeper and message-
taker after his successful discharge from the Corps. But (except for an occasional three-way) the sexual part of our friendship ended early when I realized that—unlike Mike and the other prime candidates—Fred was innately
gay and would have become openly so, even if we'd never met. (The poor
guy would end up haunting the bars and offering himself without charge to

his former johns—who, heartlessly, nicknamed him "Freddy Free-Love".) But he proved the most loyal of employees and, even today, I still miss his gift for organization and his quiet stewardship.

Servicing Old Stars and Casting New Ones

Methodical Fred had helped to keep track of the celebrity johns and their needs—a crucial task, given my growing weekend workload as MC for studio tours and host of a syndicated radio show. By 1971, the volume of incoming talent had reached eight or ten per weekend, to which were added other guys who'd decided on return engagements of their own. In the process, I had turned from L.A. Representative into the Sorcerer's Apprentice. But, even if I'd been able to summon the self-control to end my involvement, my phone number now graced the Rolodex of every military-loving celebrity in Los Angeles.

Today, it's tempting to drop hints about the identity of the names on Vin's and Abner's lists. But let me take the coward's route and tell you about three who've *died* in the interim. The most generous of them all was short, wiry, and black: a multitalented entertainer who ran with a trend-setting pack of boozers and womanizers—certainly not a public image that included his secret need to bottom for well-hung Marines. He'd rented a "safe house" for his encounters, well away from his wife. And there he'd watch through a one-way mirror as his recruiters' candidates romped naked in the pool. From that vantage point he'd choose his partners, like picking lobsters from a restaurant tank. The winning candidates, if they could perform, would get $200 a shot.

But, by contrast, many celebs on The Game proved tightfisted, some preferring to think the pleasure of their company ought to have been payment enough; some struggling to meet the cost of a celebrity lifestyle on declining income. Take the case of a middling-famous character actor, age about sixty at the time, with a sagging face discolored by drink. His thing was serial peter-puffing—ideally, four or five at one kneeling. But, at home, the man had an unsuspecting wife and two college-age kids to support on an income from his incidental role in a faltering detective series. For him, $15 a pop was the going rate, except when bartering for a truly huge exception. Gary Boyd was such an exception, and I can still see the old actor sitting in my living room, his face magenta with fury as Vin whipped Boyd out the door with the excuse that, sorry, he'd been promised, fully loaded, to a hugely successful actor known for his long-running series of courtroom dramas. Later that night

(I heard indirectly) my frustrated friend showed up drunk at a straight producer's party for married couples. Spotting a handsome young actor across the room, my friend reeled over to him and introduced himself as the man who gave "the second best blow job in Hollywood." Despite the sudden silence all around, the startled young actor just had to ask, "Who gives the best?"

"Oh, Perry Mason, without a doubt," came the loud reply.

Pre-1970, servicing the stars had been the easiest way for troops to make extra money and to dabble in a bit of Hollywood glamour. Post-1970, however, even bigger bucks became available for those willing to do their thing on-camera. For, in that year, thanks to a string of Supreme Court decisions, America's porn industry had come out of hiding. And, to fill the need for the all-male version, a dozen little gay-oriented studios had sprung up in Southern California, each vying for the hunkiest and least inhibited of young performers. In those days, before the gymnasium craze of the eighties, "hunkiest" usually meant active-duty military. Thus, Vin, Abner, and a string of their new imitators now competed for film studio finder's fees. As a result, it's no exaggeration to say that Marines and sailors constituted a majority of the young models appearing in all-male porn between 1970 and 1977. But often that fact wasn't obvious, because some of the guys had been AWOL for months when filmed—time enough for their hair to grow out. This "majority" claim is just a hunch. But, in a tall stack of cartons stored in a climate-controlled locker, I've got courtesy copies of many of those films. These show dozens of young servicemen at work— all of whom had passed through my unofficial agency during those years. If ever photographic proof is needed that "America's servicemen were sexier in the 1970s," I know where to find the evidence.[5]

Dodging Scandals, Busts, and the Mann Act

Given such photographic evidence on display in the sex shops of the day, you'll wonder why the Naval Investigative Service or the FBI didn't try to stifle military prostitution and why we civilian customers didn't feel imperiled. The second part of that puzzle was solved by Vin's lawyer and by mine. The two pointed out that the military code applied only to those in service, not to their civilian contacts. This assumed that we contacts hadn't "suborned" desertion or prostitution and that we hadn't knowingly harbored any fugitives. Those dangers—plus the great bugaboo of the 1970s, the drug bust—led me to hand each new arrival a printed card:

Welcome. We want you to have an enjoyable and profitable time during your visit. It should be a safe time, as well. So, first, if there's a problem about your military status, please wait to discuss it when your hosts can arrange for a sympathetic attorney to be present. Second, if you're carrying illicit drugs of any kind, please don't tell your hosts about them. Finally, we know that you're here of your own free will and you're not expecting payment. Even so, at the end of your visit, we'd like you to accept a donation that should more than cover your expenses.

Some of my fellow military mavens called the card "dishonest"; I preferred to think of it as "a flower arrangement of the truth." The attorney really existed, for instance; he'd willingly take his fee in trade, and he had good contacts in the judge advocate's unit. But his "sympathy" varied inversely with the amount of a would-be client's body hair. ("A glabrous Marine? I'll be there faster than you can say 'habeas corpus.'") In any case, the card would have proved useless in a violation of the Mann Act (forbidding the crossing of state lines "for immoral purposes"). True, I'd heard reports of thousand-buck weekends in Chicago, during which servicemen sent from California would make it with a long list of Midwestern johns, including local magnates and a U.S. senator. But I'd shied away from the whole deal. (The closest I came was to shelter a heart-stopper of an ex-paratrooper whose client list included powerful johns all across the country, such as one Roy Cohn, who used to fly the para to the East Coast to serve as a party favor on yachting weekends. But the young man had been bounced out of the service for mental problems, and he and I soon parted company.)

Despite precautions, however, Hollywood's all-male porn industry would eventually suffer a lulu of a scandal. This involved "the Brentwood Studio," headed by a gifted cameraman who roomed with Vin during much of the 1970s, living in the shadow of El Toro Marine Air Station. In 1976, casting one too many little film productions with Marines, that cameraman featured a pair of them going at it in a Louis XVI bedroom. A still from this scene soon showed up on the front cover of one of the studio's magazines. Unfortunately, the lone adult bookstore in Oceanside put that magazine on display. Reportedly, an off-duty sergeant caught sight of it and bellowed, "Those cocksuckers are in my unit!"

Within days, newspapers and newscasts had broken the story. And the Navy's investigators—by offering each suspect a lighter punishment if he'd name others on The Game—had a list of Marine names that was growing geometrically like a pyramid scheme. Luckily for the pimps and their johns, the Marine Corps' commandant intervened, "congratulated" the NIS for its zeal, announced that his own staff would now take over the investigation . . . then quietly ordered his staff to seal the records and end the whole matter. ("We don't need this image of the Corps competing with our recruitment ads," he's rumored to have said.) In the wake of that scandal, Brentwood ceased operations, Vin's on-base ringers stopped returning his calls, and many among the film colony's military mavens decided to make do with civilian hustlers in the future.

Sadly, I have very little first hand knowledge of today's Southern California military scene. For, in 1980, unable to moderate my military compulsion and finding that I was having to work three jobs to continue funding The Game, I'd reached the edge of a breakdown. Three years before, at age forty, I'd received a wake-up call that my hothouse glamour had begun to wilt. A long-running TV series, *The Dating Game*, had used me as an "eligible bachelor" on a couple of episodes: one in 1968, one in 1972. When, in 1977, I answered another of the show's invitations, I got eliminated by the staff at the screening stage. With the right makeup and lighting, I could still cut it as a TV pundit or an arena MC. But the buzzards were circling, in the form of younger men with better cheekbones, firmer necklines, and wider smiles. And, alas!, nobody had called me "skinny" in years. A change of scene clearly seemed in order.

Early in 1980, rescue came in the form of an offer from an oil sheikhdom to direct public relations for that country's airports. I grabbed it and (except for an occasional embassy guard) I subsisted throughout that decade on memories, cold showers, and a diet rich in saltpeter. In fact, the timing of that offer proved doubly lucky. For America's blazing sexual revolution—which had caught fire coincidentally just when I had, and which had really begun to rage in 1968, when I had—was about to be smothered by a mysterious new disease.

Stopping the Music

I can't leave the subject of "the end of the sexual revolution" without a final military anecdote. Late in 1979, a portly young producer, famous for a hit rock musical and a near-miss sequel, put out the word that he needed all available Marine beauties for a new mainstream film musical that would star an Olympic decathlete and a famous disco group. Having soon exhausted the usual sources for weekend recruitment, early in 1980 that producer applied directly to the Pentagon, with the incredible result that a cherry-picked platoon of Marines got assigned to the man's production. (Consider the mentality of 1979: by now, the Vietnam War was over and—here at the end of the Bisexual Seventies—the Secretary of the Navy had toyed with the idea of using the Village People's campy "In the Navy" as the soundtrack for a recruiting commercial.)

To the Pentagon's dismay, the production ran far beyond its target deadline. In the meanwhile, comely Marines had vanished from the streets of Hollywood. And calls to Vin and Abner got the same answer: "Sorry; every good-looking guy we can find is on loan to the film production." When finally the musical did get finished, its release coincided with the death of disco; the movie lost a bundle. As for the Marines, all those months at the studio (and at the producer's house) yielded less than two minutes of edited film. You'll see the troops romping in the "YMCA" segment, provided you don't blink.

Closing the Circle

To regret my decade of military mania would be to regret the most vital, indelible moments of my life. I had been drawn to my psychic opposites. In their company I'd found psychic "wholeness."

The conduit from San Diego and Oceanside to Los Angeles closed down in the early eighties. But today, in other liberty towns around the country, the campaign of outreach goes on, manned by wiser and less compulsive souls than I. Meanwhile, a few timid men—with needs similar to mine of thirty years ago—stand hesitantly to one side, wondering if they dare to make the first move. To them I say, reach out, brother. Your other half is out there, and he's waiting.

Wormy:
Hell Bent for Leathernecks

In ten years of hanging around barracks, I have more than once been confronted with a link between military homoeroticism and heavy metal. Last fall, I got a chance to talk with someone from the other side of the equation. The subject of this interview is a famous English "metal god." Though he has since come out on MTV, in keeping with the spirit of my books on military men he asked that he be identified here by a pseudonym.

Walking into a hotel lobby in San Diego's gay Hillcrest district I came face-to-face with a huge gorgeous red-headed Marine and a tiny gorgeous blond boy. A man in his forties with a British midlands accent stood with his back to me registering for a room. This, I decided, must be "Wormy," the front man of one of the biggest metal bands of the past twenty years. Turning around, he recognized me, and motioned to follow him and the boys upstairs.

In his room, the boys stripped off most of their clothes and rolled around on the two beds, then rolled around with each other on the same bed. Wormy inspected the furnishings and lectured his young companions. He turned to me and rolled his eyes: "Everyone has ailments. This one's on pills. And he's not supposed to drink."

Blond Boy flashed me a naughty grin. "Where's the bar?"

"And this one's suffering from sleep dep-ri-va-tion."

"I only got two hours last night," Marine Boy confessed with a sheepish grin.

"And your point would be?" Wormy demanded. "I get my sleep in before I come to San Diego." He made a dismissive gesture. "Two hours a night and I'm good to go."

When Wormy was ready to be interviewed, Marine Boy and Blond Boy took off cruising, replaced by Wormy's newest love interest, Daniel. Wormy insisted that the interview would not be unduly influenced by the presence of this blond, sunburnt, ultrawholesome, nineteen-year-old Mormon Marine, who sat with us radiating an impossible, just barely corrupted, beatific smile.

Mormon Boy sported a Curious George T-shirt, the one that depicts the cartoon monkey passed out beside a bottle of ether. Admiring him, I couldn't help but think of the legendary "ether bunny" (say it out loud), a Camp Pendleton Navy hospital corpsman said to have anesthetized Marines and raped them.

Zeeland: When we spoke on the phone you told me that you have observed an affinity between military men and your music.

Wormy: Absolutely. I think that the simplest reference is the tone and the nature of metal music, and the aggressive, strong masculine qualities that it kind of portrays. There's a lot of posturing, a lot of performance involved. I think the fact that I came out looking like I did, dressed like I did, which was very much in a kind of uniform way, particularly the leather S&M kind of appearance, coming out in a Harley Davidson—we just looked very tough, very potent, very, very sexual. And I think all of those qualities kind of intermingle in a military kind of way. At least that's my personal take on it as a gay man.

Z: Of course most of the guys that were coming to see you didn't at the time and still don't identify as gay. But there is this sexual charge that you alluded to.

W: Yeah. It's no different from a football team. It's men being men. I mean, you look into a mosh pit, and it's all these men rolling around on top of each other. And they don't think nothing of that. But mention sex and it's, "Back off. I'm not a fag. I'm not a cocksucker." I think that—without going really deep—it's got all the tribal characteristics, of like caveman quality. In its primitive form it's stripping away all of the cultural interferences. It's men being one step away from literally having a physical relationship with each other.

Z: I know that bands like yours were referred to, disparagingly, as "cock rock."

W: [Laughs.]

Z: I always found the term kind of exciting.

W: Well, it is cock rock. It still is cock rock. I mean, you look at it in any way, and it's inescapable.

Z: Is the sexual charge an important part of your own pleasure in performing?

W: Oh, totally. I get a huge sexual kick when I walk out on any stage. I'm a whore when I'm on stage. I mean, I'm looking at everything. I'm feasting on the menu. And I think no more differently from any other performer. I'm sure Liza Minnelli does the same thing.

Z: Have you ever talked with other metal singers about the sexual charge rippling through your predominately male audience?

W: No. I've never really been able to sit down and talk with some of the people I'd like to talk with and have that discussion. Because they just got really uncomfortable.

Z: Since long before it was as fashionable as it is now, Marines have been getting tattoos of violent images very much like the covers of heavy metal albums.

W: It's like being in a gang. You look at somebody walking down the street, and you know that that person is in the same kind of mental territory as yourself. It's just a way of showing the gang colors. It's interesting, the relationship between tattoos and rock and roll and sex. To go through the ritual pain of tattoos—for some people it's like walking through fire. I mean, when you see somebody with a tattoo, everybody says, "Did it hurt?" Well of course it hurt. And it's showing that you're a tough man. You can ride the pain out, man. And again, that's just another way of expressing your masculinity, through pain. That's a common feature with a lot of military personnel. Some of them want to go into battle. They want to get into a physical confrontation, whether it's a fist fight, or a mosh pit.

Z: The pain of getting a tattoo makes some people come.

W: Come? Oh yeah. I was reading an interesting book a few months ago about what men do when they've had a tattoo, and a large percentage go home and masturbate.[1] I never did. I used to go home and have a cup of tea. I find tattooing just very relaxing. My endorphins start pumping and I fall asleep. It's like a meditation for me.

Z: I asked you what has drawn military guys to your music. What attracts you to military men?

W: I think it's really an extension of all the things I personify with my work. It's wanting to be in the company of real strong, tough, masculine men. And the Marine Corps for me—See, for me it's not all sex. It's a lot of other things, like tradition, and the mind-set of being involved in an organization that requires some discipline, some intelligent comprehension of what it means to be a particular kind of a person, to do a specific kind of a job. It's all about what military service is capable of doing in terms of maintaining democracy and a free world. But I didn't know that until later on. Because in my early teens, when I first saw dress blues and stuff, it was a combination of "God, that looks so great" plus "This is turning me on. Why do I feel this way?" I mean, I was a gay man, obviously. But it was, "What's this all about?" And so I just began to look more at the reason why I was feeling that way. And slowly began to understand and appreciate why I was drawn to that particular area.

Z: Do you have any memory of this first time you were turned on?

W: Oh yeah. I was at my local youth club. And I was about thirteen. I was in the bathroom. There was a magazine left there. Just a small-size black and white magazine full of physique pictures from the fifties. It just blew my mind. First of all, I didn't know why I was feeling this way. It was the first time I'd ever seen that kind of a book. I picked it up and stuffed it down my pants. 'Cause you always stuff things down your pants. You don't put it in your pocket. Why do you do that? I suppose it's the psychological sexual connection. But I took it home, and I was just blown away by the pictures of these men. And there were like three or four pictures of guys that were in military uniforms. They weren't naked, it was all touched up. But that is my first real memory of that connection. And of course that developed as the years went by.

Z: My friend Mark Simpson wrote a piece on Morrissey and how he's gradually adopted a somewhat harder sound. Mark sees it as a way of getting the rough boys to come and see him. I wondered if you ever thought of your music in the same way. Or of your job. It is an especially cool way of surrounding yourself with thousands of men.

W: You mean that I may have chosen to do this kind of work to draw that kind of thing to me? Well, no, because the first time I ever walked on a stage, I was six or seven years old. So there was no real thought to anything sexual at that age. I was just drawn to that magical feeling that you get when you stand on the stage in front of people and they look at you. But as I progressed more through my life and music became more important, I saw, "Oh, this is a nice little side benefit." You know, all the other areas. That's when I began to dwell on it a little bit more. And particularly in my days writing with the band, a lot of my lyrics are really blatant. I'd think of a topic or idea and surround it with language that in my mind was very forward, and yet for most people—and I don't mean this in an offensive way, but for the straight community it would go [makes sound effect] right over their heads. It was just my way of having fun. There are numerous lyrical pieces that I've written over the years that contain that kind of double meaning. A lot.

Z: Can you give me one example?

W: "Jawbreaker." "Jawbreaker" is about cocksucking. Let me think what some of the words are. Things like "waiting to recoil," and—oh God. Let me think. Anyway, it was all to do with a dick. An erect dick. It was just so blatantly obvious to me, or for another gay man. He's talking about— What's a "jawbreaker"? It's a big dick. For a straight man, it's "Oh, man, are you gonna smash me in the face and break my jaw?" [Laughs.]

Z: When I was eleven or twelve, I told my parents that I wanted to have a leather jacket. My mother said that I couldn't. There were two kinds of people that wore leather, she told me. One was bikers. She didn't say what the other was.

W: [Laughs.] So she left you with a big question mark. Who was the other type?

Z: Yeah. Well, I already had an idea of what she meant, and I understood that I wasn't supposed to talk about it. You were a pioneer in adopting the studded leather look for your onstage persona, but there are those anteced-ents: the gay connection and the biker connection. What was your inspira-tion for doing that?

W: There was a motorcycle involved in the show. It was a case of wanting to wear something that looked cool with the motorcycle. So I started to wear that kind of outfit. Then it just exploded. I remember going to a shop in London called Mister S. It was the leading S&M shop. They fitted me out with everything. And then I began to design all the stuff that I wore. I just went over the top. My feeling with theater and presentation, particu-larly when you're walking out in front of a lot of people, is they've got to see you. So you wear too much. You just put too much stuff on. And so I did, you know. And I think it was that extreme appearance that started to attract the attention, and the feeling that "This not only feels good," riding out onstage with a motorcycle, but it also feels good . . . with everything else that I'm doing. It was really a moment that I think identified that kind of music with a specific look. Because up until then it didn't have one. I felt kind of good that I originated that.

Z: You were much imitated. But I saw from the video I bought that before the leather, you went onstage wearing these wild chiffon creations.

W: [Covers his face.]

Z: I was struck by the contrast between the chiffon and the leather, the soft and the hard.

W: Well that—What you were looking at preceded this whole defining moment. My sister would let me go through her closet and pull things out. "Can I borrow this?" That kind of haunts me now. But at that point none of us really knew what we were doing and what we were about. So it was like, well, let's see what we got. And I wore everything.

Z: I assume that that was before there were rumors about your sexuality.

W: Isn't that strange? I mean, if anybody was going to start talking, it would have been [during] the chiffon years. But they didn't. Soon as I stuck all this tough stuff on, they go, "Oh, he's a fag." You know? Go figure. I think it's just that as you become more well known, and you become part of the public arena, people start looking, and people that didn't know of you do start to look at you, and then the gay audience out there particularly starts to go, "Why is he dressing like some S&M leatherfag?" That's when the rumors and the speculation and the innuendo started to surface.

Z: Have you had any experiences where you've connected with people who have adopted your image?

W: Well, only in the later years. I've met people that have seen me at shows. I was talking to somebody just recently. They told me that they came to see the performance, and they were maybe like thirteen or fourteen, and they said that they saw me and they started to get these feelings, and they didn't know why they felt this way. They were feeling a sexual charge or whatever. There are numerous moments like that I'm sure in rock and roll, where, because of the importance and relevance of music at that specific stage, that you look and something happens to you. With that one individual, it was like a sexually defining moment. But I was never aware, really, that that was going on. And I'm still not aware that it goes on. If I'm out on the street and I see a nice-looking man looking at me, my first reaction is, they're not looking at me because it's who I am, and that I've got a record or they've seen me on TV, it's because they think I'm okay, you know?

Z: I think it would make it hard for you to have anonymous sex.

W: Yeah.

Z: My work is in part about the instability of boundaries between gay and straight in the military. When men are off by themselves, or if there's a certain excuse or understanding in place, then they don't see male-male sex as being necessarily "gay." And I can imagine that probably there are men that would feel able to have sex with you, and not think of it as gay, because you being a "metal god" puts everything into a whole different category.

W: That's true. There's been at least one instance when it's been with a particular person that would never conceive of having a physical relationship with another man. I'm sure that there's a lot of potentially 100 percent straight men that look at another male performer, or a sports personality or a film star, and if the opportunity was right and they felt comfortable, they would do something like that. They would have that physical moment. But there's only that one incident that I can recall. Where it was afterwards, "This is the only time that I've ever had a sexual encounter with another man, and it's because of who you are and how you made me feel."

Z: When you found the physique magazine—was that about the time when you were first becoming aware of your sexuality?

W: My teen years, yeah. I think for most boys it is. That for me was when I started to get crushes and things. There was one boy that I had a major crush on, who was like this stocky little bodybuilder. He was really mature for his age, physically. We were both fifteen, and he was hot. He was like this Italian stud. I think he's married and got about twelve kids now. But me and him was doing it after school every day. We got caught in the library annex. Because I was like the chief librarian for awhile. I had the key to an annex, part of the school property that I thought was quiet. We were doing it on the table. Then the next day we got called to the office of my English literature teacher. And he gave us six whacks with the cane. I mean, that was the first time I'd been in trouble for as long as I could remember at school. But it was like, "I'm going to give you six of the best." I'm going, "Why?" "You know why." And he never told me, but I knew why, because he supervised the library, and he must have been peeping over the window while we were doing it.

Z: How old were you when you first had sex?

W: I guess it would have been like around ten or eleven, with this other boy's brother, who was teaching us how to jack off. That was the first time. But we didn't think about it being gay. It was like, "This is what you can do, and this is how it can make you feel." It was, oh my God, you know. Then you can't keep your hands off it. I still can't keep my hands off it. [Touches Daniel.]

Z: Have you ever had sex with women?

W: Yeah. And I could still do it now, but I don't particularly want to do it. No reason to do it.

Z: Have you had longer relationships with both men and women?

W: Men, exclusively. And I've only really had, in my life, four relationships with men. Maybe five. [Nudges Daniel again.]

Z: You said that you remembered the first time you had a sexual encounter with a Marine. It happened in Pittsburgh.

W: I love Pittsburgh. It kind of reminds me of back home in Birmingham. Because it's a gritty steel town; tough, working-class, salt-of-the-earth people, very unpretentious, very take-me-as-I-am. We were at the Hilton. We'd done a big sell-out show across the street at the Enormodome. We're all in the bar afterwards. And this Marine just kind of invited himself to sit with us. He hadn't been to the show. I think he knew who we were. Like a lot of military people do, he'd rented a room for the weekend. He'd been with his girlfriend. They'd had dinner in the room, and then done the business and for some unknown reason she had left. So we were just sitting there. He was a very good-looking, strong, masculine guy. We just bullshitted about this, that, and the other. And eventually everybody left. It was just me and him. And in the hotel there was a convention of Roman Catholic priests. Suddenly he goes, "A couple of them bought me a drink." I said, "Oh really?" He said, "Yeah. But all they kept doing was staring at my crotch." "Oh really?" He said, "Yeah. Then I went to the bathroom and I kept lookin' at my dick. Anyway," he said, "I'm going to bed now and I'm in room" so-and-so. And left! What does he mean? I suppose I was a little drunk. It was in my drinking days. So I went back to the room, and I'm thinking: Roman Catholic priest . . . looking at my crotch . . . looking at my dick . . . room so-and-so. I'll go and knock on the door. I knock on the door, and he's like straightaway, "Oh, come on in." As soon as I closed the door he was on my bones as quick as a fly on shit. And I was like, "Just do whatever you want to do." We did it for hours and hours and hours. It was like nonstop. Then the next morning he left. Actually, I bumped into him in the lobby and he gave me his address. And I wrote him a couple of times, but he never wrote back. He'd done it all day and all weekend with his girl, but he just wanted to do it with a man. That was my first-ever Marine encounter and that was 1980.

Z: You fulfilled the magazine image you'd seen when you were a kid.

W: It was just unbelievable. It's still a really strong memory.

Z: Did you find that you began looking more at military men?

W: Yeah, I think I did. I used to get the map out. I'd be in the tour bus, and I'd get my Rand McNally out and say, "Is there an Air Force base nearby? Is there a Marine Corps base nearby?"

Z: How have you met military guys?

W: I've met some at shows. I've met some at rock and roll bars. [Pause.] I've met some on-line. [Exchanges smile with Daniel.] Thank God for AOL.

Z: Have any of your long-term relationships been with military men?

W: One was with a guy who was [Army] Special Forces, who is no longer with us because he committed suicide. That was a really heavy trip. He was a cocaine freak. He couldn't get off it. He'd been out of the military service for a while. We had some really unpleasant moments. We'd beat the living crap out of each other. Because I was dabbling with cocaine at the same time. And any form of hard drug is just a dead end to destruction. We had a fight one day, and I left the apartment. He had a gun tucked into his belt. He said, "I love you very much. Good-bye." And that was it. I went off into a taxi. He blew his brains out. You never stop grieving when something like that happens to you. It always comes back and slaps you in the back of the neck.

Z: It must have been especially hard, the fact that it was something you had to keep quiet.

W: Oh, we brushed that well under the carpet. We kept that away from the press.

Z: How long were you with him?

W: Three or four years.

Z: How did you meet?

W: Met me at the Four Seasons. We were playing that "We Are the World" thing. It was just one of those things when you meet somebody and you just like flip out. That's only really happened once in my life, in that respect. Although recently I'm feeling. . . .

Z: A lot of the men that I'm interviewing, they seem to share a sense of wanting camaraderie.

W: That's true.

Z: They believe they see it among Marines, and they haven't found it in other areas of life.

W: That's very true. Yeah. I just love to be around these kinds of people. When you go into the Marine Corps, they strip you down bare naked and rebuild you. They build you into a different man. You go in one way and you come out the other way. And that stays with you all your life. In all honesty, if there is such a thing as reincarnation, that's what I want to come back as. I want to be a "boot."

The next day, I met up with Wormy and the boys at the Hillcrest Starbucks. I'd forgotten to ask him to autograph some CDs for a military ex-boyfriend. I asked Marine Boy if he'd been a fan before he met Wormy.

"No," he said, "but my mom was. She was a headbanger."

As I rode off, I watched as the gym-toned metal daddy, a lightning bolt tattooed on his shaved scalp, emerged from the coffee shop and marched up the street underneath the pink Hillcrest neon sign, three beautiful young men following after him like baby ducks.

Gayle:
Double Penetration

I get a lot of mail. I didn't always. After the publication of my first book, months went by before I received even a single letter. Suspicious that my publishing house might not be properly routing my mail, I asked my San Francisco friend Bart to test them. His whimsical bogus fan letter was forwarded to me within a week. Scrawled in purple crayon, it read: "I have stabilized my belief thru your book that the Clinton Administration is using its very real power to sterilize our sex drives. We cannot function as sex machines within Clinton's killing machine. Sex drive = power drive = kill drive. Men loving men is potency. I WILL NOT BE STERILIZED!" The envelope had been opened. In subsequent months, a few genuine letters began to trickle in, all likewise opened. When I asked about this, I was told that it was standard procedure to screen fan mail—to protect authors from psychopaths.

Eventually, I started receiving more mail than my publishing house could screen. Then, in 1997, with the launch of my Web site, I was flooded with more correspondence than I could answer. A few of the messages I received were even wackier than Bart's hoax. But most were heartfelt and thought-provoking. Once in a while they were astonishing. Gayle e-mailed me:

> Gay men aren't the only military groupies around. Lots of us women out there too, and I've got a particularly bad case. Nothing I love better than slipping a strapped-on cock up a Marine's butt, especially if he's got some self-awareness and understands why he likes it.

Any skepticism I might have had about the authenticity of her boast evaporated after I wrote her back and she responded with essays on penetrating Marines, transcripts of her on-line dialogues with them, and actual photos.

Gayle and I met up for this conversation under the pier in Oceanside, California on a springtime Saturday night. The cute, intense, thirty-two-year-old ex-Catholic chain smoker talks in a tough East Coast accent.

Zeeland: Can you elaborate on what you meant by Marines' "self-awareness" about why they want you to dominate them?

Gayle: Well, first of all, if you look at sheer numbers—I've done Matthew up the ass, I've done Scott up the ass. I haven't done Greg up the ass. Just a finger. But I got him to accept that. The boy I did last week—what was his name? John. No, Jim. I did him up the ass. Let's see, the only one I haven't done was Brad, and he's in the Army. And Dan, who's in the Navy. And the Air Force guy I didn't do up the ass either. But all the Marines I have.

Z: But is that because the Marines wanted you to do that, or is it because you want to do that to Marines?

G: Matthew, that was a condition of him meeting me in the first place. When I first suggested that we get together, he asked me if I had any dildos. I said, "Yeah, I've got dildos. Who are they for, you or me?" He said, "Well, I want you to use them on me. Is that okay?" I said, "That's no problem at all. I'd be delighted." [Laughs.]

He came over at two or three in the morning to see me. In cammies, because I told him to. He comes in. I give him a beer. We talk for like two minutes and then I led him into the bedroom. We start kissing. I like guys who like to kiss a lot. And we probably kissed for a half hour, forty-five minutes before we did anything else. We both took my clothes off, and he went down on me for a long time. I actually had to finally push him off me because it was getting too intense. And then I said, "Do you still want me to fuck you up the ass with a dildo?" He said yes, so I got out the various sizes that I had. I had this like enormous butt-plug, and I had these other smaller ones. I had a jelly one; it's probably about an inch thick, I guess, and maybe five or six inches long. It's one of those softer ones; they're not that great. They cost like ten bucks or something. So I actually tried to do that with the strap-on, with my harness. And that fuckin' cheesy dildo, it just wasn't working. I was trying to push it into him and it was like slippin' off me and everything. So finally I just took the fuckin' harness off and I lay on top of him and I had my hand against his ass with the dildo, fucking him.

The whole time we were having sex, unless I asked him a question, he was *completely* silent. He never said a word. Not so much as a groan or a grunt. No sighs. *Nothing* at all. I was like whispering in his ear, "How does that feel?" He would respond to that, but very short. And sort of mimicking back what I said. "Does that feel good?" "Yes that feels good." "Does that feel really good?" "Yes that feels really good." So I fucked him for awhile, and it was pretty easy. He was really not stressed, not tight at all.

Z: Was he moving around and responding?

G: Just a little bit. But mostly very passive, letting me do all the work.

Z: Did you feel that this was his first time?

G: Definitely I felt like it was his first time with another person. But when we first started chatting, he tried to make it sound like it was just this idea he had. Obviously that's not the case. He'd been thinking about it for a long time. And in later conversations he admitted that he had been doing it with hair brushes. [Laughs.] So after I did this for awhile, I pulled it out and rolled him over and put a condom on him and got on his dick. And even then he was really very passive. His body would respond, but there was still no indication—We fucked for awhile, and I was gonna switch positions. I was gonna suggest that he get on top of me. I got off of him, and I noticed that he'd come.

Z: Without any indication—

G: Without *any* indication whatsoever! I had *no* idea that he had come. I said, "Oh! Am I hurting you?" You know, to keep fucking him after he's come—I mean, it can be very sensitive. I sort of joked about it. "You're going to have to tell me in the future." And he laughed.

After the sex was over he was very talkative. About Marine stuff, and just different things. We came out into the living room. He was like fooling around with my dog. Just cute, shoot-the-shit type stuff. But it was very comfortable.

I guess this leads to the next Marine! [Laughs.] Because there was another Marine the very next day. Who, now that I think about it, is totally forgettable. I did not fuck him up the ass. The second Marine was another one that I met on-line.

Z: Which is in fact how you've met all these guys.

G: Yes. Matthew's the first guy I've ever met that didn't [first e-mail me] a photo. Usually I'm insistent that they have to have a photo for me. I want to know what they look like, 'cause guys' opinion of their own looks is often far different from a woman's opinion of their looks. Guys always think they're better looking than they are. Matthew's description to me was, he's twenty-seven years old, he's about six two, maybe six three. Sort of a slim build. I'd say he probably weighs no more than a hundred and sixty or so. He doesn't have bones stickin' out on him or anything, but he's very slender. I said, "How about your face?" He's got brown hair and brown eyes. "Would you say you're attractive?" He's like, "I guess I'm okay." I'm thinking, "Oh well, fuck it. He's right nearby. If he comes over and I don't like the way he looks, I'll think of some way out of it." [Laughs.] So he comes over, and he's really very attractive. You've seen his photo. He's very good-looking.

Z: I thought so.

G: But in an unconventional way, I think. He's got great hands. I really like men's hands. He's got like long fingers, some vascularity. I'm really into vascularity on men's hands. And he's got a great cock. It's not very, very long, but it is fat. Which I prefer. I find if it's too long it slams into my ovaries and it's not pleasant.

Z: In reading the transcripts you sent me, I noticed that you ask all these guys why they want to be dominated, and their typical response is, "I don't know. I never thought about it."

G: But Matthew knows why he likes it. You've gotten that from the conversations with him, haven't you?

Z: Well, you tell me why he likes it.

G: Because it makes him feel very passive and submissive. What did he say? It makes him feel "like the most vulnerable person alive." I used to actually joke that in fact he's the perfect Marine, because he takes orders. It's like—I don't know. I mean, it seems sexual to me, this sort of Marine-ness, and his draw to it—his whole desire, and his whole approach to life seems to me to be a desire to serve. That he's naturally submissive. Of all the Marines I've met, Matthew best epitomizes what I think a Marine should be. Which is someone who wants to protect and serve. And he has a lot of honor and integrity. He joined the Marine Corps late. He's twenty-seven now, he's only been a Marine for about two years. And he had been going to veterinary school. The way he told it to me was that he just saw some stuff, working as a vet tech, that he decided he couldn't do. So he decided to join the Marine Corps.

Z: And become a professional killer.

G: And become a professional killer! Which is something we've talked about as well. He said to me one time, "I guess it's sort of sad that once I was studying to protect animals' lives, and now I'm being trained to kill people." If you ask him straight up if it bothers him, he says it doesn't. But I think about—Have you seen the movie *Full Metal Jacket*? I just watched it for the first time. The Matthew Modine character—who actually reminds me a lot of Matthew, even looks-wise—on his helmet it says "Born to Kill" and he's wearing a little peace emblem on his jacket. And the colonel comes up to him and says, "You write 'Born to Kill' on your helmet and you wear a peace button. What's that supposed to be, some kind of sick joke?" And his response is, "I think I was trying to suggest something about the duality of man, sir." And I thought to myself, the moment I heard him say that, "It sounds like a Matthew thing." I can see Matthew thinking that. I mean, he writes poetry. He loves animals. And he's very committed to a sense of honor. That's like the most important thing to him. So the night we met, we were talking about why he joined. 'Cause I always ask them why they join. And why the Marine Corps in particular over another branch. And he said, "Well, I investigated them all, and it was the last chivalrous part of the armed services." It meant a lot to me at the time because I had done this whole course in English literature, on the knight in literature. And one of the things we studied—and I think this may actually have led to my fascination with these types of guys—we studied the soldier poets of World War I.

Matthew's never let me read any of his poetry, but I know he writes it.
Z: But how does *honor* tie in to your desire to fuck them? I mean, do you want to *dis*-honor them?
G: Dishonoring them is definitely part of the turn-on. Or maybe not so much dishonoring them as much as unwinding them. These guys tend to be tightly wrapped and very controlled and I enjoy seeing them outside of that state. I have a gift, I think, for making them feel comfortable, like I am the one woman they can tell all their dirty secrets to, things which to me aren't even slightly shocking or outrageous but apparently are to the sorts of girls they date and take home to Mom.
Z: What do you mean by "unwinding?"
G: Look at their training. Their training is to make them very hard. They have to be the strong person all the time in their work. Yet in some sense what they do is submissive. Because they're taking orders, and they are doing things for the good of the group. One of the things they try to completely remove from them at boot camp is the idea that they're functioning as an individual. Individualism in American culture is a very dominant sort of thing. It's "I am going to do what I want to do and fuck everyone else." I have a lot of respect for people who buck that. What I've noticed about these guys is, some of them, they bitch about the Marine Corps, and you can tell they only joined so they can get their fucking college education at the taxpayers' expense, and they really hate it. But at the same time, they have totally taken into them-selves that group, protect-your-buddies thing, and I have a lot of respect for that, and it means a lot to me.
Z: But—
G: But as far as unwinding them sexually, the environment they're in leads to repressed sexuality. And I like to un-repress them. [Laughs.] People who are repressed—their fantasies start moving off into different directions from the

norm. Instead of just thinking about making love to someone, they think about stuff that they might consider kinky.

Z: I noted from the dialogues that you sent me that the guys all said that they would not want to be fucked by a man. But at the same time, you were writing things like, "I want to fuck you with my hard cock." That was the exact phrase that you used.

G: Yeah. And Matthew refers to it as my "cock," too. And he and Scott both know that I have this thing about homosexual sex, that I'm sort of into it and attracted by it and it turns me on. So they both fuck with me. Scott was supposed to go on to officer's school. He was going to do jump school first. He ended up not going because of his knees. I asked him, "Why are your knees fucked up?" He was like, "Too many blow jobs." He likes to fuck with me!

Z: Scott's the witty and glib one. He says stuff like that in a way where it's not tempting to read much in it.

G: No. But Matthew, on the other hand, *I* think that if we had continued going on the way we had been going on, if I had wanted him to suck a cock, he would have done it. Just because he was very submissive to me, and had a desire to do what *I* wanted him to do. That's a very strong desire in him to please me, or whatever woman he is with. It might have taken me a while to get him to that point, but I think eventually he would have done it. But he likes to fuck with me on this issue too. We were talking the other day, and—Matthew knows about every guy I've slept with. I tell him and he seems to get enjoyment out of it. "Did you fuck this Marine up the ass?" He gets pleasure out of hearing about that. So I've sort of been talking to him about Scott, 'cause I've been seeing lots of Scott lately as a friend. And I had always told Matthew that I really wanted to get together with him and another Marine. This is my big fantasy.

Z: [Quoting from e-mail:] "Nothing would bring me *more pleasure in life* . . ."

G: [Raucous, sustained laughter.]

Z: ". . . than having Matthew and Scott in bed with me at the same time. Here's the picture in my head. Matthew and Scott half-dressed in cammies and lying near me kissing each other sweetly and deeply. If I died a moment later, I'd die happy."

G: [Laughing, gasping for breath:] I could *die* after that! It's *true.* Because this is a big fantasy with me. It's been a big fantasy since even before I got married. My husband was bisexual, and we always figured we would find another guy for the two of us to have sex with. But the problem always was that we have completely different tastes in men. We had sex once with a girlfriend of mine. And that was very amusing. It was *dismal.* It was dismally bad! But afterwards we just bonded, me and him. We were just laughing and joking about it, and making fun of her. Because we're both evil. We're really bad. We make fun of people all the time, we have *despicable* personalities. But that was my big disappointment; our marriage ended and this never happened. And then I guess once I got onto this whole military fascination, that just seemed to me the ideal.

Z: What specifically would you like Matthew and Scott to do?

G: I want to see them kiss. That's a big thing for me. It's funny, because I've had conversations with Scott where we've talked about this in a BDSM [bondage, domination, sadism, and masochism] context. He's a dom. But we were talking about him switching and being submissive and he said that he thinks he could be roughly treated by a man, but he couldn't kiss one.

Z: The classic Marine answer. "Fuck me, suck me, but don't kiss me, I'm straight."

G: Yeah. But that's a big turn-on to me. When I was living back East—I'm very good friends with this other woman who's a fag hag just like me. We would hang out at the leather bars with this group of guys. And they knew I was into it, so they would kiss in front of me. I always got off on that. But I never actually had the nerve to ask any of them if they would be willing to have sex and let me watch. They probably would have. But maybe I thought that I wouldn't enjoy it as much if I wasn't involved. Because they were just gay, not bi. But so I've transferred this whole thing now onto these military guys, and these Marines in particular. And it just turns me on to think that these hard-bodied gorgeous men would get it on together.

It's why I'm attracted to the military thing in the first place, is that it's a male society. I mean, yeah, there's women in it, but there are too few women to make any difference, *especially* in the Marine Corps. I was talking to this one Marine in Hawaii who said that he hardly ever sees females in the Marines because they're not in the infantry. So for these infantry guys, it's just them and the guys, and the hazing rituals, and just all that stuff, guys being around each other, and with each other all the time—I think about that in a sexual manner. So I had said to Matthew, "Would you get together with me and Scott if I could arrange it?" And he said yes he would, because he wants to make me happy, and not because he would get off on it. But at the time he made it clear that he wouldn't sexually interact with him. We were sort of working out what was gonna happen, because of the fact that he's submissive, and Scott's dominant. So the other day when we were talking about Scott, I said, "I always wanted to get together with you two." And he says—because he always remembers this shit I tell him about people—"He's a dom. He'd want to beat me." I said, "No, no. He's straight, so he wouldn't be interested in anything with you." And he goes, "Oh darn." Then he goes, "LOL [laughing out loud]. I meant 'Oh good.'" Shit like that. Just *fucking* with me! [Laughs.] But I think he would do it, given the right sort of encouragement.

Z: You told me that you are no longer interested in men from the other service branches, only Marines.

G: Well, it actually goes further than that. Because I'm also not interested in Marines who are not infantry or in some sort of combat role. Like the guy I've been seeing recently, the lieutenant. He's in artillery. And that's fine. But you know, I used to talk with this guy who's like an air traffic controller. They're not interesting. It's like a civilian job! So why not just fuckin' date a civilian? And their training's different; I think that's probably what it comes down to. The Air Force—I don't know, it's possible that I didn't give the other branches a chance. The guy I went out with in the Army, Brad, he was an Airborne Ranger. I probably would go out with Army again, but here I am in California. Why bother lookin' for an Army guy when there are plenty of Marines available? Plus it also seems to me that, in the Marine Corps, they obviously take looks into account when they recruit these guys. I find them better looking. In addition to being in better shape, and having harder bodies.

Z: Although you did say that a Navy SEAL would be okay as well.

G: But I haven't had one yet, though.

Z: In one of your first messages you wrote me that, "I've always been attracted to men in uniform." How far back does this go for you?

G: I was thinking about this recently. I think I finally found the trigger. My first couple years in college my girlfriends and I used to hang out in this bar, which was pretty close to the recruitment center. So you'd see military guys in there occasionally, usually out of uniform. One day we were in there and there's this guy that I'd noticed, who was a Marine. Good-looking guy, Irish face, which I have a big attraction to. Lots of guys I go out with are Irish. Red hair. Blue eyes. And I had noticed him lots. Back then I was not very aggressive sexually at all. But one day he came in there wearing dress blues. It was a late Friday night or something. It must have been close to closing. And he was sitting across from me. I was just salivating. I couldn't concentrate on what my girlfriends were talking about. I had to say something to him. So finally I get up and go over to him and I say, "Why are you wearing your uniform in a sleazy bar like this?" He probably thought I was a total bitch. But he was like, "Oh, I was just at a wedding." So I talked to him for like a minute and a half. I said, "Well, you look very nice in uniform." Then went back over to my girlfriends. So that was probably really the first time I'd ever seen someone in the dress blues, in person, instead of a movie.

Z: None of the men in your family were in the military?

G: No, no. God, no. I mean, my father, during the whole Vietnam thing—it was a nonissue for my parents because he had ulcers. So he could never have served in the military. So the whole issue of the draft and everything was just a moot point. It's like my parents didn't even live through the sixties. It just seems like their experience of the sixties is totally removed from other people's experience of the sixties. They were married in '60. I came along in '65. I'm adopted. So they spent the first five years of their marriage with my father in and out of the hospital, and then after that I guess dealing with the fact that my parents couldn't have children of their own. When the hell was Vietnam anyway? What year did it start?

Z: Well, it really intensified around '65. And then it continued on until—

G: So then after that I came along, and my father was going to school part-time. I think by then he was pretty much over the ulcer problem, but that would totally forever mean no military service.

Z: You mentioned that you collect GI Joe dolls.

G: I do now. This is actually really new, too. I have a little niece, she's about four or five. I'm not really into kids. But she's smart. I like smart kids. I was buying her a Barbie this past Christmas, and I went into FAO Schwarz. And it's amazing, all these fucking Barbies. They're incredible looking. And then I discovered that there is a whole series of "Stars and Stripes Barbies" dressed in military attire. There's a Marine Corps Barbie and Ken. One for each branch. And then there's also a set of Desert Storm Barbies. But this is interesting: They're packaged in sets. Barbie is always above Ken in rank! [Laughs.] Because of course Mattel's whole thing in marketing Barbies is to make girls feel that they can do anything, and they can be whatever. But I don't really like the Ken dolls anyway and they just sit in the closet. I pair the Barbies with my GI Joes.

Z: So how did you first start talking to military guys on-line?

G: When I was in the BDSM scene I met this married guy, in the Coast Guard. I don't know if you call the Coast Guard the military, but it sort of started with him. And his persona in the scene was as a dom. I actually started coming on to him while his wife was there, which he thought was incredibly ballsy. So when I was talking to him a couple days later on-line— this is on one of those little BDSM bulletin boards—I said, "How would you like to get together with me sometime?" So he decided he wanted to switch and be submissive. I just seem to bring out the submissive desire in most men. [Laughs.] They all want to submit to me. They all want to take it up the ass. But actually, I'm trying to think if I even fucked him up the ass. I can't remember. But you know, I tied him up, and we did all that stuff and everything. So he came to see me three or four times. His body was incredible.

After that, I knew I was going to be going to Europe several months later, so I posted something on one of the AOL overseas boards. "American woman looking for a European overseas." I've posted all sorts of ads on AOL before, and you get millions of responses. Too many responses. This one that I posted, I only got one response. And it was from this guy who said, "How about an Irish-American soldier based in Europe?" I'm like: a soldier? I just sort of perked up. I'd always sort of found them interesting to look at, like in the movies and on TV. *Platoon,* all that sort of stuff. I think there's a cultural conditioning that they're romantic, in a way. I mean, not *Platoon,* but *An Officer and a Gentleman* and movies like that, it's just sort of a romantic image. And the uniform.

So Brad and I got together when I was in Europe. And then—I don't know. I'm always this way. I'm greedy! [Laughs.] I'm like, if one soldier's interesting, how about some others? One day I started scrolling through AOL chat rooms, and I came across it totally by accident. F LUVS MILITARY MEN. I go into that room and start chatting. And the room's mostly Marines. So that's how it came about. I met Matthew after I met Brad, and it went from there.

Z: Like me, you are, or you were, a vegetarian. But now you're an avowed "gun nut," and you own a pit bull . . .
G: [Laughs.] Well, the pit bull is actually a very sweet dog. Pit bulls just have an image problem.
Z: But they're popular with the kinds of men that you're now courting, too.
G: They're popular with all men, trust me. Nothing like a pit bull to get you attention. Especially out here in California. Mexican guys and black guys in particular always go, "Oh, is that a pit?!" When I'm out walkin' her. And she's all like [makes sound effect of goofy dog].

The gun thing is actually recent, too. My big thing is I want to get a Marine to show me how to shoot properly. I had a guy from the gun shop who was taking me out for lessons, but he was like this big unattractive fat guy, and he'd be like leaning up against my body and shit to position me. I'm like, "You don't fuckin' need to do that. Fuck off." So Greg is an expert at pistol and rifle, and he's a gun nut, too.
Z: Greg is the most recent Marine that you've gotten really excited about, a lieutenant.
G: Yeah. And Scott is into guns, and Matthew is into guns. Matthew has more than $30,000 worth of pistols and rifles and shotguns. He's into everything. They all go out shooting. You know, I said to Greg I'd like him to teach me how to shoot a pistol properly. Because Scott and Matthew are both more into the long guns. But Greg's into pistols, which is what I want

to learn. So I said to Scott, "Greg's a pistol expert," all impressed and shit. I'm easily impressed by the little things that they're good at. And Scott's like, "Oh, I'll teach you. *I'm* the one who teaches those officers how to shoot." I'm like, "Oh. Well, are you a pistol expert?" He's like, "Yeah." But then he admits that he hasn't actually shot a pistol since he like made pistol expert. So I thought that was amusing. Obviously it's Greg who needs to show me, not Scott.

But I mean, I would go out with any of them. You know, you go to a gun shop as a woman, and they're automatically, "Okay, you want a revolver." I don't want a fuckin' revolver. I want a semiautomatic pistol with a high-capacity magazine. [Laughing.] Because if someone fucks with me, I'm gonna empty the whole thing. I'm gonna have *fun* with it, goddammit! I don't want a goddamn revolver. They're not sexy. Guns are sexy. I don't find revolvers to be attractive. There's something sexy and lethal about a semiautomatic, I find.

Z: Have your political views changed at all the last couple years?

G: Yeah, I guess there is a certain shift. As I get older, I find I give less and less of a shit about what's goin' on. I used to be very idealistic. Now it's like, why was I so intense about that previously? There are so many personal things to be intense about. Matthew and I, on every issue except the death penalty, are in agreement. I'm adamantly against the death penalty, and he is for it. We were talking one day, and he's pro-abortion, pro-death penalty, and pro-gun. I said, "So in other words, you're pro-death." [Laughs.] I was anti-gun for a long time, really, until I started meeting these guys. These guys changed my mind on that. And everything I've read to date has suggested to me that in states where you can carry a concealed weapon, the incidence of violent crime, particularly towards women, has dropped significantly. And plus I just don't see a problem with going off and getting out your aggressions on the target range or whatever. I don't agree with hunting, of course. I would never go out hunting and killing an animal. And I would not date a guy who does. Matthew likes to shoot, but he does not shoot animals. He wouldn't even think of it.

Z: You talk about Matthew a lot.

G: I love him. I'll never stop loving him. It's difficult for me because he won't see me now. A couple of months before he went on deployment I moved back East, because I was having financial problems out here in California. So I moved back in with my folks so that I could pay off some of my credit cards. I'd seen him several times before I left. You know, I think I was in love with Matthew the day I met him. He's just really different. I was getting very emotionally attached to him because he's so nice, and he really gives a lot of himself. We both have really told each other lots of things which we haven't shared with other people. I feel very comfortable with him. And the sex is just great. That has a lot to do with it, too. So I went back East. I had written him a lot of letters to Pendleton, all these sort of sexual letters. I thought it was apparent how I felt about him. And I honestly thought he felt the same way. And just around the time—I had always said I was going to come back before he went on deployment. I wanted to see him again before he left. One day I mentioned it, and he said, "I don't know about that." "What?" He said, "I've been seeing someone. I have a girlfriend now." And I totally lost it.

I guess I've been waiting—he's been back about a month now, so about seven months. I had been hoping that she wouldn't wait for him. She had just met him, after all. And I sort of assume that most women aren't going to have the stamina that I have. But of course, Matthew's the sort of guy you wait for. He's the sort of guy that any woman would wait for.

Z: Maybe even some men.

G: And maybe some men would wait for him. *Anyone* would wait for him.

Z: The best sex I ever had was with a guy who became an Airborne Ranger, who ended up marrying a woman after I think he'd crossed off sex with men from the list of things he wanted to try. And one thing you wrote me about Matthew was . . .

G: Yeah. It's funny, because his response to that—One night—Sometimes, I would have to sort of seduce him into coming to see me. It would always be about, "What are we going to do once I get there?" Never just a case of, "Okay, I'll come over." "What do you want to do, Matthew?" "Okay, this is what I want you to do. I want you to stick strawberries in my ass."

Z: Or a banana.

G: Or a banana. One night I said I would shave his ass. So he came over to see me. And that was when I said that "I think that the only reason you come to see me is so you can check these fantasies off your list." And he said, "Is that so bad?"

That should have been an indication to me right there that he did not feel the same way about me that I felt about him. So when the girlfriend thing cropped up, what I found most painful about it was one thing he said. And I don't think he meant anything by it, but I really took it badly. He said, "She's a nice girl."

Z: It sounds like in getting these guys to play out their kinkiest, forbidden fantasies that you inevitably position yourself on one side of what is often called the "Madonna and whore" divide.

G: And I've had discussions with him about this, too. But I guess what always gets me is that he *wants* to come see me. He wants to have sex with me again. He wants me to fuck him up the ass again. But when we talk, he won't. He would never cheat on his girlfriend. He's monogamous and he would never do that. It's ironic, because I love him so much because he is honorable, yet I want him to come see me.

Z: Yet you weren't necessarily looking for a husband when you met him.

G: I wasn't at the time. When I invited him over, it was simply to fuck him. But it just changed because of who he is. Some of these other guys, I've just fucked them. The guy I saw the day after I met Matthew.

Z: Mr. Twenty Minutes?

G: Yes. He comes along, this little fucking Marine who's like five foot nothin'! I open the door. I'm like, I can't believe this, right? He said he was thirty years old, and he was twenty-five years old. Which now is not an issue for me. [Laughing.] I've been dating them progressively younger. But at the time, I was looking for guys who were sort of closer to my age. So he totally misrepresented himself. I never question their height. I never ask them how tall they are. He comes up as high as my tits. I'm five foot nine. And he had been so aggressive, "You're gonna *be* there when I get there, *right?*" And I hadn't got a photo of him either, but he told me he was Italian, he was from New York, that he was attractive and everything. I always find that Italian guys, when they say they're good-looking, they usually are. And he was very good-looking, but he was *too quick*. He was in and out. As soon as it was over, I could sense that he wanted to leave. So I'm like, "Okay, well, you know: *bye*." [Laughs.] So that was done, it was incredibly forgettable. I didn't have an orgasm. And I'm very orgasmic, I'm very easy to get to come. And it's funny, before he got there, I was on-line, telling Matthew that this guy was coming over. And then a half hour later I'm back on-line. Matthew's like, "He's *gone already?!*" [Laughs.] I tried to get Matthew to come back over that night. One of the things I said was, "Is the reason you don't want to come over the fact that I've already had someone else here today?" And he said, "No, that's not an issue." I guess I believe him.

The next weekend Matthew called me on Friday the moment he got back from base. He had been in the field all week long. I come home and there's this message. "Please give me a call. I'm gonna be here until eight o'clock." So I called him and he came over immediately to see me. I'd been thinking about him all week long, and hoping that he would want to see me again. Because I always think: I've seen them once and that's the end of it. I just find that's the easiest way to deal with it emotionally for me. And then after I see them a second time I start thinking: maybe something will come of this. So I remember feeling this rush of emotion, that he wanted to see me again. He told me that he had been fantasizing

about me out in the field, and that he almost masturbated on sentry duty.
[Laughs.] But that he didn't because he was afraid that he was going to get
caught. And I think that's really what sucked me into him.

Z: So that was something from his side. Most of the time, you told me—

G: I'm the pursuer. The first person to message. The person who calls
them on the phone, who invites them over, who suggests we get together.
And he, that second time, he wanted to come see me. And with Greg it was
virtually the same thing. There are so many parallels between Matthew
and Greg. And this is why I can find myself getting emotionally so wound
up about Greg. Even though he sent me that letter . . .

[Indented passages are excerpts from Gayle's e-mails to Zeeland.]

> Rather a strange first date with Greg considering the first thing we
> did when he arrived was to go over to my girlfriend's so I could have
> him lift a bunch of boxes for me. Marines really are so useful :) After
> he toted all my crates from my girlfriend's place to mine he was
> covered with sweat and since he'd brought his Dress Blues to wear
> to dinner (sweet huh?) I told him he could take a shower. So I went in
> to show him where the soap and towels were etc. and he started
> taking his clothes off before I left the room, and one thing led to
> another and I ended up in the shower with him. And he was wonderful
> . . . great kisser, very sexy and sensual and lots and lots of stamina
> and energy. We eventually staggered to my bedroom where he just
> about wore me out, a rare occurrence. We lay there chatting for
> awhile afterwards and then I told him he had to get into his Dress
> Blues. I watched him get dressed . . . the first time I ever got to see a
> Marine actually put it all together and I loved it. I loved watching him
> be so meticulous, constantly turning to check himself in the mirror as
> he progressed through each stage of dressing himself . . . pausing to
> inspect and brush off non-existent specks on the jacket, etc. I would say
> the entire process is fetishized and I wonder if it was just because I
> was watching. It's hard to say.
>
> The whole night I could not keep my eyes off him, it's like I had
> to feast on the way he looked and I also really got off on the stares
> and looks he got as we went out in public. He did comment at one
> point after this young Mexican guy nearly got whiplash craning
> around to look at him that he hates it when men check him out up
> and down because he figures they are either looking for trouble or

are "fags." I'm sure he enjoys being looked at though. After we had sex the second time, we just hung around my place, going through my laser disc collection while he commented on various films he likes and then he left around midnight or so in order to get back to base.

The next day I received from him a message which read in part: "We really got things started off on the wrong foot. You see, I tend to be pretty conservative when it comes to sex (although i doubt you would've guessed from last night), and i've never gotten involved in a physical relationship so soon after meeting someone—i'm not much for the so-called 'one-night stands.' Maybe it's part of being brought up in a Christian home, but i believe that sex is somewhat sacred and should be saved for marriage. i don't know where things are going to go between us, but i think that getting physically involved at this point only makes the way cloudier—not clearer."

G: And then he was away. So he comes back on Friday or whatever, and we're on-line, and I said, "So what are you doing the rest of the week?" I'm trying to figure out if I'm going to be able to get to see him. He's doing this, that, and the other thing, then he's going back out in the field. I said, "Oh. I guess I won't invite myself over." And immediately he's like, "Why? Is tonight too soon?" So he wanted to see me that second time. But now he's blowing me off.

Z: You said that you sometimes have to be careful not to betray *too* much interest in the Marine Corps.

G: Yeah. Greg in particular. But Matthew, too—sometimes I think that as much as he seems to enjoy the fact that I tell him about these conquests and everything, and he finds it amusing, I would not be surprised if that is part of the reason he does not feel like I'm someone he can be emotionally involved with, because I have this fascination. Even though it gives us a lot of common ground. Because he is different from a lot of the other Marines that I've met. He's really bought what the Marine Corps is selling. And he bought it before he went in. But it's like that whole Madonna-whore thing again; you're not gonna marry the woman you have sex with the first time you meet her. So, I'm careful with Greg. I did let it slip once or twice. One night we were talking on the phone. I was all irritated with someone who had been incessantly messaging me. Like, "I wanna meet you." I said to Greg, "This guy was really irritating me, so I finally said to him, 'I only date Marines.'" And I could tell Greg was like, "Oh. You only date Marines? I didn't know that." I could instantly feel that it was an issue.

Z: He felt *objectified*.

G: Yes. And then when I was over at his house the second time we got together, we were talking about that book *The Marine Sniper*.[1] And I said, "Oh, there's this woman I know on-line, that's her favorite book." And he looks at me. "A woman? Really? That's so weird." And I said, "Well,"—and I said it so casually, and I just could fucking kick myself for saying it, because of the look on his face—"she's into Marines too." [Loud, long laughter.] And I was like: Oh, I said the wrong thing.

Z: What kind of interaction have you had with these other women? Do you exchange stories?

G: There's one woman who I've been talking to for about a year or two now who's into military guys. Actually, she seems to have gone off that lately, because she's exploring the whole BDSM thing. She's been meeting guys who are strictly into that. My whole deal is like, I like to pervert vanilla. Which is why I have to go after Marines. They're pervertable. And they're kinky. They don't call it by its particular name, though. They don't say, "Well, I'm into bondage, domination—" They don't use that sort of vocabulary, they don't know about the scene, but they like the same shit. It's like that Marine I saw a couple weeks ago from El Toro. He was like, "Bring your toys over," and he wanted to be submissive.to me. Even though he'd approached me as a dominant, originally. It's like the moment [snaps fingers] they find out I have any sort of dominant streak in me, they want to submit. They want to turn over, they want to be the one who's passive.

Z: With the exception of one guy.

G: Pete? [Laughs.] He's very different. He's a cop.

Z: An ex-Marine cop. And you switched roles . . .

G: Totally.

Z: . . . it seemed pretty quickly, from what I saw from your transcript.

G: [Laughs.] Yeah. He was really incredible. I still think about the sex with him. No emotional attachment. In fact, I dislike him. I actually have fantasies about shooting him. [Laughs.] With his own gun!

As for Pete, I should explain our first meeting, since that's when he set me up for everything else that followed. First he was a half hour late, and I thought rather surly when we met. I almost walked out then. But instead we went into a bar and sat down. I remember there were several ashtrays on the table and he asked me, "Should we move these?" Well, I guess I hesitated a fraction of a moment too long and he looked at me and said "How many cigarettes were you planning on smoking at the same time?" Very snide.

A half hour later we'd pretty much exhausted all avenues of conversation since we in fact had fuck all in common and were saved by the Irish band that was too loud to talk over. He suggested we leave. I thought we'd go to his place. Instead he suggested we sit in his car and talk for a bit. We get in the car, he starts the engine. "You didn't say anything about driving someplace." "I'm just driving over here to this dark corner in the parking lot. Relax," or something like that. Like I said, we had nothing to talk about so we kissed instead, after a few minutes of which he grabbed my hand and placed it on his cock and said something like "I bet you really think you're a handful, don't you?" Then he said that he could "handle me," unzipped his fly, pushed my head into his lap and told me I better give him a really good blow job or he would fuck my ass red. I was pretty amazed this was happening but at the same time incredibly turned on, especially when he kept telling me what a bitch I was, on and on and on. What's always amazed me about Pete is that for someone who I think is of barely average intelligence he is incredibly verbal when it comes to sex, which I find a powerful turn on. After I gave him head and he came in my mouth (don't even say anything!) I sat there stunned while he whipped out his gun, pulled out the clip, unchambered the round, and then put it back in his holster, then immediately repeated the process, deciding that if he's going to carry the gun with him it was actually safer loaded. I'm sure he did all this to freak me out. He succeeded. But it was hot, too.

I saw Pete two or three more times. One of these times we actually went for a walk in a park and I blew him in the woods, he came all over my face and then we walked out of the park and went our separate ways. The various times I blew him in his car, he would usually spank my ass before or during the blow job, telling me that I was his good little bitch. Verbal abuse was a constant and necessary feature of our engagements. Sometimes he actually would just double park, putting his little police sign on the dash, walk inside my apartment and upzip himself, leaving me to make myself cum after he'd left. I loved it and hated it at the same time. Fucked in the head huh?

G: He definitely used his gun as a way to manipulate. But I almost think in a way he's typical of anyone who becomes a cop. I think the difference between men in the military and men in your average city police force is that cops—they're joining the police force because they want to have authority. And they have a lot of it. Where in the military, men have no leeway, in their job function. Their job function is to submit.

Z: Even if they are military police, there is still that big military "daddy" controlling and structuring their lives.

G: Exactly. Where cops are almost free agents.

Z: And cops don't live in all-male barracks. One thing that I'm finding among the gay male military chasers is a frequent fantasy of—

G: Barracks fantasies? I have those too! [Laughs.]

Z: Why does that not surprise me?

G: I have various barracks gang bang fantasies. [Laughs.]

Z: As a woman or as a man?

G: [Slightly wounded tone.] As a woman. Yeah.

> Remember when I told you about the hazing Matthew went through, where they dragged him off to beat his torso and two other Marines bit him? That is one of the episodes I think about a great deal. It is always popping into my head and it holds a great erotic charge for me. When he showed me his bruises and bite marks and told me the story, I commented that I wished I'd been there to witness it. He laughed and said "I know you'd love that!" In my fantasies I come across them while it's happening . . . he's nearly naked and they are all dressed in cammies, totally oblivious to me while they proceed to pummel him . . . but I move closer when the first one leans in to bite him . . . my gasp draws attention and the first biter catches my eye and smiles after he's finished. Later they bring his bruised and bloody body back to camp. I'm already there for some reason and they lay him out for me and I sponge off all the blood before running my fingers lightly across the bruised skin and bites then I lean forward and lick and suck where he was bitten. I think about those bites all the time. I think about tasting the mouths of the men who did that to him. And that's what I do in my fantasy . . . I approach each of them and kiss them long and deep, and they all end up fucking me. I don't know what it is about that episode that gets to me. I guess a combination of things: homoeroticism, Matthew's masochism (he told me he never resisted what was happening) and acceptance of it, his knowledge that I found it a turn on.

Z: What I was going to say is that you don't seem to share the same thing that many of these guys have about just being buddies. A lot of gay men seem to have this fantasy of a male camaraderie that is very, very close, but isn't the easy sex that they have access to in gay life. They're actually looking for something that is more repressed, though of course they're not really prepared to go without sex. It seems like what you were describing with Scott is that he almost wanted to put you in a buddy role. You said that that was not what you wanted.

G: No, that's not what I want. I've almost accepted the role, but—We have a great deal in common. Our outlook on life is very similar. And yet it is different from Matthew, because there are things I haven't told him that I would not hesitate to say to Matthew. But it goes back and forth.

Z: But now you're friends with Matthew, too.

G: Yeah, but we're not. Because there's always that thing. I could not see him in person. I would go to pieces. I would throw myself at him. I would be begging him. I can control myself around Scott. I'm always physically attracted to him when I'm with him, but I've accepted the sort of buddy role that he's sort of thrust me into. My feelings for Matthew are overwhelming to me. I think about him all the time. I waited for him to come home, and I hoped that that girl would dump him and she didn't. I think about him constantly, and it hurts me no end that he doesn't love me.

Z: Would Matthew become less attractive to you if he got out of the Marine Corps?

G: No. [Pause.] It would disappoint me. Actually he's been talking about not putting in his papers to reenlist. I said, "I think that would be a terrible shame. You more than anyone I've ever met were meant to be a Marine." I'm very curious about what his girlfriend thinks about him being a Marine and whether she's happy with that and everything. But I just don't want to go there in that conversation, because I know I'm going to get upset.

Z: Would you still ideally like to meet a Marine who is about your age?

G: Well, my feeling right now is that, say between the ages of twenty-six and thirty is ideal for me. Any younger than that and I have nothing in common with them. And they're not smart enough for me. They haven't seen enough of this world for me. As it is, even guys who are the same age as me, just due to the circumstances of my life, often aren't as experienced or worldly as I am. And I want to get involved again. I want to get married again. I want to marry a Marine. I'm enjoying having sex with these guys that I meet, but I'm always on the lookout for a husband. And I guess that is the big difference between me and the guy military chasers.

Z: You might be surprised. Some of the guys I've interviewed have had sex with three or four thousand military partners, but a lot of them are looking for Lance Corporal Right.

G: [Laughs.] I'm looking for the right one. I feel that everyone I meet now I sort of judge against Matthew. My friends try to say Matthew's an asshole, because Matthew doesn't love me. "He's just a jerk." I say, "I can't fuckin' listen to it. Because he's not." I feel it's a self-esteem problem. I feel that there's something wrong with me that he doesn't love me. So there's this whole sort of tragic element. My ex-husband actually thinks a lot of it is that I've romanticized what I think Matthew is all about. And in certain respects I'm sure that's true. We didn't spend that much time together. But at the same time, it doesn't change anything. So I can't listen to any of my friends bagging him. I'm at the point where I find it difficult really to talk about him with other people. And actually I find you different on that score, because I feel like you can relate to why I'm so attached to him.

Z: You know, for some reason, when you talk about him, I can really picture feeling the same way.

G: Yeah. That's what makes me able to talk about it with you. But I can't really talk about it to other people, because they look at it like he's at fault. Because he's not able to see how wonderful I am. [Laughs.] I just can't fuckin' listen to it.

The tape runs out. Gayle and I join Steve Kokker, another contributor to this book, who has been waiting at a nearby bar, the Rusty Spur, which is packed with Marines. Both Gayle and Steve are new to Oceanside and enthralled. After a drink, the other Steve drives me down to San Diego. But later that night he returns. Gayle is still there.

A few days later she e-mailed me this report:

You certainly weren't wrong about the likelihood of my finding someone interesting if I just stayed in the bar. In fact, a Marine zoomed in on me about five minutes after you guys left. After a half hour of smiles back and forth I finally had to go over and talk to him between breaks in his pool game. Once I did, some other woman decided she was going to attempt to muscle in on my turf, but it was a no-hoper. Still irritating though as she insisted on acting like she was with us the whole evening and kept throwing herself at him and trying to get him to agree to go home with her "for security." Pathetic!! Steve is so funny though. When he arrived I told him what was going on and he started pushing her barstool away from us every time she got off it to wander off. LOL . . . Then he starts flirting with MY Marine :) I had told him the Marine knew he was gay because earlier in the evening the topic of prejudice had come up and he said he was not prejudiced but members of his family were so I asked him if his lack of prejudice extended to homosexuals to which he said yes and that many of his friends were gay. (This should have been a tip-off to me of what's coming.) I'm not sure if Steve was actually interested in him or just flirting for the sake of it and to amuse me but I did suggest that I didn't want to scare the guy off as much as I would enjoy him joining us so we left it alone. Stupid me . . .

Once we left the bar the Marine took charge . . . designated himself as driver and once we were in my car asked where I wanted to go. I suggested we just drive for a bit so he said okay and then pulls into the parking lot of the first motel we came to :)

Once in the room he says he wants to get under the covers because it is "cold" and that maybe we should cuddle for "warmth." After that we didn't bother any longer with being indirect LOL. At one point I teasingly said that I thought Steve might have liked to join us and he said, "Oh, you'd like that . . . two guys," and I said that of course it wasn't me he'd been interested in. To which he responds: "I don't normally tell anyone this, but I'm bisexual!!" ARGHHHHHHHHHH! I seriously considered getting dressed again and going back to find Steve. I am such an idiot sometimes!!!

Anyway, the sex was great and rather violent and he likes to be in charge. My entire neck is covered in bite marks right now and my ass is killing me from the fucking it got and I slept for nearly 24 hours once I got home because I was so wiped out. At one point, during a break in the sex, we were discussing the bisexual thing and he said that he wished he weren't bi because he's not actually attracted to men, he just likes the sex. I asked if it was fucking guys up the ass that he liked since I'd pretty much decided he wasn't a bottom from the way things were going between us, but he surprised me and said "No, I like being fucked in the ass." I asked him if he'd ever had a woman do that to him with a strap-on and he said once and that it was incredibly hot. I asked him if it was as hot as being fucked by a guy, and he replied that it was even hotter, more exciting to him to be fucked that way by a woman. Where is a dildo when I need one!

Andrei: A Family Tradition
and
Denis: Raised on Soldiers' Milk

Steve Kokker

After eight years as a freelance writer and editor of the cinema
sections at *The Montreal Mirror* and *Hour Magazine*, Steve Kokker
made the short documentary *Birch (Berioza)*, the story of a troubling
but erotic encounter with a straight Russian soldier. In 1996, he quit
film criticism and North America to discover his roots in Estonia and
travel as an itinerant video documentary maker through Russia. He's
currently working on several video and book projects, discovering
plenty more than his roots, and doing travel writing. He can be
reached at maadlus@infonet.ee, but won't give guided tours.

The gods that govern military attraction surely noticed two like-minded
souls in Steven Zeeland and myself and decided to bring us together. His
books had kept me company and inspired me while I was in Russia conduct-
ing my own interviews for a video project about male bonding in the Russian
army. We were two military chasers compelled to analyze and intellectualize
our passions (a formidable, self-defeating task if ever there was one). We just
had to meet.

At least that's what our mutual friend, Mark Simpson, a main confidant
for the experiences I was having with a population I knew to be of some
interest to him, kept telling us. Then, coincidentally, Steven wrote to
another friend of mine in Montreal, Tom Waugh, asking if he by chance
knew of any Canadian military chasers. Tom replied that there are no such
creatures in a country as gentle and peace-loving as his (we're encouraged
to respect our soldiers' peace-keeping missions and noble pacifism rather
than harbour pervertable ideals of their virility and bravery like our war-
mongering southern neighbours do). Except for one.

I admit, I'm far from the only Canadian military chaser, but it did take leaving our seemingly demilitarized soil to develop a weakness for soldiers. Before my first visits to Russia, I don't recall any special affinity for uniforms. I was drawn to male collectives of any kind, and the army was but one example. In any case, my potential for fetishizing all things army had been dashed by military-themed gay circuit parties, and porn in which lisping gym queens draped in khaki were expected to send viewers into undiscriminating rapture (clothes most certainly do *not* make the, er, man). These sights alone no doubt stunted the flowering of my army fantasies for years.

When I first visited St. Petersburg, I found myself bowled over by the sight of all the fine young uniformed men. They were everywhere, it seemed, on every street, at any time of day. In tender navy blues, in police academy blacks, in army greens and camouflages, cadets and soldiers would strut along with airs of self-confidence, and with postures perfect enough to make me correct my own when they passed—as if rising to their attention (as if). Russian men in general attracted me, their full-lipped, effortless sensuality, their tough-guy posturing combined with a winsome gentleness when spoken to. But Russian military men took my breath away.

I was coming from a country where soldiers are only seen in public performing disaster relief duties; nice as that is, social workers and sanitary engineers in any uniform don't make for much of a fantasy. In any case, the average Canadian soldier is middle-aged and paunchy—even budding military chasers have their limits! And the American military boys on display in U.S. magazines and TV ads were not much better. First, they were inextricably linked with patriotism, honour to the flag, and other unsexy ideals I'd always, in my typically Canadian way, negatively associated with the brash side of Americana. Second, they tended to be portrayed alone, as strong individuals with chiselled jaws stretched towards the heavens. Ultimately, my attraction to the military would reveal itself to be about the collective, not the individual.

Russian cadets to me embodied the full mystique of communal army life. I'd watch with great envy as groups of them marched through tall steel gates into the courtyards of their army bases or academies. What went on inside I could only imagine. But imagine I did, coordinating visions of bunk beds, midnight card games under the glare of fading flashlights, mutual teasing while pushing down paint-chipped corridors, army jackets and caps strewn atop tightly made-up beds, rigorous drills under the watchful gaze of a sergeant, crowded, steamy shower rooms. . . . I became an ardent military admirer. And if I had turned into a cliché, I was determined to make the best of it.

For a time, a short time, I knew that desiring those kinds of men was *wrong*. Queer theorists and political line-toers who would stain their Calvins over someone's tale of bedding a straight guy would also shame young homos away from eroticizing and idolizing the symbols of their so-called repressors—this in the context of a subculture which concomitantly propagated and negated the tough, straight male as the pinnacle of sexual desirability. Somehow, falling for Brent the straight wrestler, or Eric the hunky, breeder hockey player, or Sergio the impossibly beautiful, hetero artist were not only exercises in futility, but also self-defeating, demeaning. I must have a *problem* to find these men more erotically exciting than the here, the queer, and the fabulous. It was not *healthy*. And now with my military interests, I was licking the boot that stomped on me.

I won't deny that there's something unhealthy about such obsessions. I'm convinced that a fantasy of a seemingly well-balanced, unneurotic, self-assured heterosexual is as, if not more, powerful a motivation behind many gay men's attraction to straight men as the often-mentioned "butchness" factor. Straight lovers might admit that they're attracted to what they're not physically (rugged, manly, muscular) but that also goes for what they feel they're not emotionally (together, self-confident, mature). Even though it's often a straight man's vulnerability, insecurity, or need for attention which might ultimately make him attractive or available to a gay man, there's often a need to perceive heterosexual love objects as complete, real men in order to make the fantasy fulfilling.

In the form of a decked-out military man, these qualities fuse into a stiflingly virile whole: the confident, postured strut of someone who knows where he's going and who has had to systematically strip away layers of emotional weaknesses; the sinuous body and tough stance of someone having tested himself physically and mentally; the uniform which acts as a symbol of power one can either imagine assimilating, succumbing to, or defiling as a personal or political stance; the youth with which one can imagine the same.

What struck me hardest in St. Petersburg, even more than the individual military men I'd meet, were the group scenes: cadets horsing around, walking with arms draped across shoulders, marching in formation, or simply hanging out. I felt particularly touched by the easy way they shared laughter, space, and affection (complex maybe but never complicated), and by the aura of inclusion and cohesiveness which united them. Although I later saw how my ideals didn't always hold true in reality, this vision was endlessly more seductive to me than the image of social unity offered up in gay clubs. I knew that what I secretly desired was to be a part of such a group, to belong as they do, in a world (I imagined) of fraternal affection, bonding, and the odd dip into homoeroticism. In short, I wanted to be their buddy. That partially explains my earlier romantic, affectionate, sometimes erotic relationships with several heterosexual men. I had always been fascinated by anything connected with male bonding, and frequently found myself accepted into all-male milieus where I would observe and participate in the creative processes of buddyship. I usually felt like an outsider, but was charged by being privy to a kind of male-male intimacy absent in the homo circles of which I was also a part.

My gay friends were still calling my fixations unhealthy, but were also calling me regularly to hear about my latest encounters. I'm convinced that what most homosexuals attracted to straights really seek is buddyship, something sadly missing from a great many gay men's lives. All the nights out with the "sisters" just don't cut it. Of course, gays might think they can take male bonding and go one better, by traversing that great (false) divide and actually have sex with each other. Many gay men's partially acknowledged yearning for something as atavistic as male bonding is unfortunately only understood in sexual terms, even though this bonding doesn't have anything to do with actual genital sex.

Being gay ironically precludes a kind of closeness to other men every bit as important as a traditionally defined love relationship. Gays often dismiss male bonding as mere homoerotic game-playing, as if straight men repress actual sexual desire for each other and settle for second best. Yes, men do rechannel affection into sports, drunken tomfoolery, and ritualized behaviour, yet to assume these essentially creative methods of expressing feelings are less than genuine is nonsensical. When gay-identified men look upon such behaviour from their gay-identified perspectives, it sure does look suspiciously like what they secretly wished to do with other guys back at school. But male bonding follows different rules; desire and affection between heterosexually identified men are not the same as the desire of one gay man for another, straight or gay. Projecting feelings onto others contributes nothing towards mutual understanding. Yet if male bonding, intimate camaraderie, and group belonging are what straight-chasers are really after, sex is by no means unwelcome—in fact, it's ironically what we most often have to settle for. And what a sweet consolation prize it appears! It makes it easier to believe that we're getting what we think we wanted. Of course, we're not, really—hence the "chaser" part of "straight-chaser." Reinforcement only prolongs the chase—and the illusion.

In Russia, my own particular illusions were being reinforced by Oleg, the soldier who after an evening of girl hunting sat stealing tongue kisses with me behind the back of one of the girls he'd picked up who had perched herself upon my lap; Dima the soldier, just back from the far north, who turned out to be wearing women's white-lace underwear under his camouflage pants; Nikolai the beautiful fire academy cadet I met in a *bahnia*,[1] whose underwear-posing sessions and gentle refusal of my advances after mutual massages I documented in a short video, *Berioza (Birch)*; Ruslan, who took me on a highly illegal tour of his army base at 6 a.m. one morning to see the tightly made-up bunk beds and shower rooms I'd thus far only imagined; and Pasha the stunning naval cadet with pillowy lips who I would meet outside his academy for clandestine trysts.

These guys were masculine, sensual, and, most amazing of all to my friends back in the West, often enjoyed real kissing (excepting Nikolai, alas). This fact was greeted with more surprise than even the lace undies! (I suspect that the kissing is somehow connected with the Russian tendency to open up to others without rigid needs to erect false barriers—the "I don't kiss" alibi masking neurotic fears of intimacy is not so common there.)

As I neared the end of a year-long stay in St. Petersburg in 1997, I met one of the most interesting people I'd ever come across, a military chaser extraordinaire, and someone with relatively few illusions as to what he was doing and why. I first heard about Andrei from Russian acquaintances of mine, who would call him up whenever they were hit with that very particular urge for a military fuck.

Andrei, it was said, could call upon a stable of handsome guys in uniform who'd sleep with men for money. I tried to remain calm as I took his number down, and noted "pimp" next to his name to separate him from the other Andreis I knew. I crossed out this crude reduction once I met him and saw how inappropriate the word was. Yes, he did "help people meet each other," as he liked to put it, yet the friendly, relaxed relationships he had with the guys who worked for him, the depth and complexity of his own attraction to military men, and his general sensitivity to people separated him from the Western concept of a pimp, as well as from other men in the city rumoured to offer the same service.

We became fast friends soon after we met—he brought me home to meet his grandmother, and showed me the diaries he's kept for years, which chronicle his experiences with the military in minute detail. Obsessive about the particulars of his conquests, Andrei has recorded, often by aid of a symbol key, where and how he met the cadet or sailor in question, his ethnic background, penis size, characteristic traits, and a few paragraphs peppered with quotes, observations, and descriptions of the sex itself. He has cross-referenced his hundreds of lovers according to the country or region of their origin. He also has highly treasured address books, listed not alphabetically, but by academy.

The black squiggles and coloured codes in these texts constitute an important, fascinating social history of a generation of post-Soviet young men, most of whom were on their way home from army service when he met them, many of whom Andrei would never see again. The picture they paint is of a sexually fluid generation willing to follow the guidance of self-confident older men. In that sense then, it's not so different from North America. Except in Russia, the unneurotic way of approaching sex, the pervasiveness of a male-directed army culture, and the stupefying number of young men who grow up essentially fatherless ensures that there are even more guys ready to have sex with another man.

On several memorable occasions, Andrei took me "hunting" with him. Except for the evenings he worked as an overnight security guard, Andrei could be found looking for military at the railway stations. He's hardly alone in this search—there are always half a dozen other men loitering around groups of soldiers waiting to spring an offer of food, shelter, or cash. They tend to follow the dirty old man stereotype: most seem to shop at the same trench-coat store, hang a sallow, haunted, hungry look on their jowls, and appear disingenuous and uncomfortable chatting up the wary young guys.

Andrei, at twenty-five, looks almost young enough to be one of the guys, even if, like his postadolescent Western gay counterparts, he sports a baseball cap for insurance—yet another unfortunate Western influence which has crossed the porous Russian borders. His looks are pleasant, plain, and nonthreatening. His approach is smooth and professional. Picking up soldiers and cadets is showtime for him. Time to perform. And with the precision of an actor who scripts his own lines, he plays the part so well that within the hour, he's heading back to the small apartment he shares with his grandmother in the far-off, concrete-jungle suburbs, with one, sometimes several uniformed young men in tow. "You still manage to bed them even if they come over in a small group?" I once asked him. "Where there's a will there's a way, Stevie," he replied. "I'll put one of them in Babushka's room, the other in bed with me, and maybe switch them in the morning. Or, I'll put one in the shower and make it with the other, then switch them. It's not a problem."

Andrei almost exclusively sleeps with military guys. He needs sex, often. That he's chosen military men as the objects of his desire is a product of a complex set of personal and family factors. While his situation is a unique one, his candid insights into his own behaviour highlight some of the psychological factors at play in many military chasers. The interviews which follow were all done in my rented St. Petersburg flat on videotape (for a future project), in Russian, on different days in October 1997.

The other interview which follows is with Denis, a twenty-six-year-old successful gay computer programmer. His is a portrait of a more typical St. Petersburg military chaser. The chase is half-hearted for him: frivolous adventure and thrill-seeking while satisfying unacknowledged needs. His attitude toward young army men is more representative of the military chasers I met there: he sees them as quaint sexual objects rendered more exciting by their uniform, an attitude slightly condescending and fraught with the need to feel superior. Witty, clever, and flamboyant, Denis has had several revealing encounters which he's only too happy to share. During the interview—done entirely in English—Denis wore dark glasses to protect his identity, sat very relaxed with his hands behind his head, laughed frequently and freely, and answered his mobile phone about eight times during our forty-five-minute discussion.

Andrei: A Family Tradition, Part One

Steve Kokker: A love for military men is what initially brought us together as friends. Maybe you can start by trying to explain what it is about guys in uniform that you find so attractive.
Andrei: I don't exclusively like military men, but I do like real, masculine men, and they're mostly found in the army. Naval cadets, soldiers, sailors . . . . They're real men, normal guys.
S: Does that have to do with how they act or what they wear, or is it more about how you conceive them to be?
A: Nothing to do with my imagination! I simply don't like feminine men, like at the gay clubs, mannered and full of attitude—they aren't men. I don't need gays, I need real men.

S: What is it about army service that makes them masculine?

A: Well, the army typically takes boys and turns them quickly into men, but it's also true that the army takes in lots of guys who are of frail, poor health. Most of the guys in the army right now don't want to be there, and they are in it only to avoid problems with the law, or else to get away from family troubles. Or their families sent them there to get a financial break for a few years. Our army is now a peasant workers army, and for that reason, many feel that our army should be professional. Guys with richer, well-to-do families aren't in the army—they've either paid money to avoid it, or they're studying in universities.

S: You served too?

A: Yes, during Soviet times, so I know the problems well, and can attest to the deplorable psychological atmosphere. It's even got worse since then. Even from the army's perspective we need a professional army. The guys they churn out now can't be called professional—they can't even shoot a pistol properly.

S: But isn't it true that some branches of the military have it better? Like in the academies, for example?

A: Right. Most of the cadets in the military academies are there because their parents figured it was better than sending their kids to the army.[2] There they feed and dress you more or less properly, you're not totally cut off from your family, and they pay you—miserly, but still something. And guys are not locked up like in prison, or far from women. It's unhealthy to keep young guys away from sexual expression—they are after all, young men! I know that in some other countries, men are allowed time off their base, but here, they're totally cut off for two years, and because of that guys leave the army aggressive. It stems from sexual frustration.

S: And you saw how homosexual contacts form in the army?

A: Yes, but it's all done incredibly secretively. It's a big problem in the Russian army right now. It would be better for gays and for the army itself to completely forbid them entry because the attitude is so negative towards them.

S: But that's for gays. Sure society's outlook on homosexuality here is negative, but there seem to be many men in Russia who'll sleep with other men when they feel like it and think nothing of it, and they certainly don't see themselves as gay. They aren't gay. What do you think—

A: Yes, but in the case of young sailors and soldiers, I know many who sleep with men simply because they have no money. I mean, imagine getting next to nothing for six months! It's as if our social structures are leading young military men into homosexual prostitution.

S: You think that they wouldn't do it if it weren't for the money?

A: They might try it once out of curiosity. For all of them it might be interesting. There's lots of public talk of homosexuality, so they might want to see what all the fuss is about. But to do it regularly, I don't think so, for most of them anyways.

S: But I wonder if there's something in the Russian character or in military guys particularly which makes them so easy to pick up?

A: It's simply Russian mentality. Russians are sincere, guileless, kind by nature. On the other hand, army service is very hard, so if a soldier ever gets out on the street and someone wants to help him out or give him something good to eat, of course he's happy and grateful. And remember, many of these guys come from the provinces, not from big cities, and tend to be a bit naïve, gullible. So if they visit someone, they want a bit to drink, they want to relax, they may even want to take a shower, a simple shower because they can't wash properly in the army.

S: I wonder about the tendency on the part of these guys to simply follow what another man, especially an older one, says, to follow them home or whatnot. I've noticed this tendency of guys to simply do what they're told, and I wonder if the army, instead of making independent, strong men, simply fosters dependence on command.

A: In the army, they are often given useless, stupid orders which they know they must obey. And when these guys get out, there's something unbalanced in their psyche. It's as if they only know how to follow commands. They don't know how to think for themselves. The army teaches you how to do what you're told, without thinking, and when they leave, it's hard to shake.

S: Before your own service, were you attracted to military guys?

A: No, I'm from Kyrgyzstan originally, and there the attitude towards homosexuality is very severe, very negative. Before my service, I didn't even think of it as a possibility.

S: Did you have a homosexual experience before the army?

A: I wanted to, but never did. I was too scared. Even in the army, I didn't because of fear. After my service, I returned home at a time when anti-Russian sentiment was mounting—to this day the people there don't like Russians very much and discriminate against us.

S: So when did your attraction to uniformed men develop?

A: It developed when I came here. I felt freer, and could look from a distance without fear at how guys look in uniform.

S: What's the percentage, in your opinion, of guys in the army who sleep with men for money?

A: About 20 percent. There are guys who show up in uniform at gay clubs in Moscow and sell themselves. If there's an interest, there are people willing to satisfy it. It's an elemental law of the wild capitalism that's taken over Russia.

S: This is a bit of a classical situation, though. In the U.S. in the forties, and throughout history really, there have been countless stories of soldiers and sailors sleeping with men for money.[3] Do you have a different understanding now of what homosexuality and heterosexuality mean, after sleeping with so many guys who are primarily heterosexual?

A: Every year I sleep with about 150, 155 new partners who are almost all not gay, 95 percent of them military guys. About 50 percent of these will just do it once, just as an experiment. Either because there's no women in the army, either because they see it as a way to make money, either because they know that to find gay men interested in them is easy, or because they simply enjoy doing it occasionally.

S: So what do you think of these guys? Are they bisexual, curious?

A: I see the other 50 percent as bisexuals, guys who like men, but not gays. They consider themselves hetero, but I figure them to be bisexuals. I can tell if it's something they really want.

S: And the first half?

A: Just guys who simply try it out of curiosity and decide it's not for them.

S: Can you tell to which half the guys you approach belong?

A: Not immediately, but there are a few standard questions I ask. I have my methods, I have experience with this now, and after speaking with them for a while, all becomes clear. There are times when I err, but it is seldom. There are many guys who themselves don't know what they want. They want to try it, but are scared to. Someone needs to help them. [Smiles.] Those situations are very interesting, Stevie.

S: As an example, can you describe what happened to you last night?

A: [Laughs.] Well, yes, it was one of those intimate situations. I met this guy who had served in Chechnya, he's from the Caucasus himself, had lived through some horrible experiences, and hadn't had a woman in two years! He was on his way home, but there were no tickets left on his train—I met him at the station. The army pays for their trips home, but if there're no empty seats, they have to either buy their own ticket, or wait until the next day. They never have any money, so what can they do? Anyways, he came back with me, we sat down with my grandmother, had tea, and he told us about the terrible things he'd lived through. Then I suggested to Babushka that it was time for bed, and my new friend and I went into my room, relaxed, and watched some straight porno. At first he didn't want to do anything, but it's clear that, after two years without a

woman, well, soon he was ready for everything, and all was quite normal.
So much so that he even bit me out of passion, and today my lip is all red!
S: Don't expect too much sympathy from me! Seems like you can *smell*
which guys will sleep with you. I know it comes from experience, but
from where did this experience come?
A: At first, I was pretty nervous, I had no savvy, I didn't know what I was
doing, and there were times when guys wanted to beat me up, even
strangle me. Now I'm wise to it. I'm twenty-five now. When I arrived here
I was twenty-one, I'd had absolutely no sexual experience. I made mis-
takes, and learned from them. It's still dangerous now, and I wouldn't
recommend trying to pick up these guys if you don't know what you're
doing, because the criminal situation is very severe, and there are many
who get beaten up, robbed, even killed. One mistake could be your last.
But now I practically never make any errors of judgment, and I don't make
them do anything they don't want to do. They even thank me as they leave.
[Self-satisfied smile.]
S: But you must know how to act in such a way that they don't feel like
they're doing anything really gay, you must know how to let them pre-
serve their self-concept as masculine men but at the same time have them
sleep with you.
A: I never, never tell them what I'm interested in from the start, never. It's
like an exam at a theatrical institute. If you play the part well, you don't
sleep alone, if you foul up, you go home empty-handed. Usually guys
can't tell I'm gay—I can act very manly—and if they're wondering,
they'll never ask. At home, if they don't want to do anything, nothing will
happen, no problem. But how to get them to want it, that's my job.
S: Do you think you'll always be attracted to military guys?
A: I think yes, for the rest of my life . . . however long that'll be. It's quite
possible that I might come to a bad end, who knows? I'm careful and
intuitive, but it's a dangerous situation to take a stranger home. Sometimes
there's no way of telling how they'll react. At least I never try to coerce
them. Others try to get the guy so drunk that he can't say no, or try to force
sex. That can have adverse consequences, so I never do that—if the guy
really doesn't want sex, I won't push . . . but that happens so rarely, I must
add. [Smiles again.]
S: Many who chase after military flesh probably feel the need to get their
soldiers drunk first.
A: It's not a professional approach. Many of these soldiers may want to try
something out but already are a bit nervous about it. Too much alcohol,
and either they're so out of it that they don't understand what's happening,
or else they get aggressive once the other one makes his move, and sud-

denly, they're like, "what the fuck?" It can bring out dangerous aggression or else complete passivity, and in either case, it doesn't make for a good sexual partner. Alcohol and drugs aren't necessary. You have to get them to want it themselves.

S: The tape's coming to an end. How do you feel after this interview?

A: I think I've been completely honest about how I felt and thought. It's my own personal opinion, and I'm not scared of stating it—we live in a democratic Russia. [Ironic smile.]

Andrei, Part Two

S: After we spoke last time, I started wondering, amongst other things, what personality characteristics do you think you need to project to these sailors and soldiers in order that they feel so ready to go with you? Do you feel you have to project self-confidence, or be self-assured, for example?

A: As long as it's nothing to do with sexuality, because for them, I am not a sexual object. Their sexual objects are women. First and foremost, they need to feel friendship. In order to connect, you have to be genuine, a nice, friendly guy. Above all, you need to be aware of and sensitive to their situation. To connect with them fully, you need to have served in the army.

S: You try to show that you're one of them?

A: Yes, that I've been there.

S: And how do you think they react to, say, a foreigner, or with someone far removed from their own realities?

A: Sure there'll be some contact, but you won't be able to connect with that part of their lives very well if you haven't lived through it, and they'll feel it.

S: Okay, but they still won't go home or sleep with anyone who happens to have served in the army, so what kind of personality characteristics do you think they need to pick up on so they feel they can do this with you?

A: I try to make them trust that if they come with me, nothing bad will happen. There are lots of criminals and maniacs around, so they have to feel comfortable. And I live far out in the suburbs. They have to sense that I want to help them out. I mean, otherwise, they'll what, sleep in the train station with nothing to eat, nowhere to sleep? I can't let that happen! I honestly do want to help them out, and they can sense it. And when they hear that I live with my grandmother, they feel safer.

S: But what about all the cadets who live here in the city, whom you meet on the streets or in the metros—they don't really need your help or a place to stay. What must you project for them to want to come home with you?

A: That's a different story. They don't need places to sleep over, what they need is friendship, companionship—male companionship. Many aren't from St. Petersburg, they're far from their families, and need people around them with whom they feel comfortable. Someone to hang out with, have sex with too, that's not a problem.

S: Have there been situations when you bring someone home and they say, hey, what the fuck are you doing, I thought I was just going to have tea with your grandmother and go to sleep?

A: Yes, and there have been some heavy times, right at the beginning. A couple of times the guys said, "I don't want to," and I said, "okay, sleep on the floor," and in the morning, they simply left. But there are others who reacted very badly. Guys with psychological problems. But that's rare, maybe one in a hundred.

S: Can you describe a time when you were caught in a dangerous situation?

A: [Takes a deep breath.] In 1994, I once brought home a soldier who was supposed to leave for Yugoslavia in two days. They chose him because he was healthy, strong, big. But, like many in the army, he had criminal tendencies, and he had gone especially to the Catherine Gardens [a well-known gay cruising area in the centre of the city] to look for a fag to rob. He arranged it so that we would meet. We came back to my flat, and I sensed that this guy might be trouble. He insisted that I was to shower after him, and there was something in his tone I didn't trust. He wanted to rob the place after locking me in the bathroom. So when he got out, I said I didn't want to have a shower. He told me, "Get in the shower," and tried to push me in. I struggled, got the front door opened, and told him to get out, that I was going to call the police. He got nervous, pissed off, grabbed a big knife from the kitchen and threw it at me. It flew literally about one centimetre from my head and stuck in the door frame next to me. After that he got scared and just ran out. He was a professional. And that's the type who were sent to Yugoslavia.

S: I've heard from a number of people that some cadets, knowing how popular they are with gays, go to the cruising areas and get picked up, only to rob them or beat them up. I was shocked to hear from one of my friends that a couple of the guys in the gang of naval cadets who'd constantly come to visit me used to entrap gays at the Catherine Gardens. And I know that at least two of them had slept with men before. They'd lead them to a darkened area, or behind some bush where their friends were waiting, then either hassle the guy for fun, or rob him, or beat him up.

A: It's a dangerous life in general for gays in Russia, even today. They make such easy targets. And all too often I see them becoming depressed, alcoholics, drug addicts, or suicides . . .

S: Do you consider yourself gay?

A: Yes.

S: But you often speak in a negative, derogatory way about gays, about the way they act, how you don't want much to do with them. Yet at the same time you consider yourself one of them?

A: I understand that I'm gay, Stevie, but I'm ashamed of the kinds of gays who behave "badly." They shame other gays like me who behave normally. I'm more of a secretive gay, and act more like a heterosexual. But there are the kinds of gays who are like, "Hello darling! Ooh, sister!" [Places a limp hand under his chin and flares eyes.] Like women. I don't like to see this, because these are the people that society sees and thinks of as gays, and from that comes the negative stereotypes. They spoil our reputations.

S: If you said that in public in America you'd probably be attacked, because the argument would be, this is the way they want to behave and should be free to do so. If you don't want to just let them be themselves, you'd be the one seen as prejudiced, as the enemy. Not to mention a *self-hating* enemy. That's a favourite concept out there.

A: Well, that's not true, because in America it's only in certain cities, in certain areas where gays are free to act openly like that. In England it's only in London. But still in those countries gays have been visible and open for twenty years. In Russia we've had democracy only five years, we don't need that kind of behaviour here. In any case, even in the West, even after twenty to thirty years, society still reacts negatively to excessive effeminacy outside the ghettos of the big cities. It's a myth to think otherwise. If they want to act that way, then [they should] do it only in the clubs and bars reserved exclusively for gays. There's no need to act like that on the streets, and no need to provoke people into being against you.

S: But ideally, do you think it would be a good world in which people like that could act just as they wished? Isn't it *your* problem if you don't like that behaviour?

A: No, I mean, if everything was allowed and free and open, there would be other problems. . . . There are subcultures for that. And these guys are in the minority, but they're the ones children see and grow up to think badly about. I'm not saying that it should be outlawed. Please, there are discos for that, clubs, bars. But on the streets, at work, no! Those are the kinds of people who get beat up on the street. I think the way I behave with my cadets is actually helpful because they'll know that there are normal, regular gays out there and next time they meet one maybe they won't be mistrustful or negative towards them. Their first experience will make a strong imprint.

S: So how do you strike a balance between showing that you are interested in them, but not exactly in that way?

A: I don't have to say anything! A soldier who hasn't had sex in a long time, who's had something to eat, watched a porn video maybe, had a bit to drink, when I put them in the shower, it's all set!

S: Like what happened yesterday?

A: Yes, well, I picked up a very nice-looking border guard from Novgorod who had just finished his service and was on his way home. It was a classic situation: he'd had no girls since before his service. So we watched some porn, then jumped in the shower, and by the time I offered to wash his back, he already had a full erection, and could hardly contain himself. It was all very quick and very pleasant. Later on, once he'd calmed down a bit, we did it again, and it was even more pleasant.

S: Do you ever see that these straight guys become troubled over having had sex with you?

A: Sure, sometimes, but no more than 10 percent of them. I'd say 50 percent react very well to it, 10 percent react badly afterwards and torture themselves over it, and about 40 percent, well, they simply don't care one way or the other; bisexuals.

S: In your opinion, are Russian men less neurotic about having sex with guys than say, straight foreigners you've met, or from what you know about Western men?

A: Let's just say that Russians are kind-spirited, open-hearted, and there's a strong tendency to avoid insult—if they feel that the other person wants something, they won't want to offend them by refusing. That goes in general for all Slavs. But in the West, it's a completely different mentality. There it's more egotistical and individualistic, people think primarily about themselves. "I want it, and I'll use someone else to get it if I have to."

S: So how many people have you slept with in your life?

A: In all? As of yesterday, there have been . . . [pretending to think about it] six hundred and six.

S: And in this year alone?

A: One hundred and thirty-six *new* partners so far.

S: Of those six hundred and six, how many have been military guys?

A: [Without hesitation.] Five hundred and four. [Seeing Steve Kokker's eyes widen.] Five hundred and four military guys. Well, I truly like military guys, not gays.

S: [Recovered.] Does it make any difference to you if that guy happened to be a gay military guy as opposed to simply a cadet trying sex with a man, with you, for the first time?

A: Absolutely, a big difference, because gay military cadets entered the army to be around men and are hoping for lots of sex in the absence of women. They aren't comfortable around other gays; they're afraid of competition.

They usually aren't very attractive and they don't turn me on. Maybe for one night, but no more. To quote Freddie Mercury, "I can have sex with anyone once—but only once."[4]

S: Do you ever feel the desire to repeat an evening with any of your conquests?
A: If all the standards that I require were there, then sure, maybe two, three, five times. But if he was just normal, typical, only once.
S: And I guess your first time with someone is always the best?
A: Absolutely, it's always very vibrant, strong sex . . . strong orgasms.
S: And why do you think that is?
A: Because new is always interesting—every guy is interesting in his own right. It's the process itself.
S: And what do you get out of that process?
A: Enormous pleasure. Just knowing that I'm opening up a straight guy gives me great pleasure.
S: Do you consider yourself to be *giving* these guys something interesting and pleasurable as well then?
A: Yes, [laughs] well, let's say that I give these young guys sexual wisdom.
S: A parallel to Lenin disseminating wisdom to his young pupils?
A: No, I like to think of myself as the Mother Theresa of the St. Petersburg military! [Both laugh.] I think it's useful for them—everyone should know what gay sex is all about. It gives me satisfaction to know that through their experience with me they'll think more positively about gays in the future. These guys will go back to their little provinces, raise families, have friends, and will be able to say, well, it's not that bad after all, to know a gay.
S: But what else do you get out of these experiences? I'm wondering specifically about the fact that you like military. Uniforms can be seen as some kind of symbol, whether of power, of masculinity. Yet when they're with you, they're unclothed, intimate, vulnerable, maybe even passive, so—
A: First of all, I can say that the uniform acts like a magnet to me. I see a uniform and right away my attention is caught, bang. After that, I look at the guy and decide if he's worth it or not. Not everyone looks good in uniform. Power? I don't know about that. As soon as he takes off the uniform, he's just like me. With his clothes off, he's like the emperor with no clothes, and that's even better.
S: What is?
A: When he's naked in my bed.
S: And the uniform ceases to mean anything then?

A: It's only at the beginning; it's my first impulse. Uniforms are to me like lighthouses to a ship, orienting me, showing me the way. I look for masculinity, for "macho" men, strong, handsome—the ideal for many gays, especially for passive gays, like me. I consider myself more passive than active in terms of what I like sexually.

S: Still, your behaviour to get these guys is nothing short of active.

A: Ah, yes, and actually in bed I tend to be more active than they are, come to think of it. I don't know, I feel dominant when I'm teaching them.[5]

S: But if you still consider yourself passive, you don't feel that you look for masculine power—

A: I do!

S: I mean for yourself.

A: Yes, for myself.

S: But on a more psychological level, do you look for something—

A: That I don't have myself?

S: Yes.

A: [Smiles.] Well, maybe I do. Sure, I think I look for what I'm not. I don't consider myself strong and big and masculine and handsome. Just normal. But opposites attract, for people as in physics. It's more interesting that way. It's symbiosis.

S: And why do you think it's so important for you to have so many different partners, and to keep track of exactly how many you've had?

A: I one day just started counting, and simply decided to keep track over a long-term period. Sometimes you hear people, like in Hollywood, boasting that they had two, three thousand. I don't think two, three thousand is all that much really. I've already had over six hundred, and that's only in the last five years. I know that it can be dangerous, what with AIDS, but I try to do things as safely as possible. I try. In Russia, a lot of people never use condoms. Everyone fears AIDS, but everyone also understands that pleasure is sometimes stronger than that, that those impulses can be so strong, there's nothing you can do. I always have condoms with me, but with military guys it rarely works that way because everything happens very, very quickly when you're breaking them in.

S: You could always carry one in your pocket!

A: Yeah, but if I enter the bathroom with a condom, do you think I'll get anything? That's not serious, Stevie. If he's standing there, excited body and soul, ready for sex—these are impulses we're talking about—condoms will kill all that [makes a limp motion with his hand to pantomime falling erection]. Sure I'm scared of AIDS like everyone, but, as we say here, "he who's afraid of wolves never enters the forest," and "he who doesn't fear AIDS doesn't jerk off."

S: Is there ever a time when you feel love, or being in love?

A: There's this boy who I love very much right now, but at the same time I'm hesitant to call it love because that implies something very serious, a great responsibility. And I don't ever want to hurt anyone because I know that I'm simply not able to sleep with just one person. I have an extremely strong sex drive, and need the kind and quantity of sex that just one person couldn't fulfil. I need to have sex at least twice a day, sometimes four times, and I haven't yet found someone strong enough to keep up with me.

S: But because of your work schedule, there are many nights when you can't have sex. How do you feel on those days?

A: I start to get nervous, anxious, and think about sex a lot. I get visitors to my workplace as well, you know, but, if for whatever reason I can't. . . . Masturbation doesn't help, it's not serious, I just try to keep myself as busy as possible. But I'm an "erotomaniac" and therefore always thinking about sex. I think I'll always be that way. Who knows what'll happen. I may end up getting killed because of a mistake I make, I might get AIDS, maybe end up a drug addict, though I never drink or take drugs at all. My only drug is sex.

S: Are you ever actively afraid of something bad happening to you?

A: I can't say I feel fear, I'm just conscious of the possibility. Already I've had a number of acquaintances hurt and killed because of bad pick-ups. But, what to do? Nothing ventured, nothing gained. Life would be boring if I were afraid to do anything. Life itself already offers big risks and dangers, especially in our economic and social climate.

A: Were you ever concerned about this strong desire for so much sex? Do you understand it?

S: Before, I was worried. I didn't comprehend why I needed it so much, but now I understand. Until the age of twenty, I never had sex with a man, but always wanted to. Until then, I only had sex with women. Maybe if I had had sex when I was fifteen, sixteen, with guys, I'd feel more peaceful. I'm making up for lost time, trying to get what I didn't then.

A: You think if you had had even 1,000 partners when you were younger, that you'd have inner peace now?

S: The time you start having sex is important—when you're young you have so much energy and you need a place to expel it. Anyway, it's in my genes—my mother was Russian, but my father was Greek, and I think a lot of my physical needs come from his blood.

A: You also mentioned to me earlier that you learned something about this kind of behaviour from your mother.

S: [Face clouds a bit. A brief pause.] My mother was a dominant lesbian. She was big, strong. And she also loved uniforms. Inside, she was more of a man. She wanted to join the army. She often wore male military uniforms, around the house, to parties. Her dream was to be a man, and my dream also is . . . [voice trails off and looks to the side, stroking his chin] to be a real man, although, who knows, maybe it's to be a woman. But she came to a very sad end. When she was twenty-eight years old . . . she committed suicide. She wasn't able to express herself openly at all. It was still the Soviet Union then and society looked very negatively upon lesbians. She wasn't able to find a proper lover, and she lived in Kyrgyzstan in a conservative environment. At first she started drinking, and it all ended in suicide. Quite a few of her lesbian friends also died that way. What's the point of living when you can't be yourself, when everything about you is forbidden?

S: And she also had many lovers.

A: Yes, many. But, what's many? Compared to me, compared to what she could have now, she had few, but for her, then, there, it was many.

S: Did you ever suffer from depression?

A: I felt it when I was living there. When I wanted to do things I felt I couldn't.

S: Do you remember seeing your mother dressed in uniform?

A: Yes, I even have photographs. She was a strong lady, athletic, into boxing, swimming, cycling, had very short hair.

S: Sorry if this sounds simplistic, but do you think there's a link between your passion for men in uniform now and the memory of your mother and her passions from back then?

A: Yes, I think I inherited something from her genetically. [Starts chewing lip.]

S: But you also remember seeing her dressed up in those same uniforms that you are now so strongly attracted to.

A: Yes, I think psychologically there's something there too, because when I was growing up, my mother wasn't my caregiver, it was my grandmother, to whom I'm forever grateful. But I saw how my mom lived, how she wanted to be a man, whereas I felt more like a little girl. Now I'm attracted to other men. That's how I see that the gene for homosexuality was passed to me from her.

S: So it's a mix between genetics and—

A: —Psychology, but first and foremost, it's genetics. When my mother died, I was ten years old, and by that time I already understood that she didn't feel herself to be a woman—she didn't even have any maternal instincts. She didn't care for me much. I don't think she even considered me her child. Well, maybe she did but she didn't show it, she couldn't, it wasn't important to her.

S: Do you remember wanting attention from her?

A: Sure, like all kids want attention, help, and love from their mothers, their fathers. But my parents for me lived in the person of my grandmother—she brought me up, had respect for me, and to this day doesn't interfere in my life. She thinks that if she'd interfere I might end up like her daughter. If you forbid something, there'll be tragic results. She tried to control her daughter, and it ended in suicide.

S: You think she knows what you do?

A: She assumes, for sure, she understands. She saw it all before. I'm sure she has a complex as well, feeling that it's her fault, that her daughter got it from her, that I got it from my mom, that it all started with her. For that reason, she doesn't interfere, only tries to help me as much as she can. [Pauses, looks down.] I love her very much, and she loves me too.[6]

S: Where was your father all that time?

A: Oh, my father, I never . . . I know he's somewhere in Greece now, somewhere. . . . I never had any contact with him, or if I did I was so young I don't recall it. I only know him from a few photos, but my grandmother threw them all out.

S: And for your father, did you ever feel a strong desire to know him?

A: Not so much, I just would like to talk to him, to ask him why he did it. He just ran off after sleeping with my mom once. She had been a virgin before then, and after that never slept with another man. She was only seventeen at the time. Then he went off into the army and she never heard from him again. At that time, there was complete ignorance about sexual matters. No one used condoms, there was no information about contraception, what tablets to take, even what tampons were, nothing. You went to the pharmacy and everything was shrouded in secrecy, taboo. During the Cold War, it was like the Dark Ages here. And so lots of kids were born like that, with no father, or no parents. My father was a very irresponsible, bad man to just have sex once and disappear, like smoke. And because of him, my mother's life was destroyed—mine too.

S: Because . . . ?

A: I never had a complete upbringing, never knew masculine strength and power. Maybe if I had had a father as caregiver, things would be different now. I'm sure I'd still be gay, but different. Because if a child only receives mother love, that's not complete, there's an unbalance, especially for a little boy.

S: You relied on yourself for life education?

A: Pretty much. I never asked anyone for anything. I had to be independent quite young. I was working by the age of thirteen, at the local post office. There simply wasn't any money in the family.

S: When you feel in love, like with that young guy right now, is there any glimmer of desire on your part to be dependent on that person?
A: No, that's not love, to feel dependent upon or depended on. Dependence doesn't bring equality. It's unhealthy. I never want anyone to be dependent on me, and never want to feel dependent on someone else. I only want freedom.

Andrei, Part Three

S: There's a subject we've been avoiding, and this time I'd like to ask about the special kind of work you sometimes do—how it came about, how you originally thought of it.
A: [Tries to conceal worried look. Pause.] You mean about Max, Zhenya . . . ?
S: Yes.
A: It's not really work, I'm just trying to help these guys make some money because I know what a miserly sum they live on. And I haven't been paid at my job for two months now. I don't think of it as work, only helping.
S: But how did you come up with the idea?
A: It was a couple of my cadets who once asked *me* if I knew any men, any ways to make money, and I, I'm just the middleman.
S: So the first time—
A: —It was them who asked me. They'd asked me for money, and I had to tell them I didn't have any. Then, "Do you know anyone with money? Someone who might pay a bit?" After that, I . . .
S: . . . You tried to . . .
A: . . . Help them out, organize things.
S: How did it happen the very first time?
A: I just called up an acquaintance of mine, someone I knew. He came over to my place, met the cadet, looked him over, and . . . that's it. [Pause.] But, Stevie, people go to jail for work like this, and I don't want to get mixed up in that—I just help people get together, nothing else. The men are often shy about meeting soldiers, who really need money. The army pays them next to nothing. Many of them have poor parents. And I only help them do what they themselves want. I don't want to do it full time, professionally. That would be aiding and abetting, prosecutable by law, and in any case, it's a dirty business, for me and for them.
S: When was the first time you hooked people up?
A: [Frown.] Maybe a year ago, just over.
S: Not that long then.
A: [Pause.] What to do? Last year they paid out very little, this year too. On TV they say, sure, this year all wages will be paid. . . . Nothing's ever paid.

S: At the same time, is it interesting for you, meeting new people, getting into new kinds of situations?

A: Well, it's interesting to see how the guys react, how they get along with each other, that's about it. Overall, I don't really like it . . . it's a bad thing. [Scrunches face, looks away.]

S: Bad how?

A: People should meet each other on their own, it's better that way. If people get used to someone else introducing them to others, they'll never be able to do it on their own. People with lots of money, they lose the ability to connect with others on a genuine level, they're used to buying everything. But love, friendship, intimacy, you can't buy those. It's an illusion to think otherwise.

S: I'm sure you've seen those illusions many times.

A: I have, and I don't need to be near that in my life. It's just the money.

S: Do you ever see men fooling themselves into thinking that these cadets or sailors really do like or love them?

A: Very often! The men are often very sentimental, and say, "Oh, I can tell he really likes me by the way he looks at me." They construct this love in their minds. When they see a good-looking guy, they immediately think, I'll buy them this and that, and they'll love me. They lie to themselves. And later, when their eyes are finally opened and they realize that they aren't loved, then comes the depression, the alcohol. . . . *C'est la vie.*

S: And after that they no doubt start over again from scratch.

A: Yes, later, when they've recovered and forgotten a bit, after a few weeks, again it starts, wasting money, going around in circles.

S: One of the reasons you don't feel comfortable with what you do is because you're involved in that whole world?

A: Yes. First of all I feel uncomfortable because I feel ashamed about it. I mean, I do help people out, but . . . if the cadets had money, and if I had money, this wouldn't be happening. But what are my options—go out and rob, become a prostitute? I've got my principles. I was brought up not to cheat people, to have respect, not to lie. . . . If there was a million dollars lying around, I'd never take it.

S: So sometimes you feel bad about this—

A: I get depressed sometimes about it, ashamed. In all conscience ashamed in front of myself, in front of God.

S: Does it ever happen that you feel good about setting up two people who really like each other? Are there cases when nice people simply get together, and there are no lingering complexes and bad feelings, when you feel more or less okay about it?

A: Maybe 20 percent of the time. Maybe 20 percent of the men don't build illusions and fantasies. But 80 percent of the men don't themselves understand what it's all about and what is entailed. They don't understand that to the prostitute, it's just a job, it's just money, that they'd have no use for them otherwise. And if they're not even gay, they have even less use for them. But I wouldn't call this real prostitution.

S: What's the attitude on the part of the cadets and soldiers to these men who pay for them? How do they feel about what they do?

A: I think the guys from big cities, they're fine with it, at peace with it. It's just work, maybe. Many could care less either way. But the guys from the villages, it's more difficult for them, they search themselves, worry over it. . . . It's difficult for them all. It's not so simple, or easy on their consciences when they ask themselves what they're doing and why. [Fidgets with hair.]

S: Do any of the cadets ever blame you for feeling bad about themselves?

A: Not so far, because, if they agree to it, they've usually asked to do it in the first place. Some just work occasionally, but others call me all the time to make money. For them, the work isn't painful, they're used to it.

S: And for others, it's painful.

A Yes. [Pause.] Sometimes I find it hard to understand them, when a young, good-looking guy tells me they need money, money, money, and can I help him make it. If you're educated, ambitious, I think there are other ways to find money. It's easier to understand the less educated ones in that respect.

S: And how long do you think you'll keep doing it? If you got a good job—

A: If I made a *minimum* of $300 a month, and if I got paid every month, I'd quit doing this. For me it's a kind of moral trauma. But I make $100 a month at work, and that's only when they pay. Out of that I must pay for the apartment, electricity, food, and help my grandmother. Winter is coming and I don't even have a proper jacket. My cadets are in similar situations. This society is forcing people into dishonesty. To work, and to work honestly, yet not get paid? What's that? Russia is a country of paradoxes—you can work well for a year and not get paid for it. Why do you think we have such a criminal situation now? Because salaries are not being paid. It's completely wild, and the West doesn't understand—people say, if you don't get paid, just quit your job, walk out. But right now that's impossible.

S: Before we finish up, I also wanted to ask you about this very special talent you have of knowing exactly what's inside a guy's pants just from looking at him. You're really quite good at it!

A: Ah [smiles, visibly relaxes]. That comes from experience, from practise. I can look at a guy, assess several factors, and in five seconds I know what he's got. Ninety-five percent of the time I'm right on. I look at the ears, the nose, nostrils, eyebrows, lips, hands. Just a quick look, and, like a computer, I process the information.

S: And you don't only know the size of his dick, right?

A: That's right, I'll know if it's thick, thin, long, short, left- or right-leaning, big headed, curved. . . . That's all from experience.

S: Experience and good memories. And you also are able to suggest where people who like big cocks should be traveling to.

A: [Laughs.] Yes, well, the Archangel region is particularly excellent, so is around Vologda—there are many guys there . . . [drifts off dreamily] with . . . very big members.

S. And St. Petersburg?

A. [Frowns disconsolately.] St. Petersburg is a city of immigrants and migrants. People come through here from all over, it's not great for that . . . but not far is Novgorod, and there it's much better.

S: Why are large penises so important to you?

A: Oh, [smiles] a small dick is boring, I can't feel it. If it's a friend of mine, I could care less what he has in his pants. But if it's a sex partner, it's important. And if it's my boyfriend . . . I don't know, I wouldn't be able to love someone with a small dick. I just couldn't. There wouldn't be any harmony. Love is fine, but sex is very important; they form two halves of the same whole. So, I don't need small dicks [smiles devilishly].

S: What do you say about people who say, yes, I like big dicks, but if I loved the person, it isn't important?

A: Lies. Of course you can love the person. But if you aren't satisfied physically by him, you'll look for another eventually. Love can go away awfully quickly.

S: I doubt you only receive *physical* pleasure from your encounters. It's also psychological too, how you fantasize about what a big penis is and what it means—it's also about your conception of a big penis, not only how it physically feels.

A: Yes, it's psychological, but a small penis doesn't excite, doesn't stimulate fantasies and emotions. But from big penises [eyes raise heavenwards], a sea of fantasies can arise! A small one, it's like a finger swirling around in a mixing bowl. It's not interesting.

S: What about that soldier from Kaliningrad who you picked up last week? He had an extremely small dick and you still got great pleasure from him.

A: [Pause.] You're forgetting. About Freddie Mercury. Once, I can get pleasure from anyone, even if he has a small dick—but only once. After that, forget it. If the guy is just a gay civilian and he has a small dick, then even once would be too much.

S: Can you imagine yourself in a loving relationship with a nonfeminine gay?

A: Yes. Masculine gays I have no problem with—I've probably already slept with all of the ones in this city. I lived with someone for two years, until it ended very sadly. Who knows, maybe in the future I'll find what I want, though I doubt it.

S: You have a tendency of speaking negatively about your future sometimes.

A: Stevie, life is such that it knows no reason. I'm trapped in a job I don't like, I have nothing of my own to speak of. . . . Sure, sometimes I get depressed and feel the need to do something about it quickly. It's hard to see the purpose of it all.

S: From what I've seen in Russia, it seems to be the tragedy of your generation.

A: Maybe yes. I feel as if my youth is slipping through my fingers, that I'm not getting anywhere, like a fish swimming against the current. It wouldn't take much for me to feel at peace, just a comfortable apartment and a good job. But, in this time of economic crisis, I don't see how that's to be.

S: Would you say you're fatalistic? You're always very realistic about what's around you, I know, but you've casually mentioned before how you wouldn't be surprised if you came to a bad end.

A: Life here is dangerous, not at all easy. I could get killed by one of my cadets. Or I could get sick. I more or less believe that nothing ever changes for the better, only for the worse.

S: That's your philosophy.

A: [Cites proverb:] No, well, "fate will show what happens." Who knows. I'm hopeful about the future, more or less, but something's got to change. There are days when everything seems black. I was sick recently and spent two days in bed with a cold, and all these dark thoughts entered my head. Still, people called to see if I was okay, to wish me well, and that was nice to hear. It means somebody still needs me.

Denis: Raised on Soldiers' Milk

Steve Kokker: When did you first realize that you were attracted to military men?

Denis: Look, this is what gays look like in Russia: something in between a man and a woman, wearing Versace, nice perfume, talking like, 'Ooh la la la!" Excuse me? I like real men, and to me, men in uniform represent true manhood. They're young, strong, not fat. That's one reason I like them. The second is that it's an exciting challenge to make such a guy—muscle-bound, tough, in uniform—have sex with you. In a gay sauna, it's very easy—snap! Everyone wants you. Okay, not everyone, but many, and after a while, it gets boring.

S: How does it make you feel when you succeed in getting a military guy?

D: I think, like, "You too, honey!"

S: So you like to think that these strong, tough guys aren't so different from you, that they'll fuck a guy just like you?

D: Yes. In Russian we have a saying that translates like, "There are no straights, it's just a matter of enough vodka!" To me it's obvious that if you know how to do it, you can make something good with many of these guys.

S: There seem to be so many bisexuals here—any ideas why?

D: I'm no Einstein to know all about that. But, there are a few theories to explain sex between men in Russia. One is that about 60 million men have gone through gulags and prisons here, and it's no secret that there is constant sex in jails. Another is that people don't have much confidence anymore, especially in the military. In the last ten years, we have gone from a superpower to a third world country, from thinking we are one of the best to opening our eyes and understanding that we don't have it so good. Maybe that's one small reason why people become soft and easy to open up. And thirdly, for many years, this type of sex was forbidden, and now that they hear a lot about it, it makes people curious to try it, to see if it is really so bad, or so good. I've picked up military guys who've told me, "Yes, it's my first time, I wanted to try." And we [gays] allow them to try!

S: And—

D: But I should say that it's not so easy to pick them up! They are like bottles, and if you can't find the way to open up their souls, forget it! You can be easily beaten up by them if you try to catch them. But if you find the way to understand them you can get very nice results.

S: So what do you have to do?

D: You must be very interesting for them, and also you must show that you understand them, not just that you think they have beautiful bodies. In Russia we do it this way, first open their hearts and souls, and then there might be something else to be done.

S: Can you give an example of some military guy you've met?

D: Oh, there've been so many! Okay, one day I had had a fight with my boyfriend, he was very mean to me, and I went out for a walk. Outside I saw a cute guy in uniform, standing by a kiosk, buying cigarettes. It was maybe 11:00 p.m. I just asked him, "So, you're a soldier?" We started talking, we came back to my place, I offered him a massage, and gave him one. Very nice body. Then, after some vodka, we had 100 percent gay sex, it was wonderful.

S: To you, was this guy gay or bisexual?

D: In that case, I don't know. He had come to my place, relaxed, had some good food, we were having a good time. . . . In the army they get pushed all the time. It just happened!

S: But do you usually think afterward, "Ah, he's really gay and just doesn't know it yet?"

D: No, he's straight, and probably won't have this kind of experience again.

S: How do you search for these guys?

D: Oh, that's a big subject. Once I had this friend, just a friend, but he knew what I liked, and I don't know how he got this, but he gave me a present one day, an official document permitting me to enter into one of the military academies, where 2,000 future officers were living, eating, sleeping. Can you imagine! So I cut my hair short like a cadet and for four or five months, I would go there almost every night.

S: What would you do there?

D: Oh, talk with guys, meet people. Sometimes I had real sex inside the barracks; yes, well, what to do? It was a black day when I lost that slip of paper.

S: So you have to be interesting and interested to get them. But do you also have to be masculine, or act in a certain way?

D: That's a difficult question. It's like asking, how do you drink wine? With big or small sips? Every person is special, and there are special ways with each of them. I have one friend, he's very la la la, very like a girl, and he says to people, "Oh, I want to suck you," and things like that. I asked him, "Why do you act so badly?" and he replied, "The faster they know what you want, the faster you get somewhere." That's one way. The other is just to behave normally. To me, it's amazing how there are old guys, fifty-five or sixty, who sleep with young cadets. What do they see in these grandfathers? I asked these men, and they said, "Oh, the boys come here and open their hearts to me, and I make them feel that I take care of them, and after that, maybe they are just thankful, it just happens." But I don't know how these young kids can sleep with these old trolls, excuse me.

S: But it at least gives one hope for the future. Can you remember the first time you were attracted to uniformed guys? Was it after your own service?

D: It was in university. I had a friend who I liked very much, and he went into the army, and when I saw him after that, I felt very strongly for him, and I didn't understand what it was that I liked so much—his body, his face, or the uniform. I was not gay, but quite straight then. But I felt there was something special, like the smell of his boots and his jacket, or looking at his belt. I don't know. All these small details made me quite excited.

S: So your attraction developed out of a very personal experience for you, and not from what you'd see around you on the streets, for example?

D: Well, since I was a child I have seen many military parades during holidays. In the Soviet system, we grew up with the military all around. It was like a cult of the uniform. Military guys would make school visits, for example. Contact was very close. And don't forget that my own father was in the military! [Laughs.] Yes! I grew up near the Russian-Finnish border, and the person who raised me was a soldier. Yes! My father was a border guard, and we lived in a small settlement, maybe forty guys. No kindergarten, no fresh meat, nothing, we had only what soldiers had. And my father ordered one soldier to look after me, and this poor guy had to get my milk every day straight from the cow! You can say that I was raised on soldier's milk. I don't know, I've always liked men in uniform. In general in Russia we like the army. I mean, we have compulsory service, and there is a strong connection between the army and the common people.

S: Did you ever have sexual fantasies about that soldier, or others, when you were young?

D: When I was young, my sexual fantasies were about girls, and I realized them. But when I understood that I was g-a-y gay, I tried to realize those fantasies in practise.

S: Any fantasies about soldiers?

D: I used to like to watch the American pornos and watch the American soldiers making sex with each other, that was nice. About five years ago, when I didn't understand if I was gay or what, some special feelings would bring me to the local saunas where once a week the guys from a local military school would be washing themselves, and I would watch these beautiful guys washing—my god, it was paradise! But I was nervous then. One old gay tried to wash my back!

S: Does it make a difference to you if you know if a soldier is gay or not?

D: It's important that they don't act like girls, that they don't have gay intonations. But I like when they know how to make good gay sex. [Smiles.]

S: How about a good-looking, masculine civilian, and a good-looking, masculine soldier standing next to each other—which would you prefer?

D: Both!

S: No difference?

D: [Bites nails, thinks.] Okay, first I'd make an appointment with the military guy, and then set up a second appointment with the other.

S: Aha, so you'd call the military guy first.

D: Well, yes, I think military is better, more exciting.

S: Before you said that it's exciting to think that you can get one of these tough guys in bed with you. Do you ever feel that it's some kind of power trip on your part, that you had control over a guy who's supposed to represent power?

D: Yeah, yeah. These feelings come in the morning, after everything happened. I think, "A-ha, you too!" That guy who fifteen minutes ago was such a tough, brave, straight man on the streets was fucking with me! So many straights may say bad things about us gays, but when I have sex with them, I make the levels equal. It's a sociological experience!

S: Ah, I see, you do all this as a scientist.

D: [Laughs.] No, no scientist, I like to have sex. But it's great when you can mix sex with a sociological experiment. It should be a model for all scientists!

S: But it sounds like there's a bit of revenge involved in your feelings about these guys.

D: Maybe yes, but the real revenge will be when I can walk into a military school and point out in front of everyone and say, "You, you, and you have slept with me!" That would be great! But, speaking of revenge—To me it's amazing when you go into a military school, and you talk to some guys, and they don't know you're gay, but sometimes the ones you don't talk to suddenly come up and try to get your attention, as if to say, "Hey I'm a nice guy too!" It's like a competition develops between them. Incredible.

S: Have you ever been nervous when you try to pick these guys up?

D: I'll tell you my first experience with them. It was many years ago, so many. I went to the train station, where many gays go to try and pick up soldiers. I said, okay, if they do it, so can I, and I had no idea how to do it. But you know how at a casino, first-time players always win something. Well, either God or Satan sent me two guys that night. One of them was like a prince! The other was very ugly, but it's always that way. I went up to them and started talking, and eventually we all came back to my place. I made a nice meal, watched videos. And there was only six hours left before they had to take a train home. I thought, "What to do?" There was only one room in my apartment. So I put the ugly one in front of the video, and I brought the other to the bathroom and said, "Please, wash. You must be dirty; you're from the military," and he said, "Yes, yes." Then, without any shame, he took off all his clothes in front of me. And I said something stupid like, "Oh, maybe I want to wash too. I haven't yet today," but we were a bit drunk, so who cares? When I tried to make something, he was ready for sex. It was beautiful. He kissed me, everything. And he was not gay! My god! And then he left, as soldiers always do. And should, maybe. But now I have a nice new Pentax, and started a photo file so that when I'm on pension and am a teacher at a special gay school, I can show the students my experiences.

S: Ever any bad experiences?

D: [Explodes in laughter.] Oh yes! Many bad stories! One guy had been to Chechnya, and I started to do something and he said, "What are you doing? I was in the war!'' I understood he was a little crazy inside. He didn't beat me, but started to get very angry, hysterical. But he slept on the floor and left the next day.

S: Ever any violence?

D: No, the most they've told me is, "Sorry, I'm not gay; leave me alone." And I say, "Okay! No problem. I'm not gay either, I just like to have sex with men!"

S: Do you think there's anything passive about that? That they wouldn't react more aggressively?

D: Well, to me it's very interesting that you can pick up a straight soldier, and the role that they like in bed is passive. Incredible! For me it's good because I'm active, but for our other gays it's a tragedy when they pick up a soldier and he wants to be passive in bed.

S: Do you hear that a lot?

D: Yes, yes. Two or three out of five want to be passive. Can you imagine? This big, muscular guy and he shows his back to you! That's okay, I can make with his back something good. Oh, another interesting story. Once with my friend we picked up three guys who just had come out of military prison, which is worse than regular prisons. Real nice guys, real strong. Not only did they have military experience, but *jail* military experience! One was the leader, beautiful. He had ruled an entire cell in jail, very tough. So we talked to those guys, they understood that we wanted sex, and they said it was possible for $100. I said, "$100? Come on!" Okay, so we made a deal for $50. We came back to my place, and this leader told the others to stay downstairs while he came up. He was really a brave guy. Upstairs he asked me in his deep voice, "Do you have ladies' underwear?" What? "No," I said. "Find me ladies' underwear!" he growled. Okay, he wants me to wear ladies' underwear; for him I will, why not? So I go to my neighbour, it was very funny, and made up some stupid story about my friend who wants to give his sister a present but has no money, and she gives me a pair of stockings. And for me it was a shock when this great, big, strong guy then took off his clothes and put on those stockings! I could not believe it! This guy who ruled the jail and fucked those other prisoners was inside a passive boy. "Fuck me," he commanded, and I did.

S: He gave you the order.

D: Yes, and I did it. He sucked me too, only he didn't want me to suck his dick because he wanted to be absolutely like a lady. After that, I couldn't go to work for two or three days. I was in shock. Until the day I die I won't forget that. But those days are gone now. I have a jealous boyfriend. Still, that hasn't stopped me completely. There was that sailor last week. But that's another story![7]

Maynard:
Servicing Sailors

Editing this book provided a welcome excuse to fly to San Francisco for Fleet Week. It was five years to the day since I left Naval Air Station Whidbey Island, Washington, and my petty officer third class boyfriend Troy, whom I met when he was stationed at Naval Air Station Alameda, California, for San Diego, via San Francisco. (The alternate title of this chapter is "Following the Fleet.")

When it closed in April 1997, NAS Alameda was the last major military installation in the Bay Area. Some speculated that the Navy pullout was a direct result of the popular notion that San Francisco = gay.[1] (They thought their sailors would be safer in San Diego and Seattle.) But every October the U.S. Navy returns. After all, the military's "antigay" policy has long included a "queen for a day" clause.[2]

Riding the Oakland airport shuttle across the Bay Bridge, I discerned, high up in the pink-brown haze over the city skyline, four F/A-18 Hornet aircraft. As I tipped the van driver and found that my keys still fit the lock to my old friend Bart's Castro apartment, I heard his voice baritone-booming down the stairwell, poking fun at my self-referential conceit by reading aloud from *Sailors and Sexual Identity*: " 'On my way to Southern California I stop in San Francisco. I try to get some sleep in Bart's bed, but Navy Blue Angel jets have followed me. It's Fleet Week.' "

Bart used to lecture that my desire for military boys could only be explained as internalized homophobia. During the year I lived in San Francisco (1991-1992), he was militantly queer nationalist. Having at age thirty only just escaped our hometown of Grand Rapids, Michigan, he quickly wormed his way to the epicenter of gaydom. Bart worked as a doorman at a Castro bar (he is mentioned in the first edition of Betty and Pansy's *Severe Queer Review of San Francisco*[3]), humped Jerome Caja[4] on cable TV (so energetically that he knocked off the radical drag queen painter's falsies), and while cruising Dolores Park in a Skyy vodka stupor, accidentally set his car on fire.

These days, Bart finds it harder to be dogmatic. And he goes to bed at ten. After saying goodnight to him, I wandered the streets.

The big gay bookstore on Castro Street is open until midnight. At the checkout counter, I had to wait while the clerk made an announcement over the store's intercom. "A Different Light will be closing in ten minutes. Please make your final selection and bring your purchases to the cash register. If you're cruising, we just want to let you know: it's okay. There's no need to feel guilty or embarrassed. Why should you be furtive and ashamed? This is San Francisco."

I paid for my three-volume copy of the collected works of the Athletic Model Guild *Physique Pictorial*,[5] took it back to the Travelodge, and masturbated.

Sex was not something I expected to find on this trip. After four years in San Diego, I thought that coming to San Francisco for sailors would be like coming to San Francisco for the sun. But the next night, I still made my way to North Beach.

The streets were teeming with uniformed sailors and Marines, many of them drunk. A trio pissed in an alley, a couple squared off to brawl. Others stood clustered under the neon looking almost like Tom of Finland drawings come to life, hands tugging at conspicuous bulges. I followed two Marines into a men's room. The huger of the men, standing before the mirror, uttered the first words I heard a Fleet Week military man speak: "*Damn* I look good in uniform."

Prowling one sex shop after another I grew depressed. These days, young military men travel in packs of three to nine. And the sanitized adult video arcades of San Francisco are geared for tourists, with $3 minimum token purchase, surveillance cameras, electric eye beeper devices, and blinding banks of fluorescent lights. Inevitably, inexorably I ended up at the last refuge of sleaze, a strip show on Kearny. There, in the dark back corner, I found my old sailor-chaser buddy, "Maynard."

Maynard has been hard hit by the closure of Bay Area bases. For years he fed off Navy trade. Now, his sole sexual sustenance is this annual event, and that has proven increasingly dismal. But—he told me when I called him up from Bart's—he still takes off work so that he can spend every night of Fleet Week on the streets—all night if necessary. "The drive," he calls it. He likens himself to "a salmon, swimming upstream against almost impossible odds."[6]

Maynard did not appear overly happy to see me swim up beside him just then, so I wandered back outside and trolled the block, stopping to admire a dense tangle of almost fifty jarheads and squids gathered before a dance club, aware that I was staring at them a little too hungrily. I went into a bar and had a beer, but though I followed two sailors into the toilet ("Come on in, man. There's another head in here.") they were all buddied up and I didn't talk to any.

I decided I'd just say good night to Maynard. Back at the peep show, there was no sign of him. Almost as an afterthought, I tried the door to one of the occupied video booths. It was unlocked. A short, blond sailor peeped out at me.

With the door secured behind us, the sailor undid his thirteen buttons. There was lint in the belly button of his smooth flat stomach. . . . Afterward, he drunkenly threw his arm around my shoulder—for a second I thought he might even kiss me. Instead, he just said, "Thanks, man. How are you doing tonight?"

Resisting the compulsion to interview, I uttered the only word I said to him. "Good."

"Take care," he told me.

The sailor was gone as I staggered back onto the street. Immediately I found Maynard. He was ready to talk to me now. "So, not too much going on yet. How about with you?" he asked, doubtfully.

Dazed, I told him.

"Oh." He looked incredulous, and a little hurt. "Maybe that means there's hope for me."

I felt salmon survivor's guilt. But later that Fleet Week Maynard had an adventure of his own.

Dear Steve,

It's a funny thing about sailors. My years of experience chasing them and catching them and comforting them and mentoring them and being rejected by them has shown me that, generally speaking, many of them are just awkward kids. They come from all types of towns and cities, situations and backgrounds. They are full of wonder and eager to learn new things. But they can be very afraid. These beautiful young men are scooped up by the U.S. Navy, thrust into a regimented existence, mothered like children and ordered to trust only the fellow sailor. Is it any wonder that, like a rebellious child, the brave ones reach out and try to stay in touch with the civilian world, even if it's just for an evening or an hour, and even if it means letting some military chaser gorge himself on their private parts? It must be good to be temporarily treated like a prince. It means access to a private home, a stereo and videos of their choice, an oasis from overcrowded berths and barracks. Besides, as I can immodestly say I proved to many young men, the sex can be great. Sailors quickly become accustomed to being objects of desire for sex and/or money. As they dock their ships in strange ports and dock their dicks in strange bodies, these free-spirited, free-spending young kids are much-sought-after prizes . . . targeted by the female prostitutes or barflies in virtually any port . . . or the gay military chasers in virtually any town adjacent to a naval base. It's just nature's way. If there is a collection of handsome and available young men gathered in one place, there are gay men who want to have sex with them. It may be crude and in some ways disrespectful to reduce all of those wonderful individuals to objects of lustful worship. But, in fact, it seems that most sailors want it that way. I saw few serious, long-term friendships or relationships grow from the many casual encounters I experienced or heard about.

Nebraska Boy Scores in Memphis Game Room

As a small boy, I used to draw pictures of muscular, studly males who could save the world from all types of villains. To everyone else my creations were just superheroes, or cowboys and Indians, or other heroic figures, but to me they were the first stirrings of much stronger desires. I don't recall drawing pictures of sailors as a child. In fact, growing up in western Tennessee, the sailors I saw were not romanticized figures who sailed on mighty war vessels. They were just loud, unruly man-boys that I saw strolling at the mall or walking around town. My first sexual encounter with a man was not with a sailor. It was with a young guy from rural Tennessee and it happened at the age of sixteen on a Greyhound bus, at night, under a blanket, hurtling down I-40. Sailors came about seven years later.

As a young adult, I started to give more notice to those handsome young men clustered together north of Memphis. The Naval Air Station at Millington was what the Navy calls an "A school." It was one of the first stops for new recruits headed for permanent posts on other bases or ships. The boys looked good enough to eat, but I was still mostly shy and had no idea of how to approach any of them for sex without getting my teeth kicked in. Then one of them came to me.

I had recently moved away from home and into my first apartment. Believe it or not, it was just a coincidence that my new place was two blocks from a YMCA that was a drop-off and pickup point for Navy buses that shuttled sailors back and forth between the base and Memphis. The YMCA was very small, with just a swimming pool and a few offices. I don't believe it even had overnight rooms. But it did have a proximity to Memphis State University and all the bars and game rooms near the campus. One night while drinking beer and mentally undressing some of the many beautiful college-age men in one rather loud establishment, I noticed this great-looking guy who was by himself and playing pinball. I soon decided that he was not a college student, but instead a Navy man (the haircut was a major clue). I thought it would be fun to at least talk with him, so I introduced myself. I was not new at picking up men, but at this time I didn't consider myself an expert either. For every success story there were dozens and dozens of rejections. I had connected with most of my quick-time lovers in places where such propositions would be expected: gay bars, porno movie arcades, the woods in Overton Park, etc. I had never scored in these straight, mostly student-popu-lated, neighborhood bars. And while I had seen a few sailors in these places before, I never expected to actually talk to one.

Memphis is very much an automobile city and sailors often traveled in cars, in groups. But, here was one Navy man all alone and extremely cute. "Well, here goes." I strolled over and struck up a conversation. Unlike California today, in Tennessee in the late 1970s, you could expect a person to at least talk to you, even if he realized that you were cruising him, and even if he was not interested. A few nice words could be exchanged before he would indicate his lack of interest and then you both would go on your way. That's the most I expected to happen this time. Instead the young man was quite friendly. I bought him a beer and played pinball with him. I told him I lived a couple of blocks away. Before long we were walking to my apartment to enjoy more of each other's company. I still wasn't sure just how intimate we would be.

"Bill" (I don't actually remember his name) was a beautiful corn-fed youngster from a small town in Nebraska. Blond hair, brown eyes with medium to slender muscles built by hard work, not that gym-toned look that you see in the city these days. Despite his Navy regulation haircut, straight dangling bangs hung across his forehead as a reminder of some earlier scene when he was probably a stereotypical picture of the sexy farm boy working in the fields. But Bill was not some hayseed. He was quite articulate, as I found out when he asked me directly if I wanted to have sex with him. What a shock! It seems that he knew early in our pinball-and-beer encounter at the bar that I was attracted to him. He was curious about man-man lovemaking and decided it was time to act. He wanted me to show him everything. What a dream come true! While I thought I was picking him up, this hot nineteen-year-old, still fresh and pure to the world, had been busy picking me up.

My dream boy had previous experiences with girls but said I was the first guy. You couldn't tell by what happened in my bedroom that night! Lots of sweet oral sex, giving and receiving. The fucking came naturally, top and bottom. He was affectionate and loving and cuddly. It was like years of his inhibitions had suddenly melted to the floor at the side of the bed. We enjoyed each other for hours before we had to get up and drive back to the base so he would not be late for school. Bill said he had a great time but that he still had to decide if this type of sex was right for him.

I never heard from him again.

"Do You Know Your Fly Is Open?"

When Alameda was a Navy town (the Naval Air Station there officially closes this week, two days from when I'm writing this), I cruised around in my car and picked up sailors. One night as I was driving back and forth along Atlantic Avenue, the main road to the naval base, I saw this really cute blond sailor kneeling on the sidewalk. I passed by a couple of times. He seemed to notice me, but there was no real reaction from him. By the time I turned my car around, he was gone. Then I noticed that he was no longer on the main street, but had walked onto a less busy street that leads into the Navy housing community. I drove up next to him and got my first good look at what a handsome young man he was.

Sitting in the car, engine running, I engaged him in some meaningless conversation about finding a good place to drink or dance. He was very polite and a little drunk. But he also knew I was full of it and just using any excuse to talk to him. He told me he lived in the Navy housing and his wife did not like him drinking, and that he had just stepped outside to get some air and to avoid an argument. After a while, I realized that the button fly on his jeans was open. So I asked him, "Do you know your fly is open?" He touched himself a little, pretended to unsuccessfully close his pants and mumbled something I could not hear. Then I said, "Let me help you with that." As I touched his pants, I realized that he was not wearing underwear. To my surprise, I put my hand on a nice hard cock through his open fly. Before this, I suspected the guy was just being polite, and I was still not sure how I would raise the subject of giving him a blow job. I remember saying, "Oh, what's this!" I took his cock out through the open fly and gave him a nice, slow blow right there in the street with him leaning on the roof of my car. Occasionally, other cars would pass by, and he would step back a little bit so it appeared that we were just talking. After he shot his load, we talked a little more and he said he should get back inside; his wife would be wondering where he went. We shook hands, thanked each other for the sex, and said good night.

USS **Nimitz:** *An Old Faithful Ship*

This old aircraft carrier always makes me think of a guy named David. He was cute, tall (about 6 feet), Caucasian, brown hair, in his early twenties, and he loved to play pool. He was married to a black woman and never cheated on her with another woman, but another man was something else because it "really wasn't like cheating." By the way, I'm African American. Race had nothing to do with David becoming friends with me or with him marrying his wife. I met him in North Beach in San Francisco and we just took a liking to one another. He came to my apartment in Oakland and after a few beers decided to have sex. It was the usual with most "straight" or bisexual sailors: some hugging, mutual rubbing, a slow blow, then I'd drive them back to their ship. David's ship was based in Washington state and it stopped in San Francisco Bay an average of once a year. For several years, he always gave me a call when he was in town.

A sailor I picked up and got to know in Alameda named Philip was also married to a black woman and just liked black people a lot. He was this white kid, a little stocky, with black curly hair. He called me occasionally to come over to my place. He loved to stretch out on my bed and let me suck his dick.

Almost all of the sailors I sucked were white or Latino. I was more successful with white guys because they seemed to be more open-minded when it came to experimenting with man-man sex. I know this is a generalization, but negative encounters and rejections indicated to me that black and Asian straight sailors were not as receptive to my propositions. In fact some were quite offended when I raised the subject. On the other hand, I realize that some of the white sailors accepted my proposals as part of a white-black fantasy, and that's okay. But generally speaking I believe race was not an issue in the overwhelming majority of my sexual encounters with sailors. Most of the guys were "just curious" or "experimenting" and the fact that a black man's mouth was on the receiving end of their dick was not a factor.

"You're Still Out Here?"

I was standing in San Francisco's North Beach, just off Broadway, outside the live nude dancing theater that was a favorite cruising spot of mine, when I recognized him. He was a handsome guy with brown hair and a nice smile. Although I had not seen him for a couple of years, I immediately remembered his name. "Steve!" I said, greeting him warmly on the sidewalk.

"You're still out here, doing this?" he replied.

"Come watch a movie with me," I asked.

"No thanks," he said. "I can't believe that two years later you're still out here picking up guys."

I felt bad about the rejection. I felt worse about missing out on sucking the cock of a man that I had serviced at least four or five times before. I had met him in that same neighborhood two years earlier. He came over to my apartment that first time. The sex was good. Over the later months, he'd call occasionally. More good sex. Then like all sailors, he disappeared and I never heard from him again until I saw him that night. I knew he considered himself straight, but apparently he no longer bent.

"I Tell My Mother Everything"

I don't remember this sailor's name. In bed, after sex, he mentioned that he could hardly wait to call his mother and tell her about this new experience he just had. He had never been with a man before. As good as it was, it was just a blow job, and I couldn't believe it was the kind of thing anyone would call home to Mom about. "I tell my mother everything," he said. "She and I are very close." Now, this was no wimpy mamma's boy, but a handsome, strapping young man that any woman or man would be pleased to have. I liked his style and told him that it was good to actually meet a man who was in touch with his tender side. He declined my offer to be his bed buddy or sex slave, and since I never heard from him again, I don't know if he ever told Mom about me.

The Third Pass Along the Embarcadero

For me, Fleet Week is celebration time. Every year in October the people of the San Francisco Bay Area let the Navy know how much we appreciate the long association and the many years of service. For us cocksuckers, this is a special time to let the Navy men know how much we appreciate the many years of servicing them.

Fleet Week lasts only four days or so. During the good old days (the 1980s), most of the ships involved in the festivities were visiting from other ports, and all the sights and sounds of the City were brand new to the raw recruits. The streets were filled with handsome young men in their tight dress blue uniforms. It's a wonder I got any sleep at all during Fleet Week. If I was lucky, I was up all night having sex. If I was unlucky, I was up all night *trying* to have sex. A popular all-night dance club was located near my favorite XXX video arcade in North Beach. Sweaty sailors who struck out with uninterested girls in the club came next door to watch girls dance at the nude theater. Some of them went right into movie cubicles to be serviced by some of the scores of cock-chasing "queens" that swelled the population of North Beach during Fleet Week.

I often had my share of that action; quick, dirty, no muss, no fuss. But sometimes I wanted more. Besides, I knew from experience that many sailors had to work the next day and usually headed back to their ships at 2:00 a.m. when most bars closed. At that hour I surrendered my station at the XXX arcades and took to my car, driving up and down the Embarcadero, the San Francisco boulevard that runs along the bay from Fisherman's Wharf to South Beach, south of the Bay Bridge. Many of the Navy ships were docked along there.

During Fleet Week 1988, I saw a well-built sailor walking along the boulevard. I circled, pulled up next to him and offered him a ride. He declined. I guess he was nervous since he was alone and the Navy brass had probably given him a long lecture about crime and being careful of predators. As a stocky black man who is very attracted to inexperienced white guys who live virtually every moment in a prestructured environment, I am often faced with the challenge of convincing sailors that I want to give, not take.

I made another pass and waved at the handsome man who had rejected me earlier. At least he was not rude as so many sailors are. Then I made another pass, and I noticed that the young man had stopped walking and was just standing there. I approached him again and asked if he would like to party with me. To my surprise, he accepted. He later told me he did not go with me the first time because he wanted some time to see "what I was up to." He went home with me and I sucked his cock almost until the sun came up, and then safely delivered him back to his ship in time for duty. He even gave me his mailing address.

I wrote him once. No reply.

"If I Do This, Will You Stop Following Me?"

Fleet Week has been mostly disappointing during the 1990s. The sailors still come to visit, but there is little or no sex to be found. Several Fleet Weeks came and went and despite my best efforts I had no sexual adventures to report to my friends. From what I could see, most of the other cruisers also went hungry. We just stood around and talked about the good old days as we watched scores of beautiful young men bypass the XXX arcades and ignore all our friendly advances.

Like every Fleet Week, the 1996 events started on a Saturday with the parade of ships and the public tours. Also, like every Fleet Week, I began my cruising on Saturday afternoon, giving the boys a few hours to get off duty, get something to eat and then hit the streets. Absolutely nothing happened. Frustrated, I went home at dawn Sunday morning, got some sleep and came back Sunday afternoon to continue my mission.

Surely another Fleet Week would not go by without me sucking at least one sailor's cock. That afternoon, I met a really nice guy named Jim, a tall sailor from Southern California. He didn't mind hanging out with me and talking, but he rejected all of my sexual propositions, insisting that he was married and 100 percent straight. He loved bondage games and had a mistress who satisfied that need in him, but sex with a man was out of the question.

Jim was very attractive—okay, gorgeous—despite his big ears. Since nothing else was happening I sat and chatted with him in a North Beach restaurant for a couple of hours before I gave him my phone number, shook his very masculine hand and said good-bye. I told him to call if he changed his mind, since he would be in town another couple of days. But if there's one thing I've learned over the years, it's that sailors never call.

Monday evening the North Beach XXX arcades were mostly empty. Even most of the cruisers had given up. Then this really cute sailor wearing shorts, a T-shirt, and a baseball cap came into the nude dancing theater. He went back and forth between the dancing girl booths and the video booths. I followed him like a puppy dog. To have him would mean the end of a very long drought. The guy noticed me and appeared irritated. He left. I followed. He stepped into the bookstore/arcade next door. I was right behind him.

He studied the magazines for a while, occasionally cocking me an annoyed expression. He made a move like he was going to go into the back room where the videos are but instead he left the store. I pursued him again. He turned the corner onto Broadway and walked quickly down the sidewalk with me hot on his tail, I mean trail. I knew that this was going overboard. I could have been accused of harassing the guy.

When he was forced to stop and wait for a red light, I approached and said hello. He ignored me and crossed the street. Discouraged, I turned to go back the other way, but saw him enter another arcade. I went into the store. We looked at each other and I slipped into the back room (I already had plenty of tokens for the movie machines) and I motioned for him to follow. After a little hesitation, he followed me into a movie cubicle. He said: "Look, if I do this, will you stop following me?" "You bet," I said. I pulled down his short pants and underwear. His legs had this cute soft down covering. So did his butt, which I rubbed as I sucked his cock, which was hard as a rock before I even touched it. He wanted to make it quick. I wouldn't let him. Each time he was close to coming, I would make use of my years of cocksucking experience and back off, allowing him to cool down. Finally he begged me to let him pop. When I had toyed with him enough, I rolled a rubber on his dick and let him do the work. He fucked my mouth like it was a San Diego whore and fired into the condom. We hugged. We dressed. Then he opened the cubicle door just a crack, peeped out and said, "Wait a few minutes until I'm gone. And don't follow me!"

My luck with sailors had changed for the better. Content, I went home. There on my answering machine were six messages from Jim, the handsome bondage-loving sailor from the previous day. He had changed his mind and thought it was time to expand his experiences. He was sorry he missed me. A month later, Jim's wife called and left a message wondering why my phone number was on her husband's telephone bill. She asked me to call her. I can't tell you how tempted I was to call the number she left and try to connect with Jim again. But I would never do anything that would harm a man's marriage.

"I Won't Be Your Bed Buddy,
but I Have Nowhere Else to Go"

Years of recreational sex with sailors taught me many things about them, about me, and about life. Including this valuable life lesson: No matter how much you like a guy, and no matter how many times he lets you suck his dick, don't get emotionally involved. He'll only make you cry.

This sailor's name was Bill. After numerous sexual encounters we became friends. He was a plain-looking blond, boy-next-door type from Pennsylvania. Nice smile, naturally muscular body, and an easygoing nature. He was about nineteen when I knew him; I was about twenty-seven. It was the early 1980s, before the fear of AIDS, fear of crime, and fear of military drug tests dampened the Navy party spirit. Bill loved to smoke pot. So did I (mostly on weekends). When his ship was in port, he would call me once a week to come over and have sex and smoke a joint. Bill seemed to like me and the conversations we had. He told me about his family, his hometown, and the girls he had fucked. He was polite and thanked me for my sexual services, but otherwise he didn't talk much without me coaxing him. After a few months, it was time for WESTPAC (a six-month Western Pacific tour). Bill left and honestly I didn't expect to hear from him again. He was a sailor, after all. A few weeks later, the phone rang and there was Bill asking if he could stay with me a few days. It seems he had sampled the weed in the Asian ports. He had already been caught on the Navy piss test twice before. Bill was flown to Treasure Island and given a bus ticket back to Pennsylvania. How could he face his father, an ex-naval officer?

I took him in, comforted him, slept with him, and sucked his dick every chance I got. Like any nineteen-year-old, he watched a lot of TV, made a lot of phone calls, and played the music too loudly. But that was okay. We obviously had something going. He liked me, I liked him. Maybe this was it, my lifelong dream of meeting the right guy just as he was getting out of the Navy and settling down to live happily ever after.

We were sitting comfortably at home one evening, him on the sofa, me on the floor snuggling his leg. Bill looked at me and said that he was really glad that I was his friend. Well, it wasn't "I love you," but it was nice to hear. Then he finished the sentence. "But I can't stay here and be your bed buddy." He tried to explain that he was grateful for me helping him, but that he was straight and after more than a week of goofing off he needed to head on home. By now, I wasn't really listening. I was crying like a baby. And I never cry over these guys. I never expect to develop any sort of relationship. I consider it a long-term involvement if I even see them more than once.

Bill didn't know what to say except "Stop crying." I walked to the store. When I came back, the crying had stopped. I can't explain that burst of emotion. It wasn't like Bill broke my heart or anything. Although I hoped for a serious connection, I never really expected it to happen. When I play the lottery I don't break into tears as I clutch my losing ticket at the local 7-Eleven. So, why cry? That night Bill and I clicked our beers and went to bed. The next day we hugged goodbye at the bus station in Oakland. He went home to Pennsylvania, taking my fantasy with him. I went home to my life.

Jacksonville Biker Tired of the Hustle

The first time I saw Joe he was walking across the street in San Francisco near the North Beach XXX video arcades. His friends were still in the nightclub trying to score some girls. He was anxious to go home. Handsome, tall, lanky, about nineteen years old with brown hair and earnest eyes, wearing a bandanna to hide his close-cropped hair, Joe was one of those sailors who never wanted to look like a sailor. He carried himself in a confident, self-assured way—almost cocky. He paced next to his car, smoking a cigarette in the cool night air, waiting for his friends to give up the hunt. But I had my sights on him.

I introduced myself and he was friendly. Before long he explained that he mainly liked girls, but if I was cool I could give him head in exchange for a little cash. Since I wasn't looking for love and trade was okay when I could afford it (and more efficient than the long chase), we had a deal. I sucked him off in the arcade, gave him my number and offered my services anytime. A few days later he called. I serviced. He called again, and again. Before long we had a regular business arrangement going, and he came by the house an average of once every two weeks. Sometimes he was heading back to his base in Vallejo on his motorcycle and since my house was on the way, he'd drop by, occasionally at odd times, even the early morning hours.

He took to calling me "Maynard" for reasons he could never explain. (Did I remind him of the *Dobie Gillis* character? If so, why?) Joe told me a lot about himself, how he first started getting his dick sucked by guys when he was a teenager in Jacksonville, Florida. (There was a rest room in a park: "Just stick it through the glory hole and you never even had to see the face of the guy doing the sucking.") He had joined the Navy looking for adventure and a change of scenery. He hated it and often spent his days scheming up ways to convince the Navy he was crazy and should be discharged immediately. So far, it was not working.

The sex was a way for Joe and me to become friends. Joe seemed to have a great time when I sucked his cock but he also claimed to be quite a ladies' man. He claimed he managed to become a pet of sorts to some women at one of the North Beach strip clubs and that they sometimes let him hang around after closing. Some of the girls, he explained, needed to fuck after a long night of sexy dancing and Joe was glad to do what he could to help. Well, it's possible. He hoped to get a job at the strip joint as a bouncer as soon as he convinced his C.O. to kick him out of the Navy. Joe said he was tired of hustling to make ends meet. A job at a strip joint would be the answer to his prayers. Soon after, Joe called me and came by with good news. He was getting out of the Navy. They never bought into his mentally disturbed act, but apparently they grew tired of the game and just let him go. But there was no job waiting at the strip club. Joe—last seen packing to return to Florida.

Reluctant Orgasms

It probably goes without saying that many of the sailors I sucked off did not have that in mind when they first agreed to spend time with me. Of course, I never forced myself on any of them. And if a guy said no and really meant it, that was the end of that. But if a guy said no, and I felt I could talk him into saying yes, well, what would you expect me to do? I had to try to convince them to change their minds. I felt it was my duty to make them understand that opportunity should not be wasted. That happened a lot because, after all, I was mainly pursuing men who considered themselves straight. Even most of the ones who were happy to be serviced by me were usually not interested in returning my affections, did little or no touching, had little or no interest in anal sex (top or bottom) and for heaven's sake, there could be no kissing!

Gay friends who know about my activities often ask me what I get out of such one-sided sex. It's difficult to explain. If I wanted to look for a boyfriend and a real two-way romance, there were civilian guys for that game. And if I had found it among the Navy guys, I would have been the first to thank the Maker. No, Navy men were for recreational sex, friendship if possible, and the fulfilling of my fantasies and fetishes. Hearing that, gay friends then assumed I was attracted to the uniform, in the way that some guys fantasize about cops or firemen, but that's not true either. As any sailor chaser can tell you, you rarely see Navy men in their uniforms unless you work on the base/ship or there's some special event or the guys are visiting from out of town and they are ordered to wear the uniform.

My attraction to sailors is something much more basic and perhaps inexplicable, even to myself. When they are out and about in civvies (civilian clothing) I can pick them out in a crowd with no trouble at all. The haircut? Maybe. The way they carry themselves? Perhaps. I often joked with other cruisers in North Beach about my "naval radar." I'd spot a young man a block away and instinctively, immediately, know that he was in the Navy. Many times just to prove a point (and to check on the flirting possibilities) I'd talk to that stranger to find out if my radar was on target. I rarely missed.

My insatiable hunger for sailor cock sometimes drove me to do things I'm not proud of. There were occasions when I had a young man cornered, sometimes literally, in a situation where it was clear that he did not want to have sex with me or any other man. But I didn't take no for an answer. Some men had moral objections to homosexual activity. Many of my seductions entailed discussion on the pros and cons of men having sex with each other. The ones who escaped often fell back on old reliable defenses that are not the product of logic and reason. (1) The Bible. (2) "I wasn't raised that way." I stopped debating number one long ago because I don't have a lot to say to people who give ancient tribal doctrine veto power over their sex lives. As for number two, I never understood what it meant.

I talked a lot of guys into accepting head from me, even when they didn't want it. Most of the reluctant ones usually came around eventually and had a good time as I worked my magic on their hard cocks. However, one example of a reluctant orgasm involved a sailor who came home with me and ended up locking himself in the bathroom.

I met Tim in a bar on Webster Street in Alameda. He was there with a couple of friends who left to do something else. I invited him to join me at my apartment for more drinks and conversation. I started making my moves on him and asked him repeatedly if I could give him some head. He repeatedly said no. I asked him again and again and again. I don't know if his resolve was weakening or he just panicked, but he got up and rushed to the rest room. A few minutes passed before I knocked to see if he was all right. He was very upset. "I came over because you said we would be friends," he said. "But now I'm stuck here because I know you won't give me a ride back to the base and I don't know where I am." Tim truly believed that if he did not give in to me I would strand him in Oakland and force him to walk back to the base. I would never do that, of course, and told him so. However, I continued to argue the virtues of getting a blow job as I sat on the bathtub and he sat on the toilet. I talked and talked. Tim listened and listened. Occasionally he would repeat the word no, or make a small throat-clearing grunt, but otherwise he said very little.

Finally it became clear to both of us that he would not get out of the bathroom (or my apartment) without receiving a blow job. So with his half-hearted permission, I did him as he sat right there on the toilet. He responded well enough to my soothing lips and mouth and after a few minutes his average-sized dick swelled and fired down my throat. "How was it?" I asked. Tim admitted that the physical sensations were nice but he still did not feel good about doing it. We talked a little more before I took him back to the base in Alameda.

I felt bad and realized that I should have backed off on Tim. In a way I did force my desires on him. I've gotten a lot of sailor cock by being aggressive. But what happened that night was wrong. I never used those tactics in that type of situation again. I know where to draw the line. The incident with Tim was a case of going too far.

One other case of a reluctant sailor comes to mind. I took him home. We drank. We talked. I asked to suck his cock. He repeatedly said no. However, we both eventually grew tired and since I only had one bed, he agreed to sleep in bed with me if I promised not to take advantage of him. I agreed.

During the night, I reached over and started rubbing his cock through his white jockeys. His dick was hard. He awoke and moved my hand away and asked me not to do that. Bothered, I tried to go back to sleep but I couldn't. Later I rubbed some more. This time he did not move and I suspected that he was awake. I played with his dick through his underwear for a while. I yanked back the covers, patted his slim, hairless thigh, and pulled his hard cock through the leg hole of his briefs. I moved down the mattress so I was eye to eye with his cock and gave him a nice, slow, comfortable blow. Reluctant Sailor made thrusting motions and soon spurted a nice load. Putting his penis back in his underpants, he said, "I wanted to see how far you would go. Now I know." We smiled and went to sleep.

"Well at Least I Made Some Guy Happy"

This story only happened a couple of years ago. I was desperately cruising Alameda. In recent years, as I've mentioned, it has been much more difficult to have sexual encounters with Navy men. Most of the cruisers who used to wear grooves in the pavement driving around trying to pick up sailors have long since moved on to other hunting grounds. I was one of the last holdouts. Finally, one weekend late at night, I saw a cute young guy, somewhat small in stature, standing outside of a popular Webster Street bar. He wasn't twenty-one so he could not go inside. But he was bored and had left his ship to at least walk around in hope of getting laid. He was thinking about girls. I convinced him to get some beers with me and we headed down to Crown Beach to sit and talk.

After a while, I confessed to him that I was gay and that I very much wanted to suck his dick. He wasn't interested but he was curious about why I was attracted to men and not women. I explained. He seemed to accept my reasons even if he didn't understand them. As we talked, I explained how most of the guys that I have serviced over the years were actually straight men and how they always enjoyed what I did for them even if there was no chance of romance or a permanent relationship. I told him about my strong hunger for sucking cock and that I would be very grateful if he would let me do him. Finally, I wore him down. We drove to another part of the park behind the tennis courts and I pulled his pants down right there. He was still hesitating, but I assured him that he would enjoy the blow job and that he could always have women if that's where his main attractions lie. I worked him over until he fired off his first load with another guy.

He was not as pleased as I was with how things had gone. He did not freak out, but he was bothered by what we had done and said he wanted to walk alone back to the base. I told him again that if he was uncomfortable with man-man sex he didn't have to do it again, but that there's nothing wrong with experimenting. I say this to young men not because I just want to get into their pants; I say this because I truly believe it and because I believe that all types of sex should be a source of pleasure and relaxation, not a source of guilt and anxiety. His only response as we shook hands and he turned to walk away was, "Well, at least I made some guy happy."

"I Just Want to Talk and Watch Cute Guys, Don't You?"

What about the gay sailors? I rarely encounter any. Oh sure, I know they are out there, but the sailor hunt seems to mirror my hunt for men in general: I tend to be attracted to straight guys who have no interest in long-term relationships with men, and the gay guys I like have no interest in me.

In 1980, I met Chuck in The Front Page, a gay bar in midtown Memphis. Chuck was this cute little Navy guy originally from Oklahoma. He was friendly in an environment where men tended be unfriendly unless they were cruising you. We always spoke and he even danced with me some. However, he was not interested in me as a lover. I asked him out on dates several times, but he would have no part of it. He just said he was looking for a "girlfriend" to talk with, to watch cute guys with, and to share comments on their cuteness. Well, it wasn't much but at least he would talk to me. Finally, one night I decided I had to have him. We went out to his little car in the parking lot to smoke a joint and I just went for his zipper. He protested a bit as I performed my oral services but he sat there and gave up the juice. Afterward he repeated that he wanted to just be friends, although he never gave me a way of contacting him at the naval base and he never called me. I remember seeing him again, once or twice. But that was it.

Then there was Dave, the gay Navy boy I met in Alameda, California. We first came across each other in the early 1980s shortly after I discovered the XXX movie arcade. I serviced Dave a few times and we developed a "when I see you I'll do you" sort of friendship. Then I got greedy and tried to actually get to know him. He did not have a car and was anxious to go to San Francisco to explore some of the gay scene there. I took him to a bar near the Castro and, sailor or no, he proved to be like most other gay guys that I've encountered in life: disloyal and shallow. He dumped me almost immediately. Dave was very cute, a strawberry blond white boy with a pug nose; just the type that every Castro queen seems to want. We arrived at the bar, and I had barely ordered the first set of beers before another guy started cruising Dave. Minutes later, they danced. Many minutes later I couldn't get him off the dance floor, so I just walked out. Being a nice guy, I waited by the car debating whether to just leave the SOB. Soon he came out and told me he wanted to stay and have a good time with his new friend, and could he have his WESTPAC jacket out of the car before I left. I told him I didn't appreciate being treated that way, and added that I thought he was a shithead, and then, playing the role of nice guy again, I gave him the jacket. Maybe I should have kept it for a souvenir. I never saw him again.

The Cop in the Rearview Mirror

Despite my many successes in scoring with sailors over the years, there are those times when things went wrong. Very wrong. One time in a movie arcade booth, I touched a guy without his permission and he threatened to get the police and file sexual assault charges against me. That had never happened before, and although I had only lightly and briefly rubbed the guy's crotch through his pants, I was shaken by his threat. After all, I am a professional man. I left the arcade for a while and I have no idea if the offended sailor really did get the police and attempt to carry out his threat. For years after that, I was always careful to ask permission first, or at least to touch the leg and not the groin, unless I got a clear signal to proceed.

Another time I picked up a sailor in Alameda my instincts were sounding an alarm almost from the moment he got into the car. The guy was obviously agitated. He said that he hated his life and hated being in the Navy. I had already decided that I was not going to suggest anything sexual and was in the process of driving back to a more populated area when he suddenly grabbed my shirt collar and started screaming in my face that he was "sick of guys like me," referring to homosexuals who proposition sailors. I tried to calm him down, but he raised his foot from the passenger side floor of my car and started kicking the front windshield. I drove on as he kicked away at the windshield, cracking it but not managing to punch a hole through it.

I pulled into a fast food restaurant parking lot and told him to get out of my car. Instead, he tried to grab me again. I got out and asked someone to call the police. For the next few minutes, he alternately kicked at the windshield and rifled through my glove box while I stood outside and watched along with a small group of passersby that gathered. "What's wrong with him?" one woman asked. "I don't know," I answered. "Well, I saw him attacking you," she said. "I'll be your witness." The cops pulled up. I reported what had happened. The guy got out of the car and gave his side of the story. He said I had sexually assaulted him and he became outraged when I touched him. I was furious when the cops seemed to buy that lie, but I had a difficult time explaining why I picked up a stranger. As I was about to insult the cops' investigative skills (and probably get myself in a lot of trouble), one officer suggested that we all cut our losses. If I agreed not to file charges against Crazed Sailor, then Crazed Sailor would agree to drop the sexual assault allegation against me and pay me what he had in his pocket as a contribution toward the windshield repair. He had about forty dollars and some change. It was clear that I would not get justice on that night. I took the money and was glad that I had insurance.

Then there was the weekend night I was on patrol on Atlantic Avenue looking for sailors walking toward the base. I passed this one guy, and he was gorgeous. Light brown hair, muscles, and cute. I pulled over to the curb and waited for him to walk past the car. I talked to him through the passenger side window and offered him a ride to the base. He flashed a nice smile and quickly agreed. As we slowly drove toward the NAS east gate, he proved to be friendly and talkative. All of my instinct told me that this nice young sailor knew exactly what I wanted and he was interested.

I asked if he was in a hurry to get back to his ship. He said no. I asked if he was interested in coming to my home and spending some time there. He said yes. Then, right on that note, headlights in my rearview mirror exploded into colors: red, yellow, and blue. The police were behind me and wanted me to pull over. What did I do? I wondered. I was certainly not speeding. Quite the contrary—I wanted as much time as possible to talk to this handsome guy. I pulled over. The cop explained that he had seen me pick up the sailor. As I politely asked "So what?" he went on to explain that recently there had been incidents of sailors being robbed by assailants who offered rides. The cop asked for my driver's license and then walked back to the squad car to run my number to check to see if I was a wanted criminal. Meanwhile, the cute sailor sat quietly in the passenger seat of my car, no doubt wondering what the heck was going on and how could he get out of it without some embarrassing incident that he would have to explain to his superiors.

After the cop ran my record, he walked over to the cute sailor, asked him to get out of the car and gave him some speech that started with, "Didn't your mother ever tell you not to accept rides from strangers?" Even as I was being hassled—me, this middle-aged black man who had stopped to pick up this young white sailor—I was desperately considering ways to salvage the situation. By the time I considered asking for permission to give the sailor my phone number, it was too late. Cute Sailor was gone. He had passed beyond the magic barrier that separates civilians from military personnel.

I Came Four Times—Now I Have a Knife

My doctor, who is gay, always warned me about bringing strange men home. The USS *Enterprise* was always my favorite aircraft carrier, probably because my favorite starship was named after it. It had also been around the Bay Area longer than any other carrier and I had serviced a fair number of sailors from "The Big E" and never had a problem. Until Andy. I met him in Alameda. I don't remember exactly where and how, but I took him home to have a good time. I'm sure I offered him the usual: beer, videos, and conversation. I remember it was late at night when we started to party. And after a while, I asked him to let me suck his cock and he said, "Okay."

I remember he spent most of our four hours together sitting in my easy chair in one corner of the living room, watching straight porno videos and letting me suck on his dick any way I wanted. I alternately worked him over slow and easy and hard and fast. His penis was slightly longer than average. Since we were both full of beer and it was a weekend, I was determined to give him head until one of us dropped. I got Andy to ejaculate a record-breaking four times. This may sound like a lot of baloney, but it's true. You just don't forget something like that. We drank a little more beer and celebrated the victorious end to an evening of marathon sex.

Without a doubt, this was the best episode I had ever had with a sailor. Andy was fairly cute, with that all-American white-boy-next-door sort of look to him: slim swimmer's build with little clusters of brown hair on his chest and belly. He was about nineteen years old, and I remember he told me he joined the Navy almost directly out of high school. But I can't say he had the face of an angel. It was four or five in the morning and we were worn out. Andy asked me to take him back to his ship. The drive back was just an extension of the terrific evening we'd had enjoying each other's company. As we exited the Webster Street tube, a tunnel under the estuary linking Oakland and the island city of Alameda, Andy asked me to take him by an automatic cash machine down the street. I stopped the car at the bank. Then he pulled the knife.

It appeared to be a large pocket knife of the sort you might take on a hunting trip. Andy had decided that his four ejaculations were worth two hundred dollars (the bank machine's cash withdrawal limit). As he made his demand, he grabbed my wrist with his left hand and pointed the knife at me with his right hand. At first I was shocked and quite concerned. My next thought was: Why didn't I see it coming? Had my instincts finally failed me with terrible consequences? Earlier I liked him so much I had given him my telephone number and asked him to call anytime.

I opened the driver's side door and told Andy I was going to get the money from the ATM. That meant he had to let go of my arm. He did, and then he spun around and got out of the passenger's side door to come around to my side of the car. As soon as he was out, I hopped back into the car, locked the doors, put the key back in the ignition, and quickly drove away with Andy trying to hang on to my driver's side rearview mirror. He wanted to break it in a last-ditch effort to inflict some type of punishment on me. However, he failed to do even that; the mirror is designed to bend or flex if it hits something. I saw Andy shrinking in the rearview mirror.

Later that night, he called me. Wouldn't you know, the sailor who actually called me back was the one who turned out to be a lowlife. He laughed and made nasty remarks on my answering machine. I could hear another guy also laughing in the background. I made a tape of the telephone message just in case I had to go to the captain of the *Enterprise*. But I never heard from Andy again.

Repeat Performances

The overwhelming majority of the sailors who had sex with me considered themselves straight. I always understood that they were experimenting or just plain horny and desperate to get off. They came to me for various reasons. Jonathan, a cute freckled-face redhead with a short dick and who used to always say "Oh, God" when he came, often visited me and had sex with me in exchange for marijuana. This was before the Navy's zero tolerance policy on drugs. Tom from Michigan used to call me on the phone and just say, "Hi, it's Tom. I'm horny, can I come over?" He hated to masturbate and I loved to suck cock, so we were very compatible. Sometimes he managed to date girls and get some pussy. But he knew that he was always welcome to plop down on my sofa and enjoy some righteous head.

Many other Navy guys I encountered considered themselves bisexual. One tall blond guy epitomized that group. I asked if he preferred men or women. He said it didn't matter "as long as someone was down there taking care of it." This was clearly not a do-it-yourself man.

Michael from Atlanta was one of the few sailors with whom I actually dared to hope for a real relationship. We connected in one of my favorite XXX arcades in San Francisco—you remember, the one with the dancing girls. I ran into him about five or six times at the arcade over the course of about six months. Each time I serviced him in a booth his sailor buddies were nearby, either elsewhere in the arcade or next door in the nightclub. About a year passed with no encounters. Then one night he was back at the arcade, alone. He at last felt comfortable enough to come home with me. To my surprise, that night Michael showed that he liked to give as well as receive. He crawled into bed with me and we took turns sucking and fucking each other like we were born to be together. We had long conversations about how he preferred women, but back in Atlanta he had discovered that men make good sexual partners too. I was thinking that he was attracted to me and maybe there was a possibility of making something happen between us that had real meaning. I hinted around with him about my budding feelings, but he did not respond

I didn't hear from Michael for a few months. Of course, you can never locate sailors on their ships, so they always say, so I didn't have a telephone number for him. I assumed that he was no longer in the Bay Area. Then one day as I was driving around in Alameda there he was, working on an old car in a parking lot just outside the naval base. He seemed angry and frustrated. When he told me he was getting out of the Navy and going back to Georgia, my heart danced and my eyes glowed with hope. "Stay here with me," I told him. He told me I was nuts and that there was nothing for him here and he just wanted to get as far away from California as he could. Dejected and rejected, I left, never expecting to see Michael again.

Two months later, I was on patrol in Alameda looking for fresh sailor dick. Suddenly a taxicab started tailgating me and blinking its lights. I moved to the right lane to let it pass. It didn't. The light blinking continued. Finally, I stopped my car to see what was going on. The cabby pulled alongside me, rolled down his window, and waved. The hair was longer and growing into a ponytail, but there was no mistake: It was Michael. He explained that as soon as he got back to Atlanta he hated it and returned to the Bay Area to find work. He followed me home in his cab as I wondered if I should dare to reignite the hopes of finding a real lover among all of those sailor encounters.

We were barely through the door of my apartment before we were all over each other. We never even made it to the bed. Within minutes that former sailor took me right there on the sofa. Minutes later, he came. A few minutes more, he was dressed. He didn't say much except, "I'm sorry. I'm here pretending that I really wanted you when actually, all I wanted was your behind."

He left. I should have been crushed, but really, I wasn't. It was just like before; all we had was sex. And he was only a memory now, like a final chapter in a now-closed book. After all, real Navy men don't wear ponytails.

Final Thoughts on Male Bonding

As a young man in my twenties I discovered that sailors were a sexual option for me. It was logical in so many ways. They were lonely, horny, away from home, and looking for company. I was just lonely and horny. I was, if I do say so myself, an attractive guy as a young man and I was no doubt a fantasy come true for many of the sailors I sucked, both straight and gay. After all, if you're going to take a walk on the wild side you may as well walk with a nice-looking man.

During my many years of military chasing, I rarely chased an ugly guy. Now it's twenty years later and I don't look the way I did when I was twenty-one. I also hit my sexual peak during the 1970s and 1980s, before the fear of AIDS ended the sexual revolution and killed off much of the sexual experimentation that was so common when I was younger. Fear of crime has also prevented this generation from the serendipitous encounters that permitted me access to the pants of so many young men in Uncle Sam's Navy.

I'm the first to admit that I gained nothing from the encounters in the long run except many fun memories. I never seriously expected the encounters to be anything more than ships bumping and passing in the night. Everyone wants companionship. Friends say I should have used that energy to find a life partner, a gay one, instead of constantly pursuing transient servicemen, and straight ones at that. Maybe so. But I found all of my experiences uniquely exciting.

I met so many guys that I would never have otherwise experienced—and I mean emotionally and conversationally, as well as sexually. I was a good listener. They talked of their children and their wives and the girl back home or the girl they wanted to meet. And since our encounters were only brief and based on sex, I was no threat to their life plans. They talked of the reasons they joined the Navy, whether it was a mistake or whether it opened doors to a career. I related to young men who spoke wide-eyed of places they had seen and hoped to see again, and of people they had met and hoped to meet again. I helped some guys expand their sexuality to understand that it's okay to experiment in a safe and healthy way—to try things to see if you like them, and to stop doing them if you don't. Maybe they learned something from me that they can teach their wives. For some of the men I was just a set of ears, and the blow job was just a nice diversion. That's okay. Along the way I provided safe shelters for drunken sailors who could have gotten into serious trouble. Yes, I was looking for sex. But other things came with those couplings. In many cases, I came away with the nice feelings associated with two men bonding, however briefly. Although sailors serve with other males, and are trained in combat to even die for other males, taboos prevented them from enjoying the touch of other males. I hope I served a purpose, even if for only a few minutes or hours, to show them it was okay to enjoy another type of male bonding.

I felt no immorality when I gave those young men sexual relief and temporary companionship. There was (usually) no guilt on my part. I hope the same was true for them. Lonely servicemen have needed guys like me since the first troops gathered into regiments and marched or sailed away from home.

Most of the time I got permission for what I did, and most of the time the servicemen were pleased with the result. And most seemed genuinely happy to have known me, even if our bond was fleeting. I was driven by desire and lust. But I think many of those kids needed me, at least on some level, whether they realized it or not. And I needed them. I don't know if I can ever truly explain to myself why.

Once during Fleet Week, I was taking a leak at a crowded urinal in a rest room near Fisherman's Wharf. A handsome blond sailor in dress blues was pissing just to my left. His dick was perfect and semihard. I was staring at it. When I looked up, he was looking at me and smiling. He knew I liked what I saw and he didn't mind. He seemed pleased to show it to me. Even with a crowd pressing all around us, he lingered a little before he put it away. His buddies were waiting outside.

FIGURE 1. Twentynine Palms, California, Marine: *"I'll leave my phone number with some phrase like 'Good $$$ for BJ for USMC'..."* (Dan Devlin collection)

FIGURE 2. Sailor, 1960. *"We both save them from death and are vicariously excited by death's prospects in their lives."* And sometimes death's prospects in our own lives. (U.S. Navy)

FIGURE 3. Postcard from Naval Training Center, San Diego: *"I usually found it very easy to get on the base. . . ."* (U.S. Navy)

FIGURE 4. Wrestling Marines. (© Jon-Paul Baumer, buzzcut@ix.netcom.com)

FIGURE 5. "Mud run" Marine: *"A certified masculinity . . ."* (Private collection)

FIGURE 6. Model Marine: *"a boyish vulnerability."* (© Robert Lind, rlind@cts.com)

FIGURE 7. Oceanside Marine. (© Jon-Paul Baumer, buzzcut@ix.netcom.com)

FIGURE 8. 1950s sailor: *"The Navy boys would hitchhike to go over a bridge to their ships. . . ."* (David Lloyd collection)

FIGURE 9. 1970s Marine in all-male pornography: *"The biggest of them all was Gary Boyd. . . ."* (© Bijou Video)

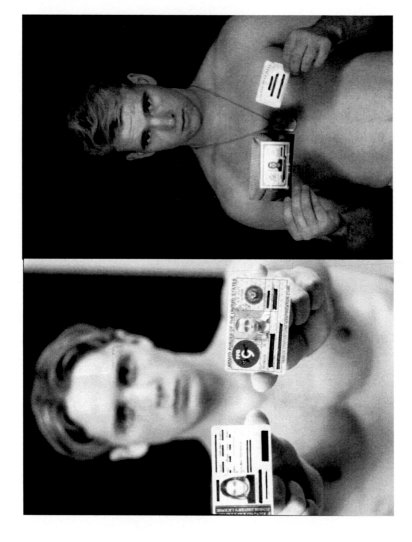

FIGURES 10 and 11. 1990s Navy and Marine Corps models. (David Lloyd collection)

FIGURE 12. *"They recalled the fresh young image of the Handsome Sailor, that face never deformed by a sneer or subtler vile freak of the heart within."* (Brian Pera collection)

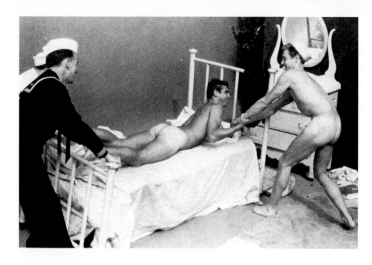

FIGURE 13. *"Most of the guys were 'just curious' or 'experimenting' . . ."* (Photo courtesy of the Athletic Model Guild)

FIGURE 14. Coast Guard cadets, early 1960s. *"What I secretly desired was to be a part of such a group, to belong as they do, in a world of fraternal affection, bonding, and the odd dip into homoeroticism. . . ."* (U.S. Coast Guard Academy)

FIGURE 15. *"I'm attracted to the military because it's a male society. . . ."*
(© Norman Eales)

FIGURE 16. Andrei and friend, Kronstadt 1997 (note reversed headgear).
(© Steve Kokker)

FIGURE 17. Pasha: *"Russian men in general attracted me, their full-lipped, effort-less sensuality, their tough-guy posturing combined with a winsome gentleness when spoken to. But Russian military men took my breath away."* (© Steve Kokker)

FIGURE 18. Latvian paratroopers, Pirita beach, Tallinn, Estonia. (© Steve Kokker)

FIGURE 19. Depiction of any person in this work should not be construed as an implication of said person's sexual desires, behavior, or identity. (D. Clemens)

FIGURE 20. Pulp. *"'Giving them a loan,' or 'tiding them over 'til pay day'—that is one way of rationalizing. . . ."* (Private collection)

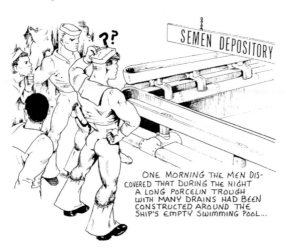

FIGURE 21. Cartoon. *". . . the association of masculinity with potency, with aggression, with being on top, with large genitalia, with buckets of semen."* (© Stephen, courtesy of Winston Leyland)

FIGURE 22. Latvian paratroopers, Pirita beach, Tallinn, Estonia (II). (© Steve Kokker)

FIGURE 23. Marine. (David Lloyd, courtesy of The Kinsey Institute for Research in Sex, Gender, and Reproduction, Inc.)

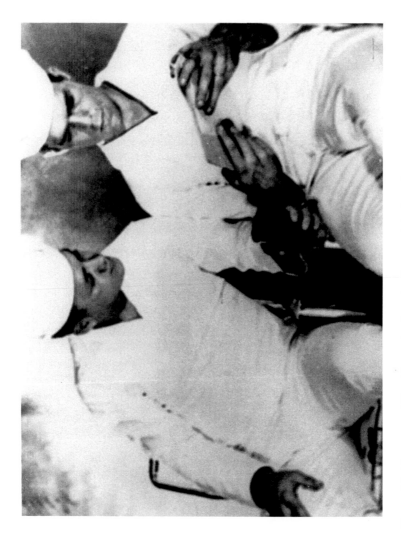

Figure 24. (Courtesy of The Kinsey Institute for Research in Sex, Gender, and Reproduction, Inc.)

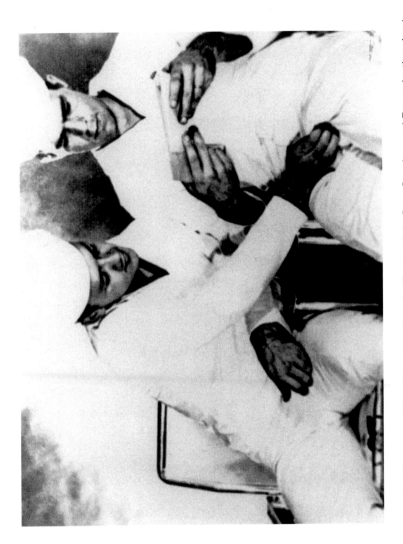

Figure 25. (Courtesy of The Kinsey Institute for Research in Sex, Gender, and Reproduction, Inc.)

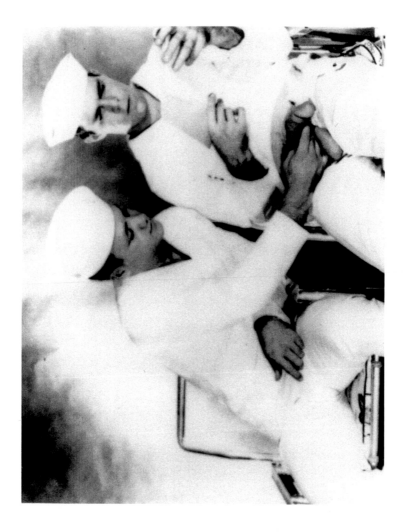

Figure 26. (Courtesy of The Kinsey Institute for Research in Sex, Gender, and Reproduction, Inc.)

FIGURE 27. (Courtesy of The Kinsey Institute for Research in Sex, Gender, and Reproduction, Inc.)

FIGURE 28. (Courtesy of The Kinsey Institute for Research in Sex, Gender, and Reproduction, Inc.)

Cory:
Bury My Heart at Twentynine Palms

Cory is a forty-nine-year-old entrepreneur originally from Montana. He has been the publisher of a big city gay newspaper, and he has had two long-term relationships with gay professional men. Now, he lives alone with his dogs in a Mojave high-desert military town.

Cory: Gay boys, to me, are just not sexually interesting. They're a total waste of time.
Zeeland: Why?
C: I'm a homosexual because I like men. I'm really turned on by masculinity. I'm attracted to it, I admire it, I like to be around it. And gay men don't give that off. They give off an ersatz masculinity.
Z: Even the younger, "roid-raging," "hypermasculine" gay men?
C: Particularly those men. They are so bogus. I'm not interested in statues. I'm interested in heroes. And for me, the Marines, the sailors, and often the other three branches, are filled with men who are heroes. Guys who got their muscles the old-fashioned way. By doing work, by playing sports. By being *men*. I like being around them. I mean, I live in Twentynine Palms because of the ambient testosterone that's just in the air. I couldn't live in a gay ghetto. There's nothing there for me.

Most of the men who enter the service are not only great physical specimens. These are people who often have old-fashioned values that I grew up associating with the best men. Men who believed in virtue. Who believed in honor. Who had a sense of personal integrity. Who had a commitment to something bigger than themselves, like our country, or the cause of freedom that they think our country represents. It's just—I'm awestruck by every new crop of Marines that comes into town. And how the tradition of service, and the sense of selflessness, sense of gallantry continues. I want to be surrounded by men like that for the rest of my life. I love them. I admire them. And I'm glad that I get the chance to be with at least some of them.
Z: But how do you meet military guys?
C: By going to places where Marines hang out, like Marine bars, rest areas, and rest rooms at athletic fields. I'll leave my phone number with

some phrase like "BJ for USMC." Occasionally, "Good $$$ for BJ for USMC." Usually I'll leave a name that is not my own. That way, I can tell where the person is calling from. So if somebody is calling for "Mike" I know they saw the number at The Virginian, which is a bar in Twentynine Palms. I know if they saw "Brad," they're calling from The Stumps, another bar. If they're calling for "Jason," they got the phone number up on Interstate 10, at either the rest area or the truck stop, which are both places where Marines and sailors coming back to Marine Corps Air Ground Combat Center [MCAGCC] will lay over, take a piss break or whatever. Also, leaving messages on phone dating lines has been effective.

Z: What kinds of phone calls do you get?

C: It's as varied as the callers. Oftentimes a Marine or sailor will call up and not say that he saw the number on a wall. He'll say a buddy gave him the number. I'll try to discern just exactly what he knows and what he's looking for. That's sometimes difficult. He's started the conversation not being forthcoming, so I realize that he may not want to tell me everything that's on his mind. Some want to get off. Some want to get paid for getting off. Some aren't sure, and they want to talk about it.

Very seldom do I get any harassing calls. The closest I get is some drunk guy calling me, maybe with his buddy present, and they're sort of playing a game. Those conversations usually end pretty quickly.

But you're always surprised. I think that part of the excitement is that you don't know who's going to choose to call. I mean, it can be anyone from a twenty-one-year-old lance corporal who's away from his girlfriend and is horny and maybe got sucked off once in an adult bookstore, to the guys who are well along in their career and have a wife and kids. A lot of the older guys want to be submissive. They want to blow somebody, they want to get fucked. There are a lot of Marines that seem to have that fantasy about taking a more feminine role. Not a majority, but certainly a substantial number. I would say that the average guy, though, tends to be mid-twenties or younger, and tends to be dominant.

Z: I assume that you have to do a lot of the talking sometimes.

C: Oh yeah. Marines, at least enlisted men, aren't usually that eloquent. And they're a little bit apprehensive. Some of them worry that they're going over to a trap, where someone's going to beat them up because they wanted to get their dick sucked. [Pause.] I forget your question.

Z: How do you express your desires to them?

C: I tell them that I'd love to have them fuck my mouth. Or, I'll ask them what's going on; they'll say, "Nothing." I'll say, "What do you want to have go on?" They'll say, "Well, I'm feeling a little horny." And then I usually say something like, "Well, when you're horny, what do you like to have done?" Usually they want their cock sucked.

I don't want to lay *my* trip on *them*. I am very much more interested in having somebody tell me what they want, even if it might be a little bit different than how I'm feeling at that time. Because it's going to be a hell of a lot better if they're getting something closer to what they want, than if I try to make them do something else. I try to draw them out. It usually works.

Z: Do you provide them with some excuse, some way of heterosexualizing the encounter?

C: Well, money is a great way of doing that.

Z: Money enters the picture in the case of guys calling back—

C: On a money offer.

Z: But do some of the others bring it up?

C: No. No. In fact, guys who came for money don't even verbalize it. They just sort of want it to happen. The average Marine is kind of shy about it. They also euphemize by saying, you know, they really appreciate "being helped out." When you live in a Marine town, everybody knows that Marines don't make a lot of money and that three days after pay day they're broke. So it's "giving them a loan," or "tiding them over 'til pay day." That is one way of rationalizing it.

Z: What's the range of how much you pay them?

C: Anywhere from fifty to two hundred.

Z: What does that depend on?

C: What they want, and what I think they're worth. I mean, I try to make that decision when they're here. Because often it isn't verbalized in the phone call. Like I said, most Marines are shy about saying anything.

Z: So you simply invite these strangers who call you up to come over to your home?

C: No. Usually I'll have them meet me at a well-lit place in a commercial section near my home. That way I can see what they look like. I can see if they were accompanied by another car, I can see if they've got buddies in the car. I want them to be alone. And I want them to look like a Marine, but I don't want them to look like, ah—There are some Marines that I may not be interested in for one reason or another.

Z: If you don't like their looks you just leave?

C: [Pause.] I think I would be raising my danger level by interacting with them for the sole purpose of rejecting them. If they call back and ask what happened, I'll usually say, "The dog's throwing up; I've got to take him to the vet." Or, "There's a small, oily rag fire in the garage."

Z: [Laughs.] Have any of these guys ever turned mean on you?

C: No.

Z: To what do you attribute your lack of problems?

C: Good judge of character.

Z: Have you had situations where you sensed the potential for trouble after they were already in your home?

C: Yeah. I did, as a matter of fact. There was a young lance corporal from Northern California. He was getting out in about three months. Very handsome guy, totally buff. He was a fucking recruiting poster. I had seen him two prior occasions. I mean, I thought his aggressiveness—and he was real aggressive—was kind of hot, kind of Marine-like. Although it had kind of a rougher edge. One time he came over and I just had a bad vibe. He sat on the couch, and I didn't like his reaction to anything I was saying. It just seemed like he was pissed off. So I made some sort of lame excuse, I don't know what it was. Probably not an oily rag fire; he would have seen through that. But I gave him the money he would have earned if he'd stayed, and said good night. I got him out of there and never saw him again.

I had a very good friend a few years ago who tried to pick up somebody he thought was a Marine who turned out to be a plainclothes cop. Took the cop back to his room in the Omni Hotel in Norfolk, Virginia. As soon as he put his hand on the cop's knee, the cop pulled out a gun from an ankle holster and held it to his head. Said, "If you move, you're dead." Then called the other cops who were in the hallway, listening. The guy got busted for felonious frequenting for an immoral act, for attempted sodomy. He was sentenced to five to seven years in the Virginia state penitentiary in Richmond. Let me caution somebody that if they're trying to [meet military men through men's room graffiti], they should only do it in a liberal environment, like California, and not try to do it in a place like Virginia or North Carolina.

Z: How many phone calls do you get?

C: Well, it depends. I would say when I'm fully advertised, about five or six a week. Generally on weekends.

Z: You've told me that you sometimes advertise scenarios involving a woman.

C: Yeah, there are some times when I have advertised [on a] local dating line phone service. I will often advertise as a husband with a young wife, specifically looking for Marines. I make her sound real 'good. I've learned over time, talking to these guys on the phone, what they like. They like big breasts on otherwise petite women, generally. Shaved pussy seems to be a big turn-on. And women who are yet to have a kid, and women who are very sexually experimental. I mean, this is not something that's going to develop into a relationship. So they want to have somebody who gets into everything. So I will advertise that, and I will talk to them on the phone about their sexual likes and dislikes. What we finally arrive at is their total frustration that my wife just works such long hours that the three of us never get together. Sometimes that can mature into them just wanting to get their cock sucked. I'll often represent myself as bisexual enough to help her suck cock, so at least they've been warming up to the idea of some male contact. I would say that I've actually been more successful, recently, at leaving messages for men seeking women. They will identify themselves as Marines, and I'll leave them a message something along the line of, "Hi, my name is Brian. I'm at Twentynine Palms. I heard your ad. I know I'm not what you're looking for. But you sound terrific, and if you're still listening to this message, and you'd like to make a little money, discretely—or maybe *a lot* of money, discreetly—then give me a call." And I'll leave the number. Two-thirty, three o'clock in the morning, they get out of the bars. They call into the phone service to see if anybody has left messages. They get that message. Marines are consistently feeling broke. And at that hour, if he's not with a broad, then he's feeling horny, too. And sometimes that makes it enough so that he calls back. It's happened half a dozen times probably in the last six months. I don't work it all the time, but when I hear a hot Marine who's advertising himself for women on that line, I can't resist.

C: My first awareness of [an attraction to military men] was in the San Francisco Bay Area during the Vietnam War. San Francisco was not only a safe place for homosexuals to be, but it was also one of the largest staging areas for young men going to Vietnam. The entire Bay was lined with bases. Being how it was the center of the late sixties counterculture, and one of the centers of the antiwar movement, the servicemen stuck out like sore thumbs. They were the only ones with short hair in the entire town—other than some of the women. And these were the kind of men that I liked. I liked their looks. Most of 'em were very attractive, most of 'em were around my age.

I remember being nineteen and going into the Downtown Bowl on Eddy Street in the Tenderloin. The men's room had a basin, a urinal, and a toilet. There was no partition around the toilet. You sat there in full view of other people taking a piss or washing their hands. I remember coming in there, and there was a sailor, about my age, who was taking a shit. I was using the urinal. I thought he was unbelievably good-looking. I wasn't in the habit of walking into men's rooms and watching really good-looking men my age taking a dump. He struck up a conversation, asking about places to go. He was from somewhere in the Midwest. We talked, I got him into the streetcar to take him back to my tiny, tiny apartment, and I ended up blowing him. After that, I thought: this is what I really want. This is the kind of guy I really turn on to.

In the Bay Area in those days it was either hippies or military guys. And I think also there was a certain kind of simpatico, inasmuch as many of these guys were lower middle class, which is the way I was raised. I could relate to these guys. I couldn't relate to hippies from the peninsula sitting barefoot in their torn jeans and $160 sweaters.

So I went out looking specifically for military, which in those days was not hard to do. They were everywhere, up and down Market Street. I'd try to meet guys in the adult theaters. Wouldn't want to do 'em in the theater. Although if need be, if they requested, I'd do it. But generally, I wanted to meet these guys, talk to 'em, and take 'em back to my apartment. That was the strategy I developed. It worked with the guy at Downtown Bowl and sonofagun if it didn't start working in the theaters. Generally Navy. San Francisco during the war, that's what you got. But also airmen, guys going to Travis [Air Force Base]. I even met guys from the Coast Guard, because at that time the boot camp for the Coast Guard was at Government Island in San Francisco Bay.

Z: In those days, were you just looking for sex, or were you hoping for a relationship?

C: In the back of my mind I thought a relationship would be a good idea. But I also realized that wasn't very likely. The guys I tended to pick were very straight, very conventional fellas, so it would be a stretch. No, I realized that I was like a dancer at the USO. I was gonna see them that night, and then they were gonna ship out. Some of those boys I'm sure never came back. I've thought about that, about all those guys that left. It was very sad when you started thinking about it. During that time, I was so alienated by the antiwar movement. I was pretty conservative, and I was supportive of the war effort because all of these boys either supported it or were putting on a brave front. And I certainly thought we should support our troops. That was the jingo that made sense to me at the time.

I learned to do graffiti in Oakland in 1972, '73. I had a little apartment in Oakland. It was probably one of the best times in my life. Oakland is connected to Alameda Island by an underground tube. During those days, Alameda was chock full of sailors. I started graffiting up bars, and my phone started ringing twenty-four-seven, my friend. They were coming over in car caravans. Well, that's actually an exaggeration, but not much. I could have five or six sailors a day.

I thought I was in big trouble one day when I was looking out the front window of my apartment and up comes a Shore Patrol car. This SP gets out of the driver seat, comes up to the apartment and rings my bell. I thought, "Well, this is it. Although doesn't he have to get the Oakland Police to officially arrest me?" But it was just a shore patrolman who wanted to get done.

Z: Did the uniforms come to play a role in your attraction?

C: They're a nice touch. Most military men are reluctant to get involved with that, and I don't bring it up much. They're reluctant because of the symbolic nature of the uniform; they sort of feel like that may be demeaning it. You can really see it; they're sort of pained about it, if you bring it up. And I must admit, I wouldn't have it any other way. Because it is the kind of integrity reflected in that reluctance, that sense of values, that I so admire in them.

C: In the late seventies, I became eastern regional manager for a large well-known manufacturer. I was living in Philadelphia. I think one time I picked up a sailor from the naval shipyard. But it was harder to do in Philadelphia. And also I was thinking that I should be doing more important things. And more conventional things, within a gay context. For six and a half years I had a lover.

Z: A civilian lover?

C: Uh-huh. A psychologist. [Pause.] We had a brownstone on Spruce Street.

Z: Did you have any involvement with the gay community?

C: Yeah. I helped publish [a gay newspaper]. And I feel committed to the cause of equality for gay people in American society. It is something worth fighting for. I don't dislike gay men. Some of the most important people in my life are gay men. It's not a disdain for their identity. But it is a lack of sexual attraction for their identity. I'm driven to look for men who are masculine.

Z: Tell me again about how you personally rank the service branches.

C: Well, okay, but I want to preface it by saying there are some wonderful men that I think could probably make me happy for twenty minutes, or twenty years, in every branch of the service. But my favorite are the Marines, number one. Probably because of the hypermasculinity implied and expressed by both the Marine Corps' own PR, and the things they tell each other about themselves. They are a tradition-bound organization, which teaches and preaches many of the virtues that we have associated with all military, but they are all of that in spades. Marines are the land assault force for the Navy. As such, they don't have many of the refinements of say, the Army. Marines take ground. The Army comes in behind them and tries to repair the infrastructure and govern the countryside. So the Army has to have more specialties, more skills. The Marines are an assault force. Period. End of story. The bravery and aggression associated with the Marine Corps is one of the reasons why they're my favorite. Plus the fact that they have the most rigorous physical training of the five branches, which generally leaves them superior physical specimens to many of their colleagues in the other branches.

Number two for me is the Navy. Somewhat because I've had so many encounters with sailors, and enjoy the Navy. I think that they're a little more happy-go-lucky, a little more relaxed than Marines. I think they sort of believe some of their lore, too, that they're supposed to be getting in trouble when they're on shore leave. They try things. I also think the Navy's uniforms are really quite nice and sexy, and they also have a great deal of tradition, too. The thirteen buttons, the collar flap. If a man is good-looking, he looks really great in Navy blues.

The Coast Guard—and I do have to count them—would be in third place, mostly because their uniforms are similar to the Navy. And many of them are career people. Coast Guard people generally stay in. They're dedicated. And the Coast Guard can pick and choose. They only need 35,000 guys.

Z: And gals.

C: Well, yeah. But it's sort of like my vision doesn't even see the women. They're invisible.

Next is Air Force. I've had good interaction with Air Force. The problem with the Air Force is they're divided into two categories. There are the officers, who are pilots, and everybody else is an enlisted man who's a mechanic. The Air Force is also the most civilian of the armed forces. They seem to be less segregated from the community in which they're living. And tend to see their job more as a nine-to-five pursuit. Also, they probably have the least rigorous physical training of the five branches, because it's usually not required. Although the young officers are about the most stunning of all the officer corps. Many of their pilots are very handsome, certainly great physical specimens.

I had periodic encounters with an Air Force captain who was thirty years old who was a real stud. He really sent Air Force stock up in my book! And one of the most uncomfortable situations I've ever been in was with an Air Force guy at March Air Force Base who had seen my ad. He came over two or three times. About a month later, out of a clear blue sky, his wife calls me and says, "I know you've been having a relationship with my husband." I thought, shit, honey, you're gonna have to be a little more specific! Then she said, "I think you know my husband." "Really. Well, I got no idea. Who are you?" She said her last name. I said, "Why are you calling me?" She started crying, and saying that her husband had confided to her that he had done this. I think he broke under the pressure of his wife's interrogation. Talk about Air Force wuss! She said, "There's only one thing I want to know. He said that the only contact was oral contact. Is that true, or did it get more than that?" And as it turns out, it got more than that. But what I told the woman was, "Look. I don't know why you're calling me. It seems to me this is between you and your husband. I can't really add anything to what he said. I can't even verify what he said. All I can say is, the only thing that can result from you calling somebody like this is to make yourself feel worse. You'll start making yourself feel better by building something with your husband. You don't need to talk to me." That was the first and only time that the wife got ahold of me.

So the Air Force is second to the bottom, and the bottom is the Army. And I say that because they'll take anybody. It's the only one of the five branches now that will take people who do not have a high school education. It has had for many decades the largest percentage of, um, inner-city folks who join the Army. So achievement levels—they score the worst on standardized armed forces tests.

There are elite groups within each service branch, such as paratroopers and Special Forces in the Army. These elite troops certainly embody the kind of things I like about the Marine Corps. There are elite groups within the Air Force, too. I can't remember the name. And also, of course, the SEALs, the amphibious warfare guys in the Navy. I think they may be the top of the food chain, to tell you the truth. I'd put SEALs above Marines.

C: In the early eighties I returned to San Francisco. The city had changed since the Vietnam war. Certainly the military presence was less. For almost a year, before my lover came out to join me, I tried to try to get back into the groove that I'd had in the early seventies, but I didn't do as well. There were fewer servicemen in the Bay Area, number one. Number two, I was not spending as much time pursuing them. And then probably to some extent the fact that I was ten years older probably made me less desirable as well.

Things started hopping again when I moved to Twentynine Palms in 1990.
Z: Did your moving there have anything to do with your attraction to Marines?
C: It was the only reason. [Pause.] The most powerful erotic sexual medicine for me has always been, now for thirty years, military guys. I'm forty-nine years old. I came to Twentynine Palms. It was at that point that I realized, from that first nineteen-year-old sailor sittin' on a commode at the Downtown Bowl on Eddy Street, that what I wanted to do was to be with those men, and I wanted to create a life that would make it possible to do that until they took me away to the nursing home. I openly planned total immersion with the men I like being around.

I picked Twentynine Palms over Oceanside and San Diego for a number of reasons. There are very few distractions in Twentynine Palms for Marines. There is a lack of women here. Eleven thousand Marines are stationed in this town. During the course of a year, another 80,000 come through here. And the town only has 13,000 [civilian inhabitants]. So there are many times of the year when you'd think the town was under martial law. More's the pity, huh? I mean, I'd much less resent a lance corporal giving me a ticket than a deputy sheriff.

One of the things I discovered when I first moved to Twentynine Palms is that I certainly was not alone. You have many gay men who have come here to be close to the Marine Corps. Some are looking for the kind of encounters that I enjoy. Many just want to be in that kind of environment, to have that "eye candy" in front of them, twenty-four-seven. And the trick for this town has always been: how do you turn a buck out here? There's only 1,600 civilian jobs on the base. The men I've gotten to know here are entrepreneurs. The guy who used to own the most important Marine bars in town was gay. He picked hot bartenders to serve Marines. Instead of choosing girls with big tits, he chose good-looking Marines, put them in white shirts, bow ties, and shorts. At midnight on Fridays and Saturdays, he'd have the "Best Buns in Twentynine Palms" contests. These would be guys who'd be wearing their underwear, and he'd wet their rear ends. The contest was for the "girls," who would vote by their applause who had the sexiest ass of all these Marines he was wetting down.

Z: How did he do the wetting?

C: With a *hose*, Zeeland. With a hose on the dance floor. It was a little messy, but at midnight nobody cared.

The only two bookstores in town are gay-owned. And gays own various of the little businesses downtown. It's gays who are the mainstay for the Twentynine Palms art museum. We have our own art museum. There's an artist's guild. There's a writer's guild. A lot of men who have retired out of the Marine Corps stay here, and that includes gay men. They get their retirement and maybe find little jobs to do. Some commute down to Palm Springs. There are many people who commute one hundred miles a day so that they can live in Twentynine Palms, to be in this environment.

Z: Do you ever hang out with Marines, do things apart from sex?

C: Play pool. Drink in the clubs. Often have lots of conversation with the guys, but generally in the bar environment because it's the most natural place to meet anybody here. Occasionally I'll go over to Lucky Park, not just for the tearooms, but I'll watch some of the intramural baseball leagues from the base that play there. Also the intramural soccer team. And I'll tell you what: Get your heart medication when I take you to watch the intramural rugby players. Oh my God! Those guys are unbelievable. Watching Marines play rugby. A blood sport for blood warriors. Be still my heart!

Z: Some of the guys I'm talking to say that they are looking for a certain kind of buddy love.

C: Yeah, I mean, when I was speaking of the ambient testosterone of Twentynine Palms, I think that's part of it. Part of it is the possibility for interaction and camaraderie or horseplay—strong interactions, nonsexual as well—with real men. Brave, courageous, risk-taking, but dutiful, chivalrous, handsome, well-built men in their goddamned prime.

Z: Tell me what you said before about them being "like desert flowers."

C: When you live here, one of the miracles of the desert is the way the plants save up their resources so they can survive the heat of the summer. We only get about three inches of rain a year. So all the plants have to be very frugal. And the most frugal of all are the cactus. These cactus have put thorns all around themselves so they don't get eaten by varmints looking for nutrition. And then, depending upon the species, between late April and the end of June, cactuses bloom. And some of them have the most extravagant displays of color and the most complex flowers. But each plant opens up for only twenty-four to forty-eight hours and then the blossoms die. Maybe you have a large cactus plant come up with twelve blooms, and within a few days, they're all shot, they're all done. And I've compared the Marines to cactus flowers. Because for many of these lower-middle-class men, their time in the Marine Corps is very short. And it's a time at which they're in the greatest bloom of their physical powers. They often go back to their working-class life when they leave, work in a factory back in Pittsburgh or Milwaukee or wherever the hell they're from. They get their beer gut, and the wife serves them all this bad American food. And you look back at them, and just for this brief moment in the span of their life, they bloomed, they flowered. They're beautiful. Absolutely beautiful. In some ways, the inside is almost as delicate and as transitory, because there is a burst of idealism in them as well. So yeah, I do compare them to cactus flowers. One wonderful thing about living in Twentynine Palms is that as they go away, there's more that come in all the time, so that they are forever young, for the folks that live here. In some ways, particularly for a middle-aged man, it acts like a tonic on me for them to be forever young. I love them forever young.

Z: Do these phone calls provide you with what you need?

C: I have not been active enough in getting what I want. I would like more activity than what I'm getting now. And I don't chalk it up to being too old to date. Because I know that by advertising more, I could be doing better. But I'm not working at it. It's because I'm too busy doing other stuff. I'd like to be doing more. Would I like it to change in nature? The complaint

I'm making is about quantity. I think it would be wonderful to find a Marine who kept me occupied sexually, and maybe mentally also, and there was something more going on. But if that doesn't happen, I'm not going to regret it, or miss it, maybe, if I am still in the ball game with the guys that you meet once, maybe twice.

Z: What do these guys find attractive about you, apart from the money and sexual servicing?

C: It depends on the guys. Some get companionship that they don't have otherwise. They get away from the base. Life aboard base, particularly for young guys who are living in barracks and bachelor quarters, is not that wonderful. It's communal living. Getting out, going to a private home in town—for some of them that's a treat in itself. Getting to talk to someone who doesn't necessarily need to hear about the Marine Corps and whatever the hell they do. So I think that's part of it. I think some of these guys have a deference to older men who they think may know more than they do. I mean, I had the cutest Marine just before we started this conversation—I was coming out of the supermarket. And this happens all the time. He said, "How are you tonight, sir?" That's so chivalrous. Or maybe they think they're helping out a senior! At least they haven't helped me to cross Adobe Road yet. But I *won't* tell them to take their hands off me!

I think there's also a certain amount of boredom. Some guys feel they're stuck in the middle of nowhere. It's a small town. There are only a few bars. I am one of the attractions in town. I'm sort of the Epcot Center of fellatio.

Z: Have any of the guys you've met in the last few years been particularly special?

C: Yeah. A couple of 'em. One of the most memorable was Lt. Joe H., USMC. I met him on a phone line. We talked for awhile and I thought he was a really very interesting guy, and he sounded very sexy. He was a young lieutenant, twenty-five or twenty-six. And really quite dashing, if people still use that word. I invited him to the house. When he came over, I was suitably impressed. He was good sex, but he was also very nice. Joe was engaged to be married when I met him. Then that engagement was broken off. I saw him once every three weeks or so for almost a year. Got to know him, got to know about his background. Irish Catholic working-class kid, his Marine ROTC got him through college, then he took his commission. His father was a janitor. He had pulled himself up by his bootstraps. And I admired that. I admired a lot of things about him. He shared so many thoughts with me that he had never shared with anyone else. I had gotten to feel very close to him. The night my mother died, I was on the phone with Joe when she was on the operating table. I got a call through call-waiting; the hospital called and said that things had gone bad, that I should prepare myself. I knew what that meant. Joe bucked me up. It was just his reassuring tone. His . . . sureness, his confidence really made me better able to gird myself to get through that.

It was no accident that I told the funeral home in Montana that they should do the embalming there, I'd buy a casket there, and that I was taking my mother to be buried in Twentynine Palms. I bought my funeral plot next to hers. I can point out to you exactly where I will be buried, and it will be in Twentynine Palms, California. It's already paid for. You just have to ship them the body. I've been carrying around my dad's ashes since 1987, and I may inter them here also. Right now they're under the sink, I think. And that's only fitting also, because Dad was a master sergeant in the Marine Corps during World War II.

Does that mean anything, Dr. Freud?

John:
The Air Force Glory Hole Replica

I'm standing on a corner in San Diego's gay neighborhood when John walks up. Grinning, he says, "I saw you do that! I was *three blocks away* and I saw you leaning there, looking all bored, then you spotted my high-and-tight haircut. It was like you *honed in on it!*"

John's chiseled chest and vascular biceps are displayed to advantage in his tight red USMC T-shirt. His regulation Marine Corps haircut is freshly shorn. He offers to drive me to Oceanside to get my own hair cut, but I explain that just yesterday I had a regulation *Navy* haircut.

"Oh," he offers sympathetically. "Well, I can still take you to Oceanside for a haircut, if you want."

The first member of his blue-collar Midwestern family to attend college, John came very close to joining the Air Force last year. He backed out after all of his friends and acquaintances (me included) told him he was crazy to quit his prestigious Hollywood job.

This interview was taped as the handsome twenty-nine-year-old and I drove around San Diego, cruising for sailors and Marines. It was our second meeting. Six months before, immediately upon introducing himself, John handed me a shadowy color snapshot of a plywood board through which had been bored three tangerine-sized holes.

John: That picture was taken in the desert east of L.A. It's where the 10 and the 215 [freeways] meet. This buddy of mine knew about it, and he knew I'd be turned on by it, so he took me out to this deserted place, and there was this board that was a replica of glory holes someplace on Patrick Air Force Base. Some guy had placed it there. He was very proud of his time that he had spent at Patrick. I found it fascinating. I went back a second time to take pictures of it and copy down the inscription. ["This glory hole board is a replica of one that once was at Patrick AFB where I came out. Help me fill it with dirty propositions and brags about your equipment."]

Zeeland: What were you thinking when you saw it?

J: As perverse as it sounds, I was really proud of the guy. I was really turned on, I thought it was awesome, I wished I was him.

Z: How long have you been having sex with men?

J: Mostly in the past two years. In my early teens, I fooled around with neighbor kids and stuff. But it's only recently I've even made gay friends and hung out with gay guys and talked about things. Before that it was always girlfriends and straight guys.

Z: You enjoyed sex with women?

J: I still do. I don't have sex with them anymore. I'd like to, but this other thing has taken over. I'd do it again if I could find a woman who I could sort of tell what's going on in my life, if she would still find me attractive.

Z: How have you met military guys?

J: I haven't met that many military guys, actually. My first experience was with a guy who was [stationed at Camp Pendleton]. I met him on-line. He said he was a doctor. He gave me directions and told me to come down. I had no idea what to expect. I'd never been to Pendleton before. I didn't know where to go. I didn't know if I was going to get stopped or questioned. And he was like it was no big deal. He said, "Just show up at eight thirty." So I get up early and drive down there and go through the gate.

It was the most amazing experience. Just stopping at the gate, I could not believe these Marines, these MP guards—they were incredibly beautiful. Very good-looking, very hot. Exactly what you think a Marine should be: blond hair, blue eyes, in great shape. They stopped me and told me to pull over and to go inside and sign in. So I'm scared at this point, I don't know what's going on. I go inside, and there's two more even hotter guys than the ones at the gate. But they're just, you know, no big deal. Give them my driver's license, they type it in. It took a little extra time because one guy didn't know how to work the computer. I was so nervous I couldn't even look them in the eye. They probably thought I was strange because I looked like a Marine, and I wasn't a Marine. They made me sign a paper and I was on my way. I was shaking when I got to my car.

So I find the guy, where he lives. He's got a little kid who lives with him. He's divorced. It turns out he's not really a doctor; he's a [Navy hospital] corpsman. He's Asian. He didn't tell me he was Asian. I'm not turned on by Asians. The place stinks like cat urine. His hair was messed up; he was pasty from the night before; he was just in sweats; and he wasn't good-looking. On top of everything he hadn't showered. I couldn't believe I drove all this way for this. So we started talking and I'm trying to think of a way to get out of it. And I was telling him about going through the gate and how exciting that was for me. Finally I realized the only way to get out of this was just to go through with it. Which we did. Then afterward he cleaned up and he gave me a tour of the base. It was awesome just driving around and seeing all the guys in their trucks, and in their cammies. It was Friday so there was a bunch of graduation festivities. The whole base was awesome. He could see that I was really excited about it. I couldn't stop talking about it. He was getting off on the fact that I was getting off on it.

That was my first experience with a military guy. Then there were a couple instances in [adult] bookstores down here in San Diego.

Z: So this is a recent thing for you.

J: Yeah. Very recent. I guess it's been six months I've been doing it. And the thing is, I lived very close to Army bases before, and I never even thought of that as a possibility. Never considered military guys as something hot, or of interest. It was just being down here in California. Something hit me. I don't know. It just became a very real turn-on for me somehow.

Z: You said that you like to go down to Oceanside and hang out there. "He walks among them," you said.

J: Yeah. [Laughs.] I do. I go down and just get my haircut and have lunch and walk around. I don't meet anybody or talk to anybody and I feel like a spy. They're very nice when you do talk to them, but I almost never do. I'm too nervous, I guess. Too shy.

Z: You told me that "Marines are the most impressive men in the world."

J: Well, they breed 'em that way. They make 'em to be strong and proud, and they stand tall. They look good, they give 'em really great haircuts, great uniforms. I mean, just from their stature and their look and everything, they are probably the most impressive men to look at. Even to make an acquaintance with one is a privilege.

I had an encounter with an ex-Marine in a very small town in Oklahoma. I stopped at a hotel, and went down to this honky tonk bar. I had been driving for days. I figured I'd go down and have a drink. But they were playing country music and it was karaoke night. I don't know what I was thinking. I hate country music. I hate karaoke. But I go in there and there's like, lots of really good-looking cowboys. I see this one guy walk in, and he's going up to guys and, like, hugging 'em, and tuggin' on 'em. He was tough lookin' and real handsome. So I walk up to him and I say, "I think I'm the only guy not gettin' laid in here tonight." And he goes, "Oh no, you're lookin' at the other guy who's not." I said, "Really." He goes, "Yeah." I go, "You shouldn't have a problem. You're a good-looking guy." He goes, "Well, I don't think there's anybody in here for me." So we were just talking and shootin' the shit for a while, hanging out and drinking beer. He walked around, and I walked around. He came back around and we started talking some more. I said, "You know, I'm staying upstairs in 217 if you wanna come on up. We can grab some beer and watch TV or something." He goes, "All right, I might do that." And I didn't think I'd ever see him again. Five minutes after the bar closes, I hear a knock on my door and it's this guy.

He tells me he's an ex-Marine from Oceanside. He's been back for a few months, and he's thinking about going back in because there's no work in Oklahoma. And he's a cowboy, the real thing; he was working out on the ranch that day, ropin' calves. So I'm laying there in my underwear, and he's laying there in his underwear, because I told him he could spend the night because he had to get up early. And I just sort of go, "Hey buddy, do you mind if I suck your dick?" [Laughs.] I was nervous. I said it sort of under my breath. He goes, "Whatever floats your boat." He pulled down his underwear and I started suckin' on his dick. And he was way into it, and he wanted to fuck me so I let him. I can't believe I'm saying this and it's gonna be in a book! Nobody knows anything about this side of my life.

Z: What did he look like?

J: He had a moustache. He didn't have his Marine haircut anymore, but he was built like a Marine. He was very strong, white, blond hair, blue eyes. Very friendly. Great smile. Great Oklahoma attitude. I was really—I was stunned.

Z: Do you think he thought of himself as gay?

J: Absolutely not. He was talking about how he was going to get married to some local girl.

Z: How important is it to you that the men you meet be conventionally masculine?

J: Out of all the things to consider about meeting a guy, that is the most important. Looks come second.

Z: You cautioned me that you weren't completely prepared to analyze your gravitation toward the military, but is that part of it? Are you looking for masculinity?

J: I'm sure. I think everybody's missing it. I mean, I guess it's no secret that the culture is being feminized, and men are being emasculated. Jung said that at the end of every cycle the culture gets handed over to the feminine. Women begin to take power, and you see a rise in homosexuality, and the culture becomes feminized. I think all men miss masculinity. I mean, we don't go out and hunt with our bare hands. [Roaring sound of passing pickup truck.] Look at that! That's a perfect example of why those trucks exist. That guy had a big loud truck. They miss it. When you're on-line and you look at everybody's profiles, everybody's looking for masculine guys. They weren't given any kind of proper introduction to manhood. I'm no different. I look for masculine men to make my life complete somehow.

Z: I'd asked you before about your earliest memories, and you said something about a dream you had.

J: I was standing at the top of the stairs looking out at the backyard, and seeing my Dad march in cammies and boots with a blond-haired soldier. They were marching up and down the front lawn. That's all I remember. I remember being frightened by the blond-haired man.

Z: How old were you, do you think?

J: Three, maybe four. It's the first dream I can remember having.

Z: Was your father ever actually in the military?

J: Yeah, he was. He was in the Army. But by the time I was born he had been out for probably fifteen years. I remember seeing his uniform in the closet. Next question.

Z: The military wasn't something you considered as a career?

J: Well, yeah it was, actually. One of my first career choices was to be a Navy pilot. And I talked to the recruiter, and they said because I needed glasses I couldn't be a pilot. But really the military never did anything for me. It's only been in the past two years. And it's just sort of exploded.

I think it's because I'm getting more in touch with myself on some level. I'm not obsessed like some guys are, where they follow the fleet, and live outside bases. I haven't had that many experiences with military guys. But I do find them incredibly attractive. Maybe I'm just getting something out of my system.

Z: Some guys who are chasing after the military are looking for a partner, for one person.

J: [Genuinely surprised.] They are?

Z: There are some.

J: I'm not looking for a partner. I'm definitely not looking to get hooked up. Maybe someday, but right now—I'm looking for buddies.

Z: What age range are you attracted to?

J: Usually above twenty-six or twenty-seven. I would take a DI or some sort of senior sergeant or even an officer before I'd go for a young recruit. I tend to like the older guys.

John and I arrive at an adult video arcade. He has sex with a beefy dark man who says he is a San Diego fireman and former Marine. I have sex with a slender blond man who says nothing. My partner has a regulation Marine Corps haircut and drives a car purchased from an Oceanside car dealership, but does not have a Defense Department decal on his windshield. So was he "authentic," or was he a military impersonator like me and John?

Z: These military guys that you have met, what do you think attracts them to you?

J: That's a good question. I don't know what attracts them to me. Because they seem to go with anybody sometimes. They'll go with old guys, they'll go with queeny guys.

Z: Have you had any conflicting feelings about looking like them, and being taken for one of them?

J: Yeah, that kind of bugs me. I don't do it to be disrespectful to them. I do it because I like the look. I'm not trying to confuse them. I never lie about being in the military.

Z: Recently you actually almost joined the military. You e-mailed me about how excited you were at the recruiter's office, and when you went down for the physical exam.

J: The weird thing is that—I really—At first the fascination with the military was an appearance thing. And as it went on, it became more and more profound. I went from being a complete pacifist to being able to understand the need for a military, and even understand the need in certain situations to kill. I mean, I had sunk myself into it so much that I was like, "I can do this. I could join and be a part of this and make it work for me. I would be good at it. And I would enjoy it." But at the same time there was this . . . excitement about joining that was not what they want you in the military for.

I asked a lot of people about it, and not one single person, either military or civilian, encouraged me to join. Everyone said that since I was being offered a great civilian job, I should just accept the offer. So that's what I did. But I feel kind of sad about it.

Z: In trying to explain what you were looking for, you said something about a sense of belonging.

J: Yeah. Yeah. I wanted to feel that camaraderie and that sort of closeness and that protection and that sense of—there's a certain amount of vulnerability to being in the military. I mean, you're not in complete control of your life. Someone else has control over you. But at the same time, you're part of a bigger scene that's connected to masculinity and brotherhood and protection. I don't know. I found it just—the more I got into it, the more it was just driving me nuts.

Z: Do you have any special attraction to uniforms?

J: Yeah.

Z: Which uniforms, and why?

J: Well, the dress uniforms don't do much for me. They're not tailored correctly. They're tailored really square. The cammies are what really do it for me. That and seeing the guys in the brown T-shirts, seeing 'em in their sweats. And the boots.

They don't have to necessarily be in the uniform. I mean, the reason why it's attractive is because in most cases you're guaranteed that if the guy's a soldier, he's gonna be a real man. He's gonna be masculine, he's gonna be cool. They go out and they camp, and they rock climb, and they drive big macho trucks. It's something I've never really had in my life, and it's really comforting to be around that. I'm working now in a situation where I'm around West Hollywood gay guys. Some of them know I'm gay, and some of them don't. But they—I feel like I'm compromising my masculinity by being around them.

Z: You don't think there can be masculine camaraderie among West Hollywood gay men?

J: I don't know. I just don't like 'em. They have bad haircuts, they dress badly. I'm sure they think they dress great, because they're so prissy, so prim and clean and proper, but it's not the way a real man dresses. They're sissies.

David:
The Milk Run

The following interview chronicles four decades of sailor chasing by a man who in 1948 was a Henry Wallace for President delegate. David grew up in Seattle, the son of Scottish and French, Presbyterian parents. His father was a college professor. In the 1950s, he moved to Hollywood and got a job in the music industry. He attempted to join the Communist Party but escaped being blacklisted because the Communists lost his application. Like many men of the pre-Stonewall era, David eschewed sex with other gay-identified civilians in favor of uniformed trade. He estimates that he performed oral sex on more than 4,000 sailors. With several of them he developed friendships that continue today.

David: I was going to high school in World War II, and where my family lived was about four blocks from a hill on which there were several anti-aircraft batteries. With listening devices that looked like big gumdrops. They didn't yet have radar. I wouldn't know how many men were stationed up there, but barracks were built and they were living right there. From a certain side of the hill you could look right into the showers. I can remember seeing guys sort of looking out, flapping a towel or something. Nobody ever came on to me, but it was the typical conflagration [sic] of soldiers. And there was something very sexual about it. At that tender age of sixteen or seventeen, I was not about to go put the make on somebody, even if I was attracted. But it never got to the point of centering on one soldier. It was sort of a group thing. That's all I can remember about it.

My nature—I was the kind of puppy that picks up the bone and takes it home to chew on. [Laughs.] Yes, I did things in public places. But that was certainly not my preference. And usually, I would proceed to do that only if the other party stubbornly refused to go anywhere with me.

I worked the "milk run" for many years, beginning in the fifties. It was a stretch of Ocean Avenue in Long Beach. The Navy boys would hitchhike to go over a bridge to the Navy yards, to their ships. I had somebody describe it to me before I actually went down there and tried it. And it was incredible. The boys—first of all, I never alluded to sex. I would look the kid over after he'd hopped in the car, and if he looked quite interesting, I would say "How would you like to come up to my place for drinks?" The standard answer would be, "Okay. I don't have to be back until 7:30 tomorrow morning." That was *the* standard answer. Unless they were not available, in which case they'd say, "No, I have to be back to do junk on the bunk," or "I have to shine my shoes," or whatever it was, and so you knew they were not interested. Maybe they weren't interested in me, or they weren't interested in doing it, or whatever. But this kind of action was so well known on the milk run—I'm not talking about one or two obscure kids. And when I would go down there, it was never a matter of would I make out. It was a matter of getting enough of them in the car and out of the car so that I could find one that was really superb.

Zeeland: Where were you living then?

D: I was living in Hollywood.

Z: So you'd pick up sailors hitchhiking back to their ships, then offer to take them in the opposite direction?

D: Yeah. Well, I didn't usually say, "Come on up to Los Angeles with me." I'd say what I just told you, "Come to my place for drinks." On the freeway they'd usually ask, "Where are we going?" And I would tell them Hollywood, but it was only another twenty minutes. I never had anybody try to get out—at high speeds. [Laughs.] Anyway, there used to be just dozens and dozens of guys down there driving around . . . looking.

Z: Was there some fierce rivalry and competition sometimes?

D: I understand that in Oceanside that goes on today, but that's because willing Marines are relatively scarce. Remember that in the period I'm talking about in Long Beach there were willing sailors all over the place. So the compulsion to beat everybody else out of the way wasn't very strong.

There were a few Marines down there, too. And one night—for some reason or other I had parked. I recognized a friend's car. He had a big Cadillac. He was in the driver's seat, and I saw that he had a Marine sitting next to him. I went over thinking, "Well maybe I'll get to know the Marine," and started to talk. My friend was very pleasant; he wasn't clutchy about it. And suddenly I looked over into the backseat, and here is my friend's buddy doing another Marine in the backseat. The Marine had his pants down. That certainly got my motor running! So I was sort of determined—this guy with the Caddy was a hair bender. He was a hair stylist. And I knew where he lived. A little later that evening I thought, well, I'll stop by, maybe that other Marine is around. So I looked through the window, and the hair bender's roommate, who was an older gentleman, was sort of hovering over—I guess it was another Marine. That Marine's back was to me. He was sitting in a chair, naked. And for some reason or other, the old gentleman was having a long-winded conversation with him. I kept thinking, "Just get on with it and blow him." And as I walked away, I must have hit something that made a noise. The Marine pulled up his pants and came running out and threw big clods of dirt after me. He apparently sensed that he had been observed, and probably didn't know for how long. And of course I don't know what went on before I came up to the window. Fortunately I made it to the car and got away. I never could find out what that was all about.

I should add that a large number of the sailors who hopped in the car didn't want to go up to my place. They wanted to go down by the docks and have me take care of them in the car. And I would not do that. I heard too many stories about the police catching people down there. And also if some-body's out to rob you, that's a pretty good way of doing it.

Z: Did you ever have any of the sailors or other guys that you picked up on the milk run turn rough on you?

D: Not really from the milk run. During this period, I met a Marine who was hitchhiking through Hollywood—that's where I picked him up—on a Sunday night, going downtown to the Greyhound bus station to go back to Camp Pendleton. He came over and we had quite a time sexually. We sort of made a tentative date; he was to call me the following Friday. And he did. He wanted me to come down and pick him up. He said he had a buddy with him, from Montana. I wasn't too thrilled with that idea. So I called my friend Maurice, who liked servicemen, and said, "I've got a blind date for you." "Wonderful! I'll be there." Well, I picked the two of them up. I was a little bit leery. The Montana kid didn't seem like he was any better or worse than the first one. But in the back of my mind I was sort of depending on Maurice being there, and not too worried about it. So we got to my place, I fixed dinner, we had dinner. No Maurice. He never called, never showed. And I don't know what made me do it, but I excused myself and said I had a headache and was going to lie down. I did go into my bedroom, and my bedroom had a panel-ray heater that went between the bedroom and the living room. And they wouldn't know it, but I could hear every word they said. I started hearing lines like, "What are we going to do with him?" I must have really had my wits about me, because I very stealthily got out the front door and quietly closed it, and just left them there. Of course they managed to steal a few things. Nothing important, a hi-fi or something. And that was the end of that. I hate to think what might have happened.

One of my good friends, David G., had been a Marine, although he was English by birth. And he was a very strange guy. He was the man who devised the whole concept of shopping centers. Finding a piece of land, and then getting a commitment from JCPenney's or whoever. Well, he had a beautiful home over in Beverly Hills, and he used to invite me up there occasionally. I had a lot of trouble with him, because he was so pushy. Not coming on to me, but if I was to take a serviceman up there he'd be all over him. I thought of him the other night. He was a Marine queen. Oh my goodness, was he ever! Anyway, they found him dead at the bottom of his swimming pool. It's an unsolved mystery. They found him wearing his glasses, and that doesn't make any sense at all. You don't go swimming with your glasses on. X number of Marines must have come back—because this was at a time when a lot of them were just coming back from Vietnam—and they must have held his head under water. When you think about it, three big, strong Marines—that's all it would take. And I'm not going to go into further details, but there were many clues that sounded like that's what happened.

Z: You said that he had a special way of treating Marines that you thought might have contributed to someone turning on him.

D: Oh yeah. He would—I know this because I met a number of his Marines on a Sunday night, when he had fucked them silly all weekend long, and he wouldn't let them have a climax. He was a doctor. He'd had a lot of medical training. And he obviously knew that the more often and harder that he fucked them, without letting them have a climax, the hotter they'd get. That's exactly what he did.

When I used to go up there on Sundays to get sun around the pool, he had a quirk. Every time someone would come through the door to the pool—the natural tendency was to not close it. And he would immediately jump up and close it. When they found him at the bottom of the pool, the spring door was open. Interesting.

Fortunately I didn't have many bad experiences. I was lucky.

Z: The potential for danger was never part of your excitement?

D: No. I don't think I'm a danger freak. I just wanted to meet a nice kid. It's funny, I wasn't looking to meet a kid with whom I could walk hand in hand into the sunset and spend the rest of my life with. But I was interested always in meeting kids who would come back to see me regularly. And a lot of them did. Not dozens of them, but some of the nicest kids I would get to know, they would come back maybe every weekend, or every other weekend. I must say I wasn't afraid of those kids. Not the slightest. Well, it was kind of a routine in the fifties and sixties. They would have a place to stay. I would take them out to dinner at a nice restaurant. In those days, they would very seldom come out and say, "It's gonna cost you fifty dollars." Nothing like that. They would say, "Gee, I'm broke this week and payday's not for another week." So then I'd slip a ten-dollar bill into their wallet in the middle of the night, and they would find it there in the morning.

Z: Just how many sailors are we talking about? If you had to estimate.

D: Boy. In the fifties, sixties, and seventies—we're talking about three decades. I suppose—you figure it out. Probably I would average three scores a week. Average. There were certainly many weeks when I had more luck than that in Long Beach. But then there were weeks when I didn't even go down there. It just depended on what was going on in my life.

Z: What did you like to do sexually with these guys?

D: I have always been almost totally oriented to oral sex. And of course sometimes you would have a supposedly straight sailor or Marine who would surprise and amaze you by going down on you.

Z: Did you object to that when that happened?

D: No. No. I had a number of situations, particularly with sailors—There was one sailor—in fact, I pulled his pictures out to show you—who was on an aircraft carrier. [Shows Zeeland photos.] I picked him up, brought him home. He thoroughly enjoyed being blown. But then he said that he would really like to be fucked. He thoroughly enjoyed being fucked. But I never—he gave me his phone number, he gave me his address. He was on the *Constellation.* I never could get him back up to my apartment. I used to run into him all the time down in Long Beach. He'd be hitchhiking and see who it was, and he'd turn his head around. I don't know what that was all about. He was friendly enough the first time. He started to go to a gym in Long Beach. Obviously made some contacts. He was eventually photographed by a famous photographer. That's what these are. And he started to develop his body. He doesn't really have a great body; he has kind of skinny arms. But he has a beautiful butt. And he's very masculine. He was from Texas. And years later—I don't remember quite how I did it, but I contacted him. Like thirty years later. Well, he didn't remember me, but he remembered the situation. [Laughs.] He knew what I was driving at. He said, "I went that route when I was in the Navy, but I don't go that route anymore." He said, "Anyway you wouldn't like me because my body isn't any good anymore." You know.

Z: That may have been true.

D: I'm sure it was. He couldn't remember who I was. I wouldn't expect him to. I mean, the guy must have had a number of assignations.

Z: But this is one particular guy you remember.

D: Oh yes. And it was just a one-afternoon stand. Because he didn't want to see me again.

Z: Did you fall in love with these guys, sometimes?

D: Well, a few of them, yeah. There was one sailor that I carried on with for a couple of years. He was married and he came up nearly every weekend. We had good times.

Z: What kinds of things would you do, apart from the sex? I assume that sometimes there was a class difference, and with your interest in classical music—

D: I can't remember too many times when I took them to hear classical music. But I was also very interested in jazz. I can remember taking a lot of them to jazz clubs. Movies.

Z: When you picked them up, would these sailors be in uniform?

D: In Long Beach, yes. Because ostensibly they were on their way back to the ship. There were locker clubs in those days. And that's where, for a small fee per month, they could come to Long Beach, in their uniform, leave it in the locker club, and wear their civvies, and then go back to the locker club and get their uniform. But the trend in the last twenty-five years has been less and less wearing the uniform.

Z: Was it especially exciting to you to see them in uniform?

D: The only uniform that ever did much for me is the thirteen-button blues. And the reason being, that's the only uniform where you can easily have sex with a sailor in the front seat of your car. The thirteen buttons open a flap. Whoever designed that uniform must have had deadly intent. The suckee doesn't have to even open the belt, or take down the pants—the flap folds down and everything is immediately available. And I always felt that the Navy blues were more masculine, sexier. Whites are sort of—I don't know, little kiddy sailors running around with neckerchiefs. Actually, the blues have a neckerchief too. I am not really attracted to uniforms. I think that's the answer I must give you. That's not what did it for me. They were much more attractive out of uniform.

Z: Later I'll ask you why you liked the military, what qualities—

D: I can tell you right now. It's the same reason that I use a lot of military in my work, which I'm not going to get into in this discussion. They generally are in much better shape than the general population, physically. And also kids in the military are uprooted, they don't have a home, they don't have a place to go to on the weekends. And I thoroughly enjoyed playing that role. I don't anymore, because I can't do that. I don't connect with guys in the military now, except through my work. And they don't want to spend the weekend with me. I don't think.

Z: Well, you don't invite them to.

D: No. But I think those are the reasons. I've always liked healthy young specimens that are between eighteen and twenty-five, twenty-six. That's what you meet in the military. Or certainly in the Navy and Marine Corps.

Z: You haven't mentioned that they might be more masculine. Wouldn't that also be part of your—

D: More masculine than what?

Z: Civilians of the same age.

D: Well, I certainly can't compare them to guys in gay bars. Jesus!

Z: You come from an upper-middle-class family, but many of these men were working class. Was that part of their appeal?

D: I don't think I ever thought about them in terms of class. What attracted me were sexy bodies, and sharp, alert intellects. Bright boys.

Z: Dumb didn't turn you on?

D: Not really. I didn't give them IQ tests. Or Rorschach tests. That's what I should have given them! [Laughs.]

Z: You told me how the "milk run" ended.

D: Well, it subsided quite a bit. Because—I can remember very well, one kid that I stopped to talk to said, "Why don't you come back by here at midnight, and if I'm still here I'll probably go with you." What he was doing was waiting for a girl to pick him up! I can't pinpoint the date, but it was sometime in the sixties. But after that I saw more and more of them driving around.

Z: Women would be driving around picking up sailors, the same as the men were doing?

D: Yeah. Solo women. And it got to be quite a traffic jam, let me tell you.

D: I look upon gayness as a progressive disease. [Laughs.] Somewhere in the fifties was when I read Kinsey's famous study. And his basic premise—and I wish you'd put it in your book—is that males are neither homosexual nor heterosexual. They're fundamentally sexual, capable of being stimulated in either direction depending on the situation, and who's involved, and the time in the person's life.

Z: But how did these sailors you had sex with think of themselves, and what did they call themselves?

D: Oh, they thought of themselves as straight.

Z: Would you talk with them about women to put them at ease?

D: A little bit.

Z: Would they have stories or excuses they told to explain having sex with men, or was it something that wasn't spoken of very much?

D: Well, I certainly can't remember talking about their straight sex life with girls very much, except insofar as they carried on over in the Orient, or something like that. I can remember them telling me all the stories about the beads stuffed up the asshole and yanked at the moment of climax. I don't think I ever had a sailor say, "What are we going to do? Are you going to blow me? Are you going to fuck me?" You just didn't discuss it.

Z: Well, when you actually got back to your place—

D: We still didn't discuss it. We just did it. Most of the times, it was a kid that had said he didn't have to be back until 7:30 in the morning, which meant we could get up at about a quarter to seven and make it just fine. And so we would probably have drinks and watch television, and then I'd say, "Well hey, it's getting kind of late, since you have to be back there at 7:30." We'd go to bed, and they were confronted with one bed. There was no choice. So we hopped in bed. And my standard move was not verbal. It was to reach over and start playing with them. I would be very slow about it, and figure that if they didn't want to do it, they'd let me know right at that point. But that seldom happened. And of course the ones that were more with it immediately flopped over on their back, so that you could do what you were going to do easily. Often that cycle would repeat itself during the night. They would curl up with their butt in my direction—not because they wanted to get fucked, but they'd curl up that way—and then if I'd wake up at two o'clock in the morning or something like that and reach over, the same exact thing. I'd start to play with it, and it would get hard immediately. That's a totally nonverbal exchange. You don't need to say anything.

Z: I assume there wasn't usually much discussion the next morning.

D: No. The discussion the next morning almost certainly was about getting together with them again. You know. Were they free next weekend? Would they give me an address?

Z: You told me a story before about something you sometimes did when guys wanted to have sex that was other than oral sex.

D: Oh that. That happened several times. I would be lying down with an erection, and the guy would sit down on it. And then I would reach around and masturbate him, and I would tell him, "Now, when you come, I want you to jack me off with your asshole." It's marvelous, because I was in complete control. If I didn't want him to come yet, I'd sort of slack back on that. If I was ready to really have him come and get me off, I'd speed it up, and—he's all this time bouncing up and down on it. One thing has to happen right after the other. He comes, and clamps his butt around my cock and I come.

Z: So when they wanted anal sex, that was how you liked to do it.

D: Well, it was only a few times that I was able to pull that off. Because the average kid, even if he likes to be fucked, probably hasn't gotten into anything quite that complex. You never know, though. Just because someone doesn't suggest something like that the first time doesn't mean they haven't done that and more. There's a wonderful phrase: "If they know the melody, and most of the words, they've sung the song before."

D: Back in the fifties, there were certain bars in Hollywood. There was one next to the Pantages Theater, which was right next to the USO. It was wall-to-wall Marines and the gentlemen who went there to meet them. In San Diego—the original Brass Rail was downtown. I can remember going into it and it was wall-to-wall Navy. There were officers and enlisted men in there, and civilians that had come there to pick them up.

My first attention was called to the USO by the fact that on Friday and Saturday nights you would see all these Marines there trying to get into a car. I mean, you couldn't say they were hitching a ride, because where would they be going? And it got to be a classic. Because what started as ordinary middle-class cars quickly evolved into Lincoln Continentals and Cedillas and so forth. The Marines were knocking each other out of the way to get into the expensive cars. I met some very nice boys out there. They would just look in the car and if you would motion to them and open the door, they'd jump in. It was pretty much the same routine after that. "Where are you headed?" and "Would you like to have a few drinks?" I don't think I achieved quite the success rate there that I did in Long Beach. It was probably only one Marine a week.

There was one Marine—I will never forget him, because he was a very interesting guy. His name was Kurt and he was from the state of Washington. Like most of the Marines that you would encounter there, he had just gotten back from Okinawa or some other Pacific posting. In other words, they were not recruits. We hit it off rather well. He came back several weekends in a row. He was over six feet, and had the obligatory short haircut, more like a flattop. He was pure Swedish. Well, we sort of carried on, on and off, and then I found out that some obviously gay guy had bought him a car, and the very next thing he had done was smash it up. I remember thinking how glad I was that I hadn't sprung for that. And then he came over one night, and he got rather drunk, and he told me this story about some guy in Hollywood who paid him and several of his buddies to strip down, squat over a big glass table, and shit on the table while the guy laid underneath and watched.

That really turned me off. I didn't see Kurt for a long time after that. In fact, I didn't see him again until after he got out of the service. He got married and had a couple kids. Every year or two, he would turn up again. He was an elevator repairman. It was always the same routine. He would call first, and he would arrive with a six pack of beer, proceed to put away most of the beer. He spent, in bed with me, the night that his son was born.

D: During this same period my mother lived in La Jolla. I used to come down to San Diego to see her on weekends. In those days there was a whole area downtown that started with the San Diego Hotel, and then there used to be a Trailways bus station. And that old cheap hotel that's still there. Well, the bar in the San Diego Hotel used to be fairly interesting pickings for Marines. Very often I would see them come in and sit down at the bar and have a beer or something, and then they would disappear down to the john. The john had several very large glory holes. I remember one incredible afternoon when I went down there. It was just a three-seater. When you went in, you would look through the crack in between to see who was in there, so you weren't wasting your time. And I looked through the crack and just about became unhinged. There was one of the most beautiful sailors I had ever seen in my life in there. He was not sitting down; he was standing up and had a roaring hard-on. And there was somebody in the middle one. I was thinking: Did I interrupt? Was he already sticking it through? Probably he hadn't stuck it through yet; he was just tantalizing whoever was in the middle. And there was nobody in the third one. Well, I don't remember now every detail, but at a certain point the sailor opened his door to me and I went to work on him. Then we heard somebody coming, so he closed the door. The guy that was coming was a civilian. Pleasant enough guy. And we took turns blowing the sailor. Then, as luck would have it, the sailor lost it; he got so hot that suddenly it just came squirting out and there wasn't time for anybody to get over there and take care of it. I followed him out, because this one I wanted to get to know. And he would have none of it. He wouldn't come up to my room at the hotel. He wasn't hostile. He had just gotten back from somewhere in the Pacific, and he just wanted to go to his locker club and check out. I said, "Why don't you meet me after that?" He said, "No, no."

The Trailways bus station had one glory hole. And I can remember going in there on a Saturday morning. There was a beautiful blond sailor in whites in the next stall. I didn't have to do too much coaxing, fairly quickly he got up and shoved it through. Then I did the same thing; I trailed after him to try to get his name, or take him to lunch, or something. Uh-uh. No, no.

D: In the seventies, Super Pimp was sending Marines up to Hollywood, recruiting them God knows how. I think mainly on Broadway, or in the park [in downtown San Diego]. He claimed that he was very discreet, and he was very choosy about who he operated with. Right. Anything that was alive and breathing! And his standard technique was that he would give [the Marine prostitutes] a list of names and phone numbers—and mine was on there—and dispatch them on the Greyhound bus to Los Angeles, and they would just start calling. Whoever they got first that came down and picked them up, made out first. But it was usually more than one assignation. Some of the kids were very nice. I mean, really, there were a good number, and I became pretty friendly with several of them. Most of them only had dollar signs in their eyes. They would only really become friendly if they thought they could bid the fee up. Oh—one of them I must mention. Very nice boy. Marine. Portuguese. And the very first time he ever stayed with me, we went to dinner, we were driving home to Pasadena where I lived then, and he said, "Why don't you take it out?" I said, "Oh. Well, all right." So I unzipped, and took it out. I was very excited. And I started to play with myself. I leak a lot. Or did then. And suddenly he reaches down and grabs my hand and starts licking my fingers. This is from a genuine U.S. Marine! Really sucking my fingers and carrying on. From that he progressed to going down on me. He repeated this performance a number of times.

Z: It wasn't typical of what the other Marines would do?

D: Oh no, not at all!

Z: What would the other Marines do?

D: Well, they probably wouldn't do anything in the car.

Z: When you got to your place would they have to be told what to do?

D: No. I'm a repetitive sonofabitch. It was almost the same thing that I just told you about Navy kids. Stay overnight, go to bed after a nice dinner and drinks, and reach over and play with it.

Z: Even though these men had been ordered from the pimp, and there wasn't any question what they were there for.

D: Well, they couldn't be coy about it, no.

Z: You've proposed a title for your interview.

D: "I can't dance and the field's too wet to plow." [Laughs.] I heard that starting in the fifties. When I would be driving a kid in Long Beach, and I would propose that he come up to have drinks, it often happened that he'd say, "Well, gee, I can't dance, and the field's too wet to plow." It was always in that context of an acceptance, but—if you think about it, it's not overwhelmingly positive acceptance. It's like, "Okay, I haven't got anything else to do," or "I can't do anything else." Where it came from I don't know. It must be from a country song, or something. Because so many guys would use that.

Z: We've agreed that we won't discuss your present work. [Note: As this book went to press, David had discontinued the career he did not wish to discuss in this interview. Under the name David Lloyd, he worked for ten years as a professional photographer for the gay skin magazines, specializing in sailors and Marines, who he recruited through classified advertisements in the semiofficial on-base newspapers.]

D: You know, you could sneak this one idea in, the interesting point that I'm still doing the same thing. Over and over again! I'm still finding the same kind of boys, very similar in appearance, and I'm dealing with them in the same way. Giving them some money, but also—I don't know how to explain this. I deal with them with respect, as I did with the tricks. I feel kind of good about that. I don't feel that I've ever taken real advantage of some young man. I'm not trying to hold myself up as an angel. [One of my friends] used to dump all over me because he said I was spoiling them, I was overpaying them. The one thing I don't do anymore—I don't have sex with them anymore. So that isn't the same. I could. But I mean, it's just an absolute parallel. And some friends who've known me for years rather well are sort of amused. "You just can't get out of that groove, can you?" [Laughs.]

I want to tell you one last little story. There was a Navy kid who I met when I was staying at the San Diego Hotel. This boy's name was Bob. He was from North Carolina. Very reluctantly he spent the night with me. And he didn't want me to blow him more than once. Once was supposed to be it. When I continued to do it and he continued to enjoy it, he was fighting me every step of the way. Well, because of that whole performance, it seemed to me that he was about the last sailor that I would ever hear from again. To my amazement, about a week later, Bob called me. He wanted to come up to Hollywood and see me again. Fine; we developed a friendship. He came up fairly often. You know, the usual routine: his ship would go away for three months or some damn thing, and then I didn't see him because he wasn't in port. Bob was a very sexy guy. He was really my cup of tea, which is a strawberry blond with very white skin and freckles and a nice body. So time passed. He married. And we kept in touch. He was living in North Carolina. Many times when I was on business in New York, I would send him an airplane ticket and he would fly up and spend the weekend with me. Things got more intense. Up to that point, he had not been aggressive with me sexually, but boy was he starting in New York. Then he and his wife moved out to Los Angeles. There's a part that I'm not going to put on this, because one of her relatives is a very big television star. Through that, Bob started to get work as an architect. Guess who had been after him from day one to go into architecture? Everything seemed to fit. He was an artist as well. I encouraged him to go to the Museum of Modern Art, and by God they took some of his work. And—well, he's very, very successful today. He and the wife have had me over to dinner a few times. I think she knows, but I don't really know if she knows. And I'm very proud of that relationship. It's lasted thirty years. We stay in touch, we talk a couple times a year. He now owns a home in Paris, a home in North Carolina, and a home in Los Angeles.

Z: And you met him when he was just a wayward little sailor.

D: I'm not telling you this because I think it all came about because of me, no. But you asked me what I did with these kids. Many times I took them to the museum. I took them to the—it was like Sea World. I didn't take them only because I was interested in educating them; I took them because I enjoyed going, too. And in the process probably gave them something. I didn't just take.

David Hubert died on June 24, 1998. He was seventy. A military chaser to the end, his ashes were distributed at sea, three miles off the Oceanside pier.

Rick:
Aries Marine Bull-Pussy

Rick Leathers is the nom de porn of a San Francisco-based writer. He introduced himself at one of my book readings and that same night wrote me two letters totaling more than ten thousand words. This is an excerpt from those letters. Rick's first book, *Leathers on Leather,* is forthcoming from Alternate Publishing.

I will confess to a certain allergy to Marines. Every time I get close enough to a hard-muscled, sweaty, hairless-bodied, Aries Marine to smell his bull-pussy my dick gets all hard and swollen. Marriage to such a Marine is probably the only cure. Too bad San Diego is so far away, though I would really rather find one who's fresh out of the Corps and looking to settle down with a loyal man who'll appreciate him. Being forty-nine gives me the added advantage of being "papa" without really trying.

As a kid growing up in rural/small town southern Arkansas in the 1950s and 1960s, I was exposed to a certain masculine phenotype. These young men were white/Amerindian mixes, square-jawed, lean-muscled mesomorphs with small pelvic structures, generally hairless chests, clean shaven, crew cut, or flattopped head hair, clean but sweaty with highly erotic body odors, athletic, moderate to large nosed, somewhat thick-lipped, and they radiated a healthy animal sexuality. Their typical dress was a skin-tight T-shirt or western shirt, western boots, western hat, and sprayed-on jeans that displayed their rounded little butts and well-packed groins. I began having sex with such young men when I was twelve.

The thought of having sex with a human female just never occurred to me. I did have some sexual adventures with cows, heifers, and chickens, but that was typical of rural Southern boys back then. And I lived in a region where sex was a favorite topic of conversation for families and everybody else (except when the preachers were around). Sexual guilt was largely unknown.

I only realized after moving to California and being exposed to people from all over the country that my small-town Arkansas childhood was not typical of most Americans. I did manage to have sex with 60 percent of the guys in my high school graduating class at one time or another.

I was severely abused by my Christian Fundamentalist mother (blood running down my legs from her beatings, and her razor tongue ever telling me that I would never amount to anything), and my older sister often joined in to humiliate me whenever she could. This may have had some influence on my sexual antipathy toward women. Perhaps due to my disinterest in women as sexual partners, I find no interest in nelly gays or drag queens, either (though some have become, and remain, close friends).

There is no military tradition in my family. The military was viewed as a form of government-sanctioned kidnapping that proved Yankees were innately evil.

In high school, I spoke with the Navy recruiter, but Vietnam was going on and I chose college for safety. While in college a friend and I went up to Memphis, Tennessee, to visit our friend, Diane. She and her female roommate both had Navy officer boyfriends from a nearby base. These young men were the most sexually intense males I had ever encountered. I slept on the couch in the living room during that visit, and I could hear both pairs fucking their brains out all night long. While I was very active in the antiwar movement on campus, I would have gladly chucked my philosophy for a chance to hit the sheets with either of those hypermasculine young officers. When we would go out to beer joints to get tanked up, the sexual desire for these tight-muscled, sexually dynamic young men would get to be more than I could stand. I often left early and returned to Diane's place alone.

After leaving college in 1970, I moved to Little Rock, Arkansas. I was new to the gay bar scene and overwhelmed for awhile by all of the nelliness and bitchery. Then I discovered the Jacksonville Air Force Base north of the city. There were queer pilots and enlisted men everywhere. The pilots looked great in their uniforms, until they were away from the military's watchful eye; then most of them turned into screaming bitch queens. The sergeants were a little more down to earth, but not much.

One sergeant named Dave became my roommate. He was a thoroughly screwed-up mess. He brought one guy over to stay with us for awhile who was fresh out of the Navy. He was definitely of my childhood phenotype— blond crewcut, hairless muscular chest, bluebirds tattooed over each nipple, clean-cut handsome face, and eager to have sex with any man or woman who wanted him.

During a "love-in" at my apartment we were all sitting around nude when my friend, Fran, sat down beside me and leaned back on my arm. Sailor Boy came over, mounted Fran, and began to fuck her like a jackhammer. With my arm trapped under them I was "forced" to watch this action at close range. He was right out of my dreams. Oh, he was a liar, a drunk, and a petty thief (and AWOL), but I was inexperienced enough back then to feel that sexual arousal wiped out everything else.

Then I discovered the city parks where Army guys from Fort Chaffee, up river, could be had. These soldiers weren't as sexy as the tattooed sailor (now on the run from the law, my sergeant roomie with him), but they were more approachable and communicative. I did get tired of dealing with all of the guilt, shame, drunkenness, and family fears they were wrapped up in. For me, sex had always been something natural and animal-like. I didn't attach it to anything else.

Fran had had enough of Arkansas by that time and she decided to return to her Navy officer husband in San Diego. She asked me to go with her. My life was totally meaningless in Little Rock, so I packed up and we headed west.

The next several years were a chaotic time in Hell, but I learned a lot and became more urban-aware. Working in porn shops and gay bathhouses gave me plenty of exposure to the dirty underbelly of gaydom. And everywhere I turned I met, and regularly butt-fucked, Marines. [In mid-1970s San Diego] the easiest place to bag a Marine was at the Vulcan Baths. They were hard to cut out of the little herds they formed, and I rarely got the chance to really make friends with many of them, but they were the phenotype and the super-sex I desired above all else at that time.

In between Marines I made do with sailors, who were available everywhere. I dated a Navy lieutenant named Pat for awhile. He had a 10½ inch dick soft (never saw it get hard), and wanted anything and everything shoved up his ass. He was a Catholic convert and really weird, but handsome. He finally reached the point where he only wanted an arm shoved up his butt to the elbow, and I got bored with his neurotic chatter and we split.

The Marines had a long list of qualities that I admired and desired, but I didn't clearly understand this until long after I had moved north to San Francisco and lost contact with my source of available jarheads. Their pride in the Corps, and in their having earned a place in that brotherhood, was in sharp contrast to the wimpery and bitchiness of the civilian gays I was mostly around. Marines were trained to believe in honor; gays got points for who could backstab the most. San Diego's gays were small-town petty, and I would later learn that San Francisco's were urban cold and predatory.

I was drawn to the discipline that helped so many of the Marines I bedded enjoy the moment they were in, instead of demanding instant gratification. Often lonely guys, the Marines seemed genuinely grateful for any affection I gave them. I wish now that I had had the insight and inner security to have given them more. Underneath their buff bluff they were usually just nice guys with great bodies. Oh, there was an extra specialness about them that came directly from their membership in the Marine brotherhood, but deep down they were the ideal men to match who I longed to be, but wasn't back then. It saddens me that I can't remember the name of a single Marine I fucked during those years.

After my move to San Francisco in 1978, I got caught up in the Leather fantasy scene, and my memories of great sex with Marines in San Diego faded for a time. As the years passed and I saw the shallowness and infantile greed of most participants in Leather, I began to miss the simple goodness of those "Dago" Marines. I moved back to San Diego twice during the following years, but I was never able to reestablish my former hunting patterns.

I moved to Texas. I was near all sorts of ROTC cadets and Army guys, but after having tasted jarhead perfection, I couldn't bring myself to lower my standards. I realize how subjectively arrogant it is to stereotype humans, but I do find myself rating military men in the following manner: Air Force if you're desperate, Army if you're not picky, Navy if "fuck and farewell" will do, but Marines if quality sex and quality men mean something to you.

For those interested in astrology I might add that the Marine Corps was founded, "born," in Scorpio; the sign of raw sex, loyalty, male/male bonding, S/M, and secret rituals. Scorpio is a sexually submissive sign that focuses energy on the penis and rectum. Scorpio also shares with Aries and Libra a wide streak of romanticism.

Textures also seem to play a patterned role in military erotic stimulation. Soldiers prefer rough, dirty stuff like rope, shit, mud, and canvas wrestling mats. Sailors like slick things such as body-hugging nylon/lycra clothes, body oils, coated synthetic fabrics, and sex in the swimming pool. Airmen want everything suburban middle-class clean and bland, with maybe a dirty jock strap thrown in once in awhile. Marines are drawn to stretchy, sweaty, tightly enfolding things like leather and rubber. I know of no way to verify or disprove these stereotypes, but they have been around, and widely believed, for a long time.

Another odd note: In the symbology of the tarot deck, Swords (Air) are Air Force, Wands (Fire) are Marine Corps, Cups (Water) are Navy, and Pentacles (Earth) are Army, and each of the Major Areana has a military form.

Marines and Leather seem to have much in common. Perhaps the key is that by the time these young men have completed boot camp they have experienced enough physical pain that they are no longer afraid of it; at least not to the degree that most civilians are. The tight homoerotic bonding of the Corps, where physical pain is regularly experienced, would naturally eroticize both pain and male-male interaction. To get large numbers of Marines interested in Leather you would probably only have to expose them to it. Sadly, most of the Leather activity available since 1978 has been a middle-class gay parody of a once-secret brotherhood that no longer exists. In the 1950s and 1960s, I'm told that many queer Marines, upon leaving the Corps, submitted their entire beings to the control and training of experienced Leathermen, mostly in Southern California. In those days, Leathermen would often go down to the bus station and pick up Marines as they got off the bus. If they got 'em fresh, before the queens messed them up, they were ready and eager for any level of training that would keep them under a secure, self-directed man's control.

I suspect that to truly understand the role of military men in the desires of homomasculine chasers, you will need to devote some time to studying domestication, particularly the domestication of Homo sap. In all likelihood, in predomestication times most homosexual interaction between males was either rape or forced submission by the dominant males in the hunting packs. Somewhat like DIs symbolically "fucking" their recruits into submission and obedience. The presence of canine teeth and sharp frontal incisors in our mouths, plus eyes on the fronts of our heads, suggests that we began as a hunting, meat-eating species (or group of related sub-species). Our molars and our ability to digest high-nutrient plants indicates that we were omnivorous. Many insights can be gained from observing the behaviors and relationships among other omnivorous species— pigs, bears, coyotes. I might posit that gays are piglike, chasers more bear-like, and Marines share many patterns with coyote packs.

My friend, Carol, has a seventy-six pound pit bull. When I help her walk her dog I stare and stare at that pit bull's ass muscles. Every step the damn dog takes makes its rear end look just like a Marine's butt. Being fixated on butt-fucking men, a big part of my sexual response to Marines is the perfect glutes they so regularly display. Fucking, squeezing, and appreciating Marine butts is a true epiphany for me. My number two fetish is the pectoral development that upper-body PT achieves in Marines. Maybe I'm quasi-hetero in that I want a Marine man-wife to love, protect, suck/chew on his titties, and screw his man-pussy. I don't consciously see Marines as feminine, but as sexually passive and emotionally loyal the way my ideal life-mate would be. I just want him to be himself, and not a calculating gay who's always looking for drama.

There may be a fine line between military chasers and military predators. Whether this line parallels that separating us chasers from gay fantasizers would make an interesting study. Chasers want the military man's reality, while gay predators only want their image and the implied status of having "had" a military man. I've known queens who went into heat at the sight of a Marine or sailor in uniform and tittered away about "getting" them. Like their black widow mothers, they wanted to suck the life juices out of a masculine man and toss the empty husk aside afterward. While I do find many of the uniforms sexy, especially cammies, it's the man inside of the uniform, and what military training has built him into, that draws and holds my interest. Fetish-wise, I'd druther see/feel/smell a sweaty Marine stripped to the waist and wearing tight, thin, black leather pants and pull-on boots. To complete the fantasy he would have to want to be with me and develop an ever-deepening relationship. Guess that's the bottom line for me—Marines trigger my mating instinct. While I can certainly appreciate jarheads as prime pieces of ass, each time I fucked one was really an audition for the one I hope will one day complement my own personality and won't go away. To date they've all gone away.

How much of a military chaser's erotic response to men in uniform is a way for them/us to feel what it might be like to belong to a tightly bonded brotherhood? Most chasers whom I've known are as much loners as I am. I never had a genetic brother, and I have consciously envied the closeness and interdependence that I have observed in herds of Marines. My personality would never have fit in the Corps—I would have fought to the death to maintain my personal sense of independence—but I have always paid for that in a deep sense of aloneness. Perhaps that aura of an isolationist is part of what has prevented me from partnering up with a good man thus far. Marines are trained to buddy up. I have not the slightest idea how to do that; how to surrender the absolute "I" for a shared "we." A prime virtue of Aries is that if something attracts their attention, they just charge blindly at it without bothering to read any of the signs along the way. If I can get myself in an appropriate Aries Marine's path, he probably won't notice all of my quirks till we're already married.

A big part of my attraction to, and admiration for, Marines is the personal effort they have made to become more than typically self-obsessed, petty, responsibility-fearing, cynical Americans. This cultural disparity also tends to force Marines into closer dependence on each other—who else will truly make the effort to understand and accept them but their own kind?

This is probably where the role of the sincere military chaser is most apparent. We chasers care less for the military "image" than we do for the reality of the individual military man. Michael Grumley wrote in *Hard Corps*, "The essence of a fetish is its authenticity."[1] Those of us who find sex, affection, companionship, and maybe even love most desirable with military men are looking for more than a hard body in a uniform. We are drawn to what the military has made out of a man, and what he has used the opportunities found in the military to make out of himself. Deep down I suspect that we are looking for a hint of the heroic. That's an atavistic desire in our cynical age, but there is a beauty in still believing in honor and nobility of spirit. Though most military men are nowhere near that, the military is one of the most likely places where it might still be found (among working cowboys is another likely place).

Of course it can't be ignored that military men tend to be young, in good physical shape, lonely, outside of their home community's social controls, low on cash, and often inexperienced enough to be sexually manipulated by predatory men. While I may have all sorts of pseudoanthropological reasons for my attraction to Marines, the bottom line is that many of them are sexy as all hell, enjoy getting their butts screwed, can form tightly loyal bonds with a man who cares about them, and are less likely to have unreasonable expectations about their lives than most gay-identified males. Plus the love they are trained and encouraged to feel for their fellow Marines can often translate to enduring love for the man they mate with.

In a society that is all about transitory experiences and relationships, the Marine Corps' focus on stability and tradition helps Marines to see partnering up with another man as a permanent thing to be constantly worked at to maintain. Those Marines whom I was able to get to know on more than a brief sexual basis didn't expect all that much out of life, and they were damn grateful for every act of kindness they received. I don't know if the changing of the generations has affected this or not. It has been years now since I have had the chance to truly communicate with active-duty Marines. I am very curious to learn if the Marines of today—having grown up in a TV-driven, divorce- and latchkey-homed, tabloid-truthed world—are even similar to the fine young men I once enjoyed in San Diego.

Civilians and sailors were mostly out for themselves. They would have sex with a man only in order to gratify their own needs. Marines were more into sharing a sexual experience. Oh, I could get as rough as I wanted to with those little stud-puppies, but they were right there with me all the way. I liked the fire in them, and their eagerness to get ever closer. Sometimes it was like they wanted to wrap their bull-pussies around my dick and draw me up inside of them. They were "needing" young men. I think that came from the loneliness so many of them felt. Their craving for affection and attention (the seat of rough sex is the intensity that the topman is focusing on the bottom) was a key to my evolving from a military chaser to specializing in Marine chasing.

Is my Marine fixation nothing more than another baby boomer's obsession with an ideal? Does the Marine I envision even exist in the real world, or was that too crafted from the intense sexual encounters in days of yore? I don't know anymore. What was/is real, and what a compensatory fantasy? Idealism is a dangerous trap to fall into. I keep trying to believe in goodness in a world that is determined to prove otherwise.

The physical beauty of youth is still a premium value among many of the young military men of today. Those of us who have insights from over four decades of living can only act as teachers or advisors; our own sexual/affectional/mating needs are rarely even considered. That may be why I withdrew into writing about military men for porn mags—I don't have to look at the beauty I am no longer invited to touch. And yet I can't fault these young men for their attitudes; I don't want the middle-aged, set-in-their-ways men of my own generation, either. Maybe one day I'll find that Aries ex-Marine who wants to be with "Daddy." Maybe he'll be self-aware enough to not categorize me at all, but just accept me as myself.

Don:
Interview with a Pornographer

"We don't dress 'em up, pretty 'em up, and slide 'em out and call them a Marine and you know damn well that they're not a Marine." Anyone who has winced through any of too many L.A.-produced military-theme gay porn videos showcasing grievously nonregulation haircuts, mismatched uniforms, and models unlikely to last a day in even the most stereotypically gay military job specialties will know exactly what Don is talking about.

In the world of authentic military porn video, Don is both "on the edge" and in the middle. His best titles *(What They Didn't Teach Us in Boot Camp Volume I,* and *Marine First-Timers)* are not as slick as those of the biggest name in the business, Dirk "Private Collection" Yates, who captures his masturbating sailors and Marines in condos and motel rooms so antiseptic and sepulchral you can actually hear the digestive processes of the (always off-camera) videographer's apparatus. Yet Don's quickest and dirtiest efforts fall short of the jaw-dropping recklessness of Bobby Vazquez, the rabidly ribald participant-pornographer who, years after the 1993 Camp Pendleton porn scandal put him on the *CBS Evening News,* and landed him in jail, continues to crank out tape after tape.[1]

It's enough to say that Don shares with Bobby a palpably dangerous unbridled passion, but like Dirk, he tries to play a more distanced, avuncular role that keeps him outside the frame. Mostly.

The telephone is ringing as I step into Don's fluorescent-lit, cinderblock office space, which is located in a commercial neighborhood of San Diego across the street from a strip club and not too far from several military housing areas. He instructs me to have a seat on the couch while he answers the phone. With a start I realize I'm sitting on *the* couch.

Zeeland: I thought a good starting point might be what you were telling me at the video store, that there aren't any porn videos out there that do it for you, and that's one reason why you're in the business that you are.

Don: One of the reasons I produce my own videos is kind of selfish. There's nothing in the [adult] bookstore that turns me on. I'm bisexual, turned off by women because they want to control you. And no one controls me. So I'm turned on by women, but I'm primarily turned on by guys, young guys, straight guys. [Telephone rings.] Excuse me.

D: [After break.] When I go to the bookstore, out of a thousand titles, I won't find anything that turns me on. So what I do is I produce what turns me on. I like guys eighteen to about twenty-three, and I like 'em straight. And the epitome of total masculinity is a Marine. They've got great bodies, and they have great sex.

Z: What makes the sex so great?

D: Because Marines have psychological problems to a certain extent. Most of them I think are from backgrounds without a good father figure. So they like an older guy. They have to a large extent low self-esteems. So when you're nice to them in a pure personal way, they appreciate it. They're always horny. They can jerk off ten times a day and still be horny. And I think most Marines reflect what society is as a whole: bisexual. They take orders beautifully. They're trained to take orders. You tell them to do something sexually, and they basically do it. They'll do about anything except kiss, because that's queer. They're the epitome of male masculinity. And I don't get turned on by gays at all. Sailors are better to a certain extent, because they're more into the sex.

Z: What do you mean?

D: Oh, sailors don't care. Sailors will do anything. Gettin' off is gettin' off to a sailor. And my sexuality means that I don't assume the bottom position. Sailors always want to fuck you. And I don't get fucked. Rightly or wrongly, that's just not my thing. So I like Marines. They are readily available. Treat them with respect and they'll do about anything for you. But you don't get anything emotional from a Marine. After they come, a minute and a half later they're out the door. They always say, "I got firewatch tonight." The Marine Corps cannot have as much firewatch as they say.

There's a lot of guys out there like me. I mean, I'm bisexual but gays turn me off. I've got gay friends. But sexually, they do nothing for me. I can be with a Marine, and if he reaches over and starts playing with me, it's over. I don't want to perform any more, because I think I've got a gay Marine on my hands, and that turns me off totally.

Z: How do you meet Marines?

D: I advertise. Marines love to buy these swinger magazines. Because they don't have a problem with getting in bed with a man and his wife, and doing about anything, as long as there's pussy there. A lot of word of mouth, too. One Marine will refer another Marine. Or you can pick 'em up off the streets. You can pick 'em up at bars, on the beach. Anywhere. Marines are easy to pick up. They know what you want.

Z: How do you start talking to them?

D: The old standard line, "So what's happening tonight?" They'll say, "Not much." And they're going, this guy wants to suck my dick and fuck me. So we've made good communication. They know what I'm asking. So if they're interested in going home with me or to my studio, they come. If not, they say "No thank you" and walk off. Because Marines are always propositioned. You walk up to a Marine and say, "What's happening tonight?" "Not much." "Well, let's make it happen. I've got a place over here. You can kick back, drink a beer, watch a fuck movie, and just kind of take care of whatever comes up, or gets up." It's very simple. Marines are easy to pick up.

Z: I think you told me for a hundred bucks, a Marine will fuck anybody. Is that what you said?

D: Yeah—there's nothing worse than a good horny Marine. I mean, they'll fuck about anybody.

Z: So they're horny to start with, and then a hundred dollars—

D: Induces them. But when I say "anybody," that means—we refer to a girl now. When I say a Marine will fuck anybody—you give him a hundred bucks to fuck a chick, no problem. You give him a beer to fuck a chick, no problem. They just like to fuck. And if it's late at night, they'll fuck about any chick. Fat, old, makes no difference. They're just horny. They can get six nuts a day and still be horny.

Z: Do you find that they have a certain tendency to want to show off, too?

D: Yeah. Marines know that they got the bodies. And they do like to show it off. All you have to do, like when I do my videos, you just brag on their chest a little bit, or the size of their cock, and they're more than pleased. They want to show you their cock. They're very proud of their bodies. Sailors don't have the Marine bodies. But they just have another . . . mystique. Sailors are a little more honest with their emotions.

Z: I think you told me something like forty percent of the men in your videos are military?

D: My videos are "street trade," "college guys," and "military." We'd probably have to go maybe up to 60 percent military. And right now I'm primarily shooting military, because there's such a big demand. And when we say military—if I say a Navy SEAL, it's a Navy SEAL. If I say it's a Marine, it's a Marine. We don't dress 'em up, pretty 'em up, and slide 'em out and call them a Marine and you know damn well that they're not a Marine. And they're gonna talk about pussy, and they're gonna burp, and they're gonna do all the things that Marines do.

Z: Most of the videos are solo jack-off shots?

D: Yeah.

Z: What other kinds of stuff will people see in these videos?

D: One of my basic ideas is for people to get to know the Marine. So we get his name, where he's from, where he grew up, what kind of women he likes to fuck, when was the first time he got a little pussy, what he's up to. Was he at a bar, at the beach, and so forth. When you get through, you know something about the Marine himself. And then we talk him into taking his clothes off and getting a nut. It follows basically the same pattern. We'll put a straight video on so they can get excited. It helps them get off. That's our pattern, pretty much.

Z: Do you have sex with the models?

D: I don't have sex with my models. I absolutely—I don't fuck with my inventory. I treat this—this is a business. If I meet a nineteen-year-old Marine, even if he wants to have sex with me. And after awhile, most of my models are more than willing to have sex. Most young guys are bisexual. Especially if you have a girl present. But I don't have sex with my models whatsoever. Now, a lot of times—most of my couples in videos are swingers. So I can get a couple over, and I might invite six or eight of my Marine models to come over and fuck. So we have a lot of fuck parties. That trains them to fuck in a group. It also kind of rewards them for knowing the studio and everything. But I never touch my models, never will. Because this is a business.

Z: But do you meet men that come to you hoping to audition that you end up having sex with who aren't models?

D: Rarely. Rarely. This is a business.

Z: So when you're off looking for sex, or picking guys up just to have sex with, that's a separate thing for you.

D: Yes. Yes. I don't have a problem picking up guys. I'm an older guy with gray hair and a father figure in fairly good shape. And Marines and young sailors like father figures. I have the ability with twenty-five years of sales to talk them into about anything.

Z: What do you know about your audience? I think you were telling me that you get mail from men who are especially struck by some of the models, develop crushes on them, and have very involved fantasies.

D: My clientele are guys of all ages. They can be eighteen years old or they can be in their nineties. They get turned on by straight guys. They're like me. They don't really like gay guys sexually. And they've found that there's no product out there for them. So once we get 'em, they're loyal. They're looking for the mystique of the military. This is why when we video, we'll actually shoot some training bases and put it in our film. Because our clientele love the Marines, and love the young guys and so forth. And the whole atmosphere of military. And we don't trot gay guys out and call them Marines and sailors and SEALS. The Body Shoppe tapes are real. They're authentic military. The only problem is, if you've got a straight guy talking about pussy, if that turns you off—they're not gonna sit around talking about fuckin' some guy. Because they don't fuck guys. They fuck girls.

Z: How did your own attraction to military men originate?

D: I was a salesman for a publishing house. I would spend a week in Jacksonville, North Carolina, home of Camp Lejeune. Forty some thousand Marines. I realized how much fun they were, and how easy they were to pick up. I mean, you could get a dozen Marines a night. I was about twenty-six years old then. And I realized that it was great sex. Nice guys and so forth. That's how I got introduced. And I was hooked. That's basically it. The reason I got started was there were not tapes out there of straight guys. I used to do a lot of photography. I used to provide models to different studios and so forth. I was getting another college degree, doing this part-time, making a little extra money, enjoying it. Plus the fact I lived ten years in Oceanside, which is Camp Pendleton.

Z: Did your other career take you to Oceanside, or did you go there expressly to be near the Marines?

D: I had a business on the East Coast. After twelve years, I got sick of it. It was successful, but I was just tired of it. So I sold it. I was saying, wasn't there another military base on the West Coast with Marines? And a friend of mine said, "Yeah, I think it's in the San Diego area." So I got the map out and there was Camp Pendleton. I sold out twelve years ago and moved to Oceanside. To have sex with Marines. And enjoy life once again, instead of just working all the time.

Z: Well, you look like a happy man to me.

D: I'm a very happy man.

Z: And your business is expanding too.

D: Yeah. We just put out eight videos. We're starting another line. We're calling it *Marine First-Timers,* which is gonna be gang bang. We're going to use solely, pretty much, straight Marines fucking girls. We'll also use some Navy SEALs and some sailors, but primarily the Marines. Because a lot of people out there want more of those. Especially my distributor.

Z: Something that anybody looking at this is going to wonder about, and it doesn't need to be addressed at any length, and I know we agreed that you're not going to talk about your competitors, but people would of course want to know if you've felt any special threat from the military directly, or any fallout from the scandals of previous years. Is that anything that concerns you?

D: Well, we're always concerned. I mean, I know—I know the NIS or investigative service always knows who's doing what. As a general rule, the Marine Corps does not want their guys doing videos. In this business, if you're stupid—and there's been some people in this business stupid— you really can piss off the Marine Corps. If you're discreet, they don't say anything. The sailors, as long as you don't put 'em in uniform, the Navy doesn't really care where those dicks go. Just don't put 'em in a uniform and video 'em. The Marine Corps basically doesn't want any more scan-dals. If it's thrown in their face, they deal with it. So we don't put the guys in uniforms, and—If we call 'em a Marine, it's because they're out of the Marine Corps, or on their way out. So if the Marine Corps has got a problem, they're dealing with someone who's already been out of the Marine Corps. So we don't jeopardize these young Marines.

Z: Some of the guys that come to you—I wonder if they sometimes kind of want to flirt with danger.

D: A lot of the Marines don't give a damn. They're not happy in the Marine Corps. And we always tell them that there is an element of risk. We discuss this with all these guys. There's a very small element of risk. Most of them don't care. I mean, if it happens, it happens. It's never happened to me in ten years, and it more than likely never will. We try to be discreet.

Z: Have you ever been threatened—

D: No.

Z: Or attacked by Marines?

D: No.

Z: Not even verbally harassed?

D: Probably in thirty years I've had a couple incidents. And one of them [involved a Marine who] was drunk. And you don't deal with a drunk Marine. But for all practical purposes, I've never had a problem. I always— we talk about what we did very briefly, then we switch it over to talk about pussy. So once the sex act's over, you start talking about pussy. To reassure them that they're straight. And they are straight. The straightest people I know are Marines. If you want to seduce a military guy, go for the butch ones. Because they're secure in their sexuality. If you want to suck their dick, do a little something else, they don't have a problem with that. Most of the people I interview, and I interview fifteen people a day for my studio—

I have a question: "Would you let a guy suck your dick if the girl's there?"
I don't think anyone's ever said no. Almost a hundred percent of the guys
don't have a problem—they'll let another guy suck their cock as long as
the girl is there and they're getting a little pussy out of the deal.

Z: How much do you tell them? Do you show them your videos, or your
catalog?

D: Yes, we show them the videos we put out. We try to put them with girls if
we can. They understand that most of what we do is solo videos. We also
refer these guys sometimes to other studios to do straight stuff, and to other
photographers and so forth. But they know what we are. We tell them exactly
what we do. They don't have a problem with that. We're upfront and honest
the whole way.

Z: Have you developed special relationships with your models, either
sexual relationships or buddy relationships?

D: Yeah. You always do. Right now I probably got about twenty-five
models. A lot of them want to come over to the studio and talk, but I can't
develop an in-depth relationship because these guys change a lot. I don't
have that kind of time. But we try to be personal with them. They're not
pieces of meat we deal with. They're people we respect.

Z: You said something about that earlier, about how in the videos they're not
"pieces of meat."

D: If I got a nineteen-year-old Marine, he's got a beautiful body, he's straight
as an arrow and he knows he's going to be videoed—if I were watching that
video, I'd want to know what makes Chris tick, if that's his name. I want to
know he's nineteen—I'm not going to tell you that he's in the Marine Corps,
but I want to know a little bit about his family, where he grew up, the first
time he got a little bit of pussy, when's the last time he had a little pussy. You
develop a rapport with these guys. You get on a personal basis. And then the
shirt comes off, and their pants come off, and they get off. And when you're
through, they're usually laughing, and you know something about Chris.
He's a nice kid. He's a kid next door who joined the Marine Corps. And you
want him to come back and visit you night after night after night. So my
customers have Chris come over any time they want. Just by turning on the
tape. And I get letters all the time. They want to meet Chris. But we don't do
that. But Chris is a real live living person. And when you watch the videos,
you see that. So he's not a piece of meat. Chris could have a five-inch dick
and you'll think he's the greatest thing in the world. Because Chris is a nice kid.

Z: Um, do you ever develop a crush on or fall in love with—

D: Oh, I'm in love with all of 'em. I love 'em all. Not sexually. Because I
don't allow myself to love 'em sexually. They're all good kids. And we
take care of them. But they grow on you.

Z: Do you find there are differences between men from different parts of the country? Are guys from the South and Midwest different from ones from the East Coast or here?

D: They're all nice. If they're not nice, we don't use them in a video. But we find they're all really neat kids. You get ones from New Jersey and New York, they're direct. You get the ones from Texas—they'll tell you right up front they're horny. Which is kind of neat. And we've had guys from the Midwest—they're kind of shy about things. So it's stereotyping to a certain extent. But they're all nice guys. And they know what they're here for. They just want to do a video and get a little pussy, fine. Make a little money and so forth.

Z: Do some of them have serious modeling ambitions? Do they tell you that they either hope to do so-called legitimate modeling, or be in straight porn?

D: Most of them, they just want to make a little bit of money if they can, get a little pussy, and they want a copy of the tape because they like to see themselves fucking a girl. Or see themselves getting off. We've had some guys go on and do some serious work. Because Marines are always in demand. But most of them just like to have a good time, like to come to parties and stuff like that. And we always have straight parties. There's no gay action whatsoever.

Z: Do you use men from all different races and ethnicities, or are there certain preferences among your clientele for certain types?

D: The industry pretty much likes Caucasians. I use as many Hispanics and blacks as I can. I should use more than what I do, but on a business basis you can't use that many blacks or Hispanics or Orientals, because they just don't sell, and I'm in the business of selling tapes. We use as many as we can. Every black or Hispanic or Oriental, we try to put them into other studios, or we try to put them with photographers and so forth, but primarily though I have to limit them. I don't like that, but I have to sell my tapes or I go out of business. I think blacks and Hispanics are beautiful. But I have to sell the tapes, and the general society doesn't want that many blacks and Hispanics. They like pretty much Caucasians. It's a terrible reality. And I don't like it. But if I put more blacks and Hispanics and Orientals and so forth in my videos, they won't sell as well. I hate that, but I can't do anything about it. I can get out of business, but that wouldn't prove my point.

Z: Over the years, as your business has grown and you've gotten more professional, has it sometimes gotten to be a little bit more work than fun?

D: I average twelve-hour days, seven days a week. I love every minute of it. I find young beautiful military guys, talk them out of their pants, get 'em to get their dick hard, blow a great nut, and I edit it. I've got the best job in the world. So is it business? It's always business. But I got guys all day long taking their clothes off. And I don't have any objection to Marines taking their clothes off.

Z: It doesn't get to be too much sometimes?

D: Yes. I've shot Marines before that I—almost whimper. They're so young and so beautiful. And I'm so professional. And I just want to put the camcorder down and jump on 'em. But you can't do that. And they're like two inches away from you. But I don't bridge that formality. I want to.

Z: Do you feel a special link with the men who buy your tapes?

D: Yes. I've got a toll-free number, and my phone bill last month was seven hundred and fifty dollars. These guys call me toll free and we talk. You get to know your customers. And they tell you what they like. We have guys every day call us up and say, "Well, when you shoot this Marine, can you do this and this and this?"

Z: What kinds of things?

D: We've got a guy say, "Well, when you shoot them, I like to see the Marines' toes. I like to see their feet." So every video we put out, we get shots of the Marines' feet. A lot of guys like to see a Marine put a rubber on. So we do that occasionally. And it's like, ass shots. A lot of guys really like—we've increased our footage of the Marines and their asses. A lot of guys say, "You know, you ask these straight guys to play with their asses, and they don't know how to play with their asses." My response there is, "Straight guys are not ass-oriented." Gays can be, but straight guys don't know how to play with their asses. [. . .]

Z: Do any of these guys ever express an interest—Do you ever have a sense that any of them would be up for S&M kinds of things?

D: I would never ask.

Z: Although you did say—Are you going to do this video with the dominatrix?

D: Well, I went over to the military base last week. We had five Marines I was kind of being introduced to and a twenty-two-year-old, six-foot, 190-pound dominatrix lady. I mean, she was ugly as shit. She was big, ugly, and she walked in with her leather on, and her whip. And I told the Marines we're thinking about doing a dominatrix film. So she proceeded to tie 'em all up, and when she had 'em all securely tied up, she looked over to me and said, "Get out the dildos." Which was kind of comical at the time because you had five Marines all tied up on a king-sized bed. But they were having a good time, because they knew that if they played the game she would suck their dicks. And Marines are not stupid. They knew. And we had a great time for about three or four hours.

Z: And the dildos were actually used?

D: There were no dildos. There's not going to be a movie, either. I personally do not want to see a Marine all tied up being dominated by some bitch. That's not my style. And no one tells me what to shoot. And I won't shoot it. But I just thought it was kind of fun at the time, and so did they.

Z: You say that you consider yourself bisexual, and that that's how you see many of these men. Have you had relationships with women?

D: Yes. I was married for fifteen years. Two kids. I've had two relationships with guys. One lasted nine years and he was totally straight. Another lasted three years and he was totally straight. But I'm a firm believer that there's no such thing as a totally straight guy. If you're good to them, and you love them, and all the other good qualities, any straight guy will come around. I see that in the business all the time. Guys you would never suspect, they call you up and want to have sex with you. But it's passive sex. They don't want to get involved, they just want to make you happy. They want to give you their cock because you're a nice guy.

Z: Did you live with these men you had relationships with?

D: Yeah. Yeah. And they were very young. Legal, of course.

Z: Did they have sexual relationships with women at the same time?

D: Oh yeah. Absolutely. And I never got in the way of their relationships. I was always called "Uncle Don." Yet everybody knew, and all their buddies came over and wanted to see "Uncle Don." But "Uncle Don" was very faithful. He didn't play in his backyard.

Z: Was there a financial component—

D: No. No. I don't support anybody but myself.

Z: Of course there are probably a lot of men in Southern California looking for young military men to have those kinds of relationships.

D: That's out of my realm of even thinking. I consider myself a bisexual guy. If a straight guy wants to play we play. If he doesn't want to play, fine. After a while, though, any straight guy will come around if you're a decent sort of guy. But I don't support anybody but myself. No sugar daddy here, honey. So to speak.

Z: Where are you from originally?

D: I'm a mountain boy from western North Carolina. Teacher, principal. I went into sales with a major publishing house. Then after the third college degree I started making porno. And that's where I am right now.

Z: Was your family religious at all growing up?

D: No. My mother was to a certain extent. We went to church every Sunday. We were Methodists, and then after high school I was Baptist. I taught Sunday School. I've always been involved with church, except for the last few years. Not overly religious, but decent middle-class America. The family values of the mountains of western North Carolina. When you told someone something, you did it. You promise, you deliver. And I'm still carrying around those values.

Z: That's great. What is your political orientation?

D: Um. Labels. I never voted Republican, but if I had to I would certainly vote Republican. I'm conservative, but not a religious conservative. There's no label here. I can be liberal or conservative, I can be Democratic or Republican or Independent or whatever.

Z: Do you want your age—

D: I just turned fifty-four.

Z: It's a tacky question, but if you had to estimate the total number of military men you've had sex with, how many would you say?

D: That's a tacky question. But I'll answer it. [Pause.] You won't call me a slut? I'd say, in the last ten years, at least 2,000, maybe 2,500. They're easy, though. I have four or five a day knock on my door.

After I turn off the tape recorder, Don puts on a video for me. It depicts a masturbating fireman, who Don explains is really a policeman. A hand and suit sleeve invade the frame and feel up the model's chest. "Oh, I forgot about that," says Don, checking for my reaction. "That's all I did, though. Anything else would be queer." The groping hand moves further down. "Oh, I forgot I did that," says Don, flashing me a grin.[2]

Martin:
Fathers and Sons

The first time I expressed an interest in seeing my Navy boy-friend in his dress blues he was amused. "What? You wanna undo my thirteen buttons?" Troy giggled with the air of someone for whom such a prospect was new and a little dangerous. Then he saw how serious I was. After that every time I brought it up he made excuses. The uniform had to be cleaned; he was missing a ribbon; he had to wear his uniform to work and didn't want to put it on in his free time. Finally, I decided that Troy owed me enough favors. I ordered him to go home to Alameda and return to my San Francisco apartment in his crackerjacks. Troy complied, I undid his thirteen buttons—on videotape. After that I announced that I wanted to photograph him in uniform outdoors. By the time we crossed the Golden Gate bridge and I had him positioned cliffside in the Marin Headlands, Troy was in a surly mood indeed.

"Turn around," I commanded.

The drive back down the cliff was payback time. Large white numerals on the pavement cautioned 15 mph. Troy accelerated to 25, 35, 40 miles per hour, laughing as his Nissan Sentra squealed and bounced along the precipice, flirting with certain death.

"Um, Troy," I asked. "Are you upset because you feel that I objectified you?"

"What do you *think?!*" he yelled over the screeching tires.

But three years later, Troy was pleased when I used the photo I took that day on the cover of my book, *Sailors and Sexual Identity.* I sent him an enlargement of it and he had it framed and hung it on his living room wall.

That was after Troy left me for his father. His dad was terminally ill, and Troy got out of the Navy on a "hardship discharge" to care for him.

Troy's father declined to meet me. "There's nothing I can do about it," was the dying man's caustic comment when Troy came out to him. Happily, the two reached an understanding before the end. When I next visited Troy, I slept in the room his father died in. Troy dug out the scrapbooks he'd inherited. I flipped through with polite interest, until I came upon a snapshot of his father in his Navy dress blues. He looked a lot like Troy. Maybe he was even more handsome.

A few months after *Sailors* came out, my publishing house fielded a phone call from someone who wanted to purchase an enlargement of Troy's image. Martin explained to me that he was dumbfounded when he walked into a bookstore and saw the cover of *Sailors*. A year or so previously he had photographed his own Navy boyfriend in the exact same location.

Raised Catholic but now agnostic, Martin was born and raised in the rural Midwest. He spent six years in Southern California; now he's back in Middle America. Martin considers himself "a social liberal and fiscal conservative." He's of Scots-Irish ancestry.

Martin was one of the first men I contacted about this project. He kindly wrote out a reply to the questionnaire I sent him. Later our paths crossed in Seattle and I asked him some follow-up questions. Unique among the men in this book, Martin's involvements are mostly with gay-identified military men.

My father was diagnosed with cancer when I was seventeen. He lived for two years. During that time we went from fighting like cats and dogs to becoming friends. Before his illness, I did everything I could to avoid pleasing him. When the wrestling coach told him I made the squad, and Dad told me how proud he was, I dropped out.

Two years later, I was busting my butt to make him proud of me. Hunting was the rite of passage he expected to prove I was a man. You should have seen his face after I killed my first deer.

Dad was an honorably discharged Marine. His dreams of a military career were cut short by medical problems. For whatever reason, he thought I might be cut out for the military.

From about the time I was ten, my family had a spring tradition of visiting a friend in coastal South Carolina. These trips were among the rare occasions when my father and I spent time alone together. Parris Island was where my father had gone to boot camp, and it was where he sat with me for hours watching recruits being made into Marines. I can still see him sitting in that blue Chevy pickup, enthralled watching the guys sweating in the hot sun. The first several years, I watched intently for an hour, then begged to leave. But in time I learned to respect his reverence for the Corps, and I learned to endure military museums, Army-Navy stores, and every national battlefield we ever crossed.

After my father's death, I went abroad and found myself at war memorials, and entranced by Swiss soldiers and Soviet sailors. When my father's things were divided up, there was no confrontation. My brother took the guns and the tools. My sister wanted his trophy collection and his cowboy hat. I asked for his military items.

Nearly eleven years after my father's death I went back to Parris Island. I spent hours mesmerized, watching the DIs at work. A lot had changed for me during those years. I'd found myself gravitating, almost against my will, closer to several of my Dad's interests. I didn't come out to my family until after my father's death. There were countless "I love you but I don't understand" conversations with my mother. It is sometimes a real bitch being expected to fit a straight mold just because you are the first generation to get a college degree. I know my mother loves me, but she still wishes I were straight.

I often wonder how my father would react to finding out that I'm gay. I can't help but smile when I imagine Dad seeing me and one of the guys I've dated getting up at the crack of dawn to go hunting with him. Given the guys I have a knack for dating, I sometimes think he'd feel like he finally got what he wanted out of me.

It's hard to remember where the attraction to guys in the military really began. I remember taking recruiting materials from the post office as a young teenager because of the sharp-looking Marines and the long-limbed, confident sailors. I remember watching shows on TV like *Hogan's Heroes* and *M*A*S*H.*

Most of the military guys I have met have either been through mutual friends or at country or leather bars. I despise West Hollywood, so that was never an option. I seem to have a knack for meeting military men in bars wherever I am. I've also met them at happy hours, brunches, Christmas parties, at the PX, and one at an officers club.

I tend to gravitate toward servicemen, but I don't exclude civilians. I prefer Marines, but I have dated a couple soldiers, one airman, and several sailors. I am attracted to quiet, smart, and confident men. I think Marines fit this bill better than most branches. Outside of servicemen, I have had a tendency to date men in law enforcement, and my interest in country music has led me to meet an array of cowboys, farmers, and a rodeo rider or two. I think they share similar character traits with Marines.

All my sexual encounters with military men have happened within the last six years. I'd say the number is around twenty-five. For several years, I have been open to a long-term relationship. I would like to settle down, make a home, and grow together if the right person came along. I am thirty-two and have had that feeling for a while. It wasn't always that way, however, as I used to enjoy the idea of cruising and a good roll in the hay. I am not opposed to that at all even now, but I do think of the future now whereas before I didn't.

I am still on decent, or even close terms with all of the military guys I have dated. The first guy was one that I was very taken with. I was almost ready to give up my career for John. He seemed to really care about me, and he taught me a great deal about myself. We shared some great times in my Long Beach apartment, and a particularly fantastic weekend in San Francisco and Marin. He was the only guy I've taken home to Momma. Ultimately the discovery of some lies put an end to our relationship. He is still at sea and we talk a couple of times a year.

Zeeland: Tell me more about John.

Martin: I met John at a concert at the Hollywood bowl. He was sitting in the back seats next to us. We started talking. It went from there. To tell you the truth, when I met him I wasn't sure he was in the service.

Z: He had somewhat longer hair?

M: Yeah. Well, it was short, but enough to be questionable. It seems so trendy for guys to go down and get their hair buzzed. John was the reason you and I met.

Z: That's right. How did it come about that you took his picture in the Marin headlands? Did you just happen to be there?

M: We were in San Francisco together. I was up there for a conference, and so he went along. It was actually pretty nice. It was in the spring. We were both being very romantic: we were in *San Francisco!* We were running around and doing as much stuff as we could. We ended up in Marin, just because I wanted to see the view. So we walked across the Golden Gate bridge, and that's where that happened.

Z: What did John look like?

M: He was about six feet two inches, brown hair, brown eyes, about 195, fairly muscular, fair complected.

Z: What did he do in the Navy?

M: To tell you the truth, all I ever knew was that it was in "communications." Past that, I have no clue what he did. That relationship was probably mostly based on sex. We explored a lot of new territory together. That's when I started doing a lot more nonvanilla.

With Guy, the Marine from L.A., I had more of an intellectual relationship. We just saw some things very similarly. We used to fight cats and dogs on politics. But we really got to know each other a lot better before we had sex. And there was a lot more conversation after sex. Guy was somebody I could debate the morning paper with, and walk away from it friends. He was somebody I could talk to that I didn't have to explain my vocabulary to. I think that was a lot harder for me when that ended. And I was the culprit there, for ending that. I just wasn't ready. Or at least I thought I wasn't. I was scared.

I met him in Long Beach, also, at a country and western bar. We met a couple times and talked before we finally exchanged numbers. And that was over a period of about six months or so. I remember the first time I went home with him. He had a huge pickup, and there was a Bible on the dash. It scared the hell out of me! He was a really nice guy, and there was a lot more to him than I even thought after the first few times just talking to him.

He was big and beefy. Probably about six feet four inches, 'cause he was a little taller than I was. He was definitely heavier, but he was well-built. I would say he was like 220. Blue eyes. Dark complected. A smile to die for. Didn't do it very often.

My most recent relationship was with a Marine named Andy. I met him last year in a New York leather bar. He was stationed down in the barracks in DC. He just caught my eye. I was too drunk! He was bent over, and I just got a little . . . involved. And he enjoyed it. He was a big, butch Marine—or at least he thought he was. He liked to get hit.

I can play that role when I need to, but that's not my preference. Does it have something to do with his being a Marine? Perhaps. I think he likes the idea of being put in his place. But it was only at certain times, too. It was very definitely only when sex was involved. When we out and did stuff, he wanted to be calling the shots. Which I found amusing. We'd go do whatever he wanted, because I'm usually fairly passive on those things. That was fine with me. But if I wanted to be rude about it, and he'd make some kind of comment, it was always easy to make a quick comeback like, "That's all right. I'll fix it later." And I usually did.

Z: You said that you had political arguments with these guys.

M: Guy and I had a few. John and I had some. Andy and I had a lot, because he is a die-hard Republican. I had a real hard time equating a gay man with being a Republican. And we used to argue constantly. Everything from gays

in the military—We argued about that *a lot*. His position was that gays
shouldn't be in the military, and yet he was gay in the military. I couldn't
understand how he could say that and still be in the service. And it was okay
for him, ethically, to lie.

Z: So were all these guys farther to the right than you?

M: John wasn't. John, the sailor, was coming from the extreme left.

Z: How important is it to you that the men you meet be conventionally
masculine?

M: I could have done without being asked that! I don't like being negative
about a group of folks in general. But I definitely look for a man to be
conventionally masculine. I guess the direct answer is very much so. I'll
defend drag queens and effeminate men ad infinitum, but don't ask me to
date 'em.

Z: One thing that's a little different about your story from some of the
other men I've interviewed is that it sounds like most of the guys you've
been involved with identify themselves as gay.

M: It's true. Mostly because I've met them in scenes where you had to be
pretty obviously gay to be there. There have been a number of straight
guys that I've flirted with. But none of 'em ever went anywhere. I guess it
was more my problem than anything else. I just wasn't willing to make the
first move. And I'm not so sure that I would have been willing to act on
something even if I thought it was coming from the other side. Because I was
not really wanting to end up dead somewhere. Having gone out a lot in
Chicago, I used to hang out at the bar where Jeffrey Dahmer used to pick up
people. So I was very cautious there for a period of time.

Z: But I get the sense that you are uncomfortable with the whole idea of
straight chasing, apart from safety considerations.

M: Yeah, a little bit. Straight men having sex with gay men doesn't compute
in my book. Maybe it's just too much emotional baggage to deal with. It's
like, you're gay or you're straight, and I'm not good at understanding the
in-between. In the words of [Armistead Maupin's *Tales of the City* character]
Michael Mouse Tolliver, "I am a perfect Kinsey 6." If you're in between, I
can't handle it, so it's not going to go anywhere.

Z: My editor has instructed me to look for distinctions between men who are
"just" out for sex and men who are searching for a partner.

M: I'd say I've done both. I mean, the problem has been that most of the
guys that I've met didn't live close to me. John would have worked out,
except for I moved for my career. At that point, I wasn't willing to risk my
career.

Z: You seem to have reversed a common problem in military-civilian relationships. You're the one that's always moving around and going to different places.
M: Yeah. If I had my druthers, I'd settle down. And that's been the case for several years. I'd much rather be in a committed relationship. It's just been more an issue of opportunity. I've got about nine years with a company that I really enjoy. And they've been very good to me. So I'm going, "Well, given my experience, I don't know if I want to throw that away, until I'm more comfortable." Of course the catch-22 on that is in most cases my job doesn't allow me to be in a relationship long enough to say, "Yeah, I've got something worth throwing away my career for."

M: The hottest sex I ever had was with an Army captain from Texas who I met in Atlanta. This was last Thanksgiving. His name was Mark. I had seen him out at a couple of restaurants in Atlanta, and at a couple of the bars. We made a lot of eye contact, but nothing happened. His last night in town we were out at a bar, the Atlanta Eagle. We went back to my hotel room. And he brought with him a little bag of toys. A lot of leather-type things. He wanted to be pretty aggressive. I let him, to a point. He had a flogger. And I said it was okay "as long as you don't draw blood." To tell you the truth, it was more fun to watch him getting off on it. I really enjoyed that. And he was really big. So we did some fairly vanilla blow jobs and that kind of stuff, but it was when he got into his toy bag . . . there were some inflatable dildos that were a little large for me . . . blindfolding. He was really into poppers, which was fine, because that works for me too. No other drugs, for obvious reasons. It was this old hotel in Atlanta, and we just did things that probably would make the proprietor cringe. On the furniture, on the desk. I'm surprised we didn't wake anybody up, because he was actually very loud. He was very affectionate. He kissed a lot. And he really seemed to care about me. The next morning we went for breakfast and talked. It was just very fulfilling.

The most disappointing sex was a sailor from Great Lakes [Naval Training Center]. I met him in Chicago at a dinner for a local uniform club. We went out several times and he sold the masculine, no-bullshit, sailor thing to the hilt. But he was a big yawn in bed.

The most alarming sex was with Guy on the San Diego Freeway. On the freeway, on the overpass. I think it was the Anaheim Street overpass. We were standing on the railing in view of all these cars driving by underneath.
Z: What did people see?
M: They saw one guy knelt down and another guy pissing on him. In his mouth, on his face and other parts of his body. It was late enough that it was dark, so probably all people really saw were just silhouettes. But I don't think

it would have been too hard to mistake what was going on. It was probably one of those things that, once they drove past they figured out what had happened.

The ride back was more interesting, actually. Because of the smell. He was very turned on about it. Watersports is something I didn't think would be much fun, but I did have fun with it. It seemed to be a very faddish thing in L.A.

Z: Have you ever had a military guy attack you or threaten you?

M: No. I had some guys that got off on threatening me while having sex, but that's a different story.

Z: Did you ever consider joining the military?

M: I gave some thought to West Point and Annapolis for college, but my father's illness pretty much threw out going far away from home. In hindsight, a large part of me wishes I would have attended one of the service academies.

Z: You mentioned uniforms.

M: Yeah, I belong to a uniform club. So I have a lot of different uniforms, which is a lot of fun.

Z: What is your favorite?

M: Dress blues. I also have several law enforcement uniforms. It sounds really bad, but when I've gone out in a uniform I have never failed to get laid. And that sounds really cocky, but it's the truth.

There's three uniform clubs in L.A. alone. There's one in Chicago that I'm affiliated with. I don't do a lot with them, because most of that crowd, to be real honest with you, is a lot older. Mainly it's an issue of money, being able to pay for the uniforms. Unless you're in the service, most people don't have the money to put out for it. If they can find 'em. I'm trying to think what I paid for my officer uniform. It was four figures. I think as a result of that, you'll find a lot—at least my experience has been that there are a lot—of younger guys who are interested in uniforms, but unless they know somebody, it's a scene they can't afford. And most of the ones that are there—sometimes they're just uniform queens.

Z: I lived in a house in San Francisco with a man who belonged to a uniform club. He loved to look at pictures of men in uniform, and liked to dress up, but he'd never met any military men for sex. Have you observed much crossover?

M: Limited. I've met some military guys that really like wearing the uniform out and doing stuff, but they have not associated with the clubs. They almost seem to think of the uniform clubs as an unwanted fan club of sorts.

Z: How did the military guys you dated feel about this? Did you ever discuss it?

M: Yeah, we discussed it. Actually, John was house-sitting for me, and stumbled upon a closetful of things that he wasn't expecting. For him it was a big turn-on. Guy didn't want to see me in blues. There's a picture of me that was taken with a friend in blues and he didn't want to see that at all. It just turned him off. Andy liked it, though. BDUs he liked. And he liked me in my blues.

It was weird. Some of them didn't really care. There were a couple, though, that found that complimentary. There was a guy that I met in San Diego. He was in the Corps. I met him at [a leather bar]. He was really interesting about it. He spent a lot of time going through it with me. If he could find anything wrong with it, he'd talk about it. He was pretty cool. "Okay, yeah, it looks pretty good, but you might want to do this differently. If you really were in the service, you would have done this." So he took it more like a mentorship. But I think he kind of found it amusing. And there were a couple times when John "inspected" me too. If I had on a naval uniform he was very specific. He liked that role.

Z: How did you happen to start doing that? Do you remember the first time?

M: Yeah. My father, actually, is mostly responsible for that. And I don't know if it's because of our trips to Parris Island or what, but he had a lot of military clothing. We used to spend hours in surplus stores. He just really enjoyed that. One time he had a shooting sweater on, from his days in the Marine Corps. I made an offhand comment that I thought it was cool. Which blew him away. He bought me one. And from there he gave me other stuff. He had his old Corps jacket. I'd wear it around and stuff. So yeah, Dad actually started it. He's the guilty party there!

Z: You said that when he died you inherited all his Marine Corps stuff. Did that include uniforms too?

M: No, actually that's the only thing I don't have, is his uniform. My mother wanted that and kept it. I'm sure when she dies I'll get that.

Z: Would it fit you?

M: It might be pretty close. The cover wouldn't, because my head is much larger than his. But in terms of build, we are very similar.

Lance:
Come to Daddy

MARINES, VISIT DAD'S BEACH COTTAGE! DAD IS 40SOMETHING DWM, TEXAN STUD AND OVERSEXED TOPMAN.

BEEFY EVERHARD TOTAL TOP/DOMINATOR DAD I.S.O. HORNY "SONS," BROTHERS, AND HUNGRY ORAL SERVICE EXPERTS TO SERVICE MY GORJUICY EVERHARD 7″ CUT TOOL.

BOYS BE EAGER TO PLEASE AND SERVICE-ORIENTED AND VERY ATTRACTED TO REAL DADDY TYPES. ONCE HERE, ALL YOUR EXPENSES COVERED BY DAD, BUT YOU'LL HAVE TO "WORK" FOR THAT!

Lance is a bold man. His ads, which include his home address and telephone number, appear concurrently in as many as twenty different publications. Sometimes he runs as many as three different ads in the same publication.

But Lance wasn't always a Marine daddy, he confided when I sought him out at his Oceanside, California beach cottage. He used to be a "house mother" to gay men on Fire Island. In fact, he claims to have inspired a character created by his friend, novelist Andrew Holleran. Now, at forty-nine, the bulky, mustachioed Texan says that he is getting more sex than he ever did as a twentysomething "gym bunny." But he asked me whether it was right that anyone should experience so much easy pleasure. And he complained that he sometimes feels like a schoolgirl, sitting by the telephone, waiting for a Marine to call.

Lance: I started advertising about ten years ago. My advertising at that time was mainly directed at the gay audience. I started understanding how ads work. I think advertising is a legitimate means to meet people, either for love or sex, or even, as I recently have, to meet someone to play chess with.

197

I started the ads after a long-term relationship with a younger lover had gone sour. We're still friends, but the sex went out of it and it turned into a roommate-type situation. He moved to the other bedroom. I started running ads looking for romance. You know the sort. "I want to walk on the beach and have candlelit dinners." [Laughs.] Well, that was a waste of time. I would be taking people to the symphony, the theater, expensive meals, meeting for drinks at luxury places. But I was just listening to people's problems. I wasn't getting laid. So I learned to change my approach. I developed what I think is a very good system. Now, I run a very sexually explicit ad. In my twenties I was a gym rat. But I get more action now in my forties than I ever did in my twenties. Of course I've never been so heavy, either.

In recent years when I lived in Palm Springs, I started advertising in more of a bisexual publication. I met some people from [Marine Corps Air Ground Combat Center at] Twentynine Palms. That's when I started getting interested in military guys.

Mostly the kind of military men that I meet—I am not interested in the eighteen, nineteen, twenty, twenty-one-year-old just coming out, just exploring their sexuality. I find most newbies to be very poor sex. The minute they come they're like scared rabbits and they're out the door. They can't even pretend to be civilized and take your name and number. I'm more interested in guys twenty-five and up who know what they want. At Twentynine Palms I was meeting married guys who were seeing a man on the side. I had a cottage out in the desert that was fenced in. I found at that time that Marines were very good at taking orders. I had one officer who came over once. I had him pull up at night, made him disrobe after he closed the gate, and he had to appear at the front door on his knees. [Laughs.] We had a great time.

Then I met a guy who said he was a sailor stationed at Twentynine Palms. Whether he was really a sailor or a Marine I never found out. But he was from Kansas, and he would show up like every three months, when he said he really needed a dick, that he was "fuckin' starving." Of course he *claimed* that mine was the only dick that he had ever sucked. [Laughs.] But he was so talented I found that very hard to believe. Then there was a black guy who was a really muscle-bound stud that just loved to get fucked. But unfortunately he came over with very heavy cologne and his wife's panties on, which was a real turn-off for me. I wasn't interested in seeing him again.

I also would get people coming out from [Marine Corps Air Station] El Toro and Camp Pendleton who wanted to get away from the base and see someone far away. I used to have one Marine that would come out like on leave. He said he wanted to get away from his buddies. Going out to the desert was his excuse. So he would come out on what we called "dick-hunting expeditions." He would work me over and then I'd send him out to the bookstores, and then he'd come back before he went back to Camp Pendleton.

When I moved here—it was after a big trip exploring the country. I'd won a big case and had some money, and was ready to make a change. I went all over the country, looking for a possible place to relocate. Almost to my surprise I found myself here in Oceanside, pretty close to where I'd just left. I've always been attracted to Marines. For many years I've had these little flags of Scotland, Texas, and the Marines, the three things I like the best. But I didn't realize until after I got here that I could be termed a middle-aged camp follower.

I would still love to live here anyway, whether they were here or not. The fact that they're here and that it's eye candy and hundreds of 'em go by every day is a real bonus. Most of my neighbors who are white middle-class people do not like the Marines. That's one reason I have the flag and the seal in the window, and when they come by I say hello and talk them up, to show them that I'm friendly. My neighbors view Marines as riffraff. And there are some bizarre stories, living here, of crazy things that they do. Which is one reason I avoid the eighteen, nineteen, twenty-year-olds. They're more likely to explode, they're more likely to get crazy drunk, they're more likely to turn on you. "Let's kill a fag."

Zeeland: Has that ever happened?

L: No. [Face clouds.] I do get some hate mail. And I get hateful abusive phone calls . . .

Z: From what kind of people?

L: I think they're mainstream little fairies. I had some queen in San Diego put my name and phone number in the bathrooms all over town that I was selling kiddy porn. I had the vice squad coming after me because of this queen. This queen would harass me. I know her voice to this day. As masculine and strong an individual as I think I am, I am on the other hand very sensitive. I get this stuff and I just go, "Why?" It's just pretty sad. And none of it is from someone that I've done wrong.

Z: So this is not "antigay" harassment?

L: No, no, no. This is what most disturbs me. I've had more and more and more disdain for the gay community, and for the gay community values. One reason I'm attracted to military men, and to bisexual men, is that our queens have all these criteria, and all of these guidelines. I'll listen to these phone lines: [mimics effeminate voice] "You must be eighteen to twenty-two, you must be six feet tall, you must be 160 to 175 pounds. You must have blond hair, blue eyes, a cleft chin, a nine-inch cock. You must be HIV negative, warm, friendly, financially stable, have your own car, own your

own home, and be a total top man." [Laughs.] I get my best responses from
ads in *Swing, Friends and Lovers,* and *Manswing.*

Z: I noticed that you sometimes put different ads in the same issue of a
publication.

L: Yeah. Some will never see the other one. Or sometimes they'll say, "Boy,
you got a lot of ads in there." [Laughs.] There is no magic incantation. I
keep changing it from time to time. In the portfolio I sent you I included
examples of some of the ads I've run. It's just like fishing. Different lures
pull in different fish.

There are other ways to meet military people. You can meet them by
cruising the street, you can meet them in the gay bars, you can hit the bus
stops, you can hang out in the parks, you can go to the enlisted men's clubs.
But I find that the best thing about the ads is, the person is calling me at my
home.

You need to screen the person before you have them come over to your
home. Especially if you're starting with an ad which is just your phone
number. If you run ads with post office boxes, you will get very few
replies, and very little if anything will come out of a PO box ad. Mostly
those ads are people who want pen pals. Or a place to send that kind of
stuff [sexually explicit letters] I've given you that nothing has come of.
But if you want action, then you have to install an action line in your
home. If you're going to put an action line in your house, do it for a short
term. It may not be for you. Be sure you have an answering machine or the
ability to turn your phone off when you do not want to deal with it. When
you're ready to deal with it, when the phone call comes in, it's best to turn
off everything, so that you can really listen to what this person has to say.

The person must tell me *what they want to do.* If the person can't say, "I
want a good blow job. I need to suck a dick. I really want to get fucked
today," then I really doubt I want to meet them. Unless they can tell me,
[whispers] "I'm on base now. I can't really talk." [Laughs.] But if they
can't tell me what they want, I'm not interested in tea and sympathy and
cookies and blah, blah, blah. I've gone through that. I know what that's
about. No hemming and hawing! They come over here, there is a hot triple
X movie going. There's a cold beer waiting for them. And action! Okay?!
And that's been cleared ahead of time.

I don't see anybody after the sun goes down, if I haven't met them
before. I will have [repeat visitors] knock on the door in the middle of the
night. That's okay. "USMC reporting for duty, sir!" I'll get up for that. I
will not have someone come over who's been drinking. That doesn't
always work, because for instance one Marine called me and he was down
at that Rusty Scupper bar, and it was nine or ten in the morning. I thought,

well, he can't be loaded this early in the day. Wrong! Even a jaded ruin like myself can be fooled at nine or ten in the morning if they aren't slurring their words! [Deep, rolling laughter.] He'd been up all night. He came over smelling like a gin mill, and it just didn't work. He couldn't get an erection and it was embarrassing.

One reason I like military people is they don't tend to be into drugs so much. Sometimes they won't even take poppers because they're afraid it'll show up on some drug test. Considering all the pot and crack and cocaine and crystal methedrine and everything running around now, it is a breath of fresh air that that is something you do not have to worry about with the military guys. But you need to listen to them very carefully. If anything sounds strange, tell them you're busy. If they call back again, see how they sound the second time. Get them to say what they want to do. Everyone understands that this is not for money, this is just two guys having fun. That they are of legal age. If they sound very young you ask them very quickly [shouts] "And what year were you born?!" I can hear them thinking over the phone. Once I had some kid come over who looked like he didn't even have a driver's license yet. I went, "Wrong number."

Z: Have you had any bad experiences after dark?

L: I've had people pass out. I had one guy barf in my bathroom. Then you get some sort of homeless people that need a place to stay. Just bad news. Also, the guys that I like to play with, especially married guys, daytimes are better for them. Because they have family life.

I gave you my "log." March was the best month. I met seven Marines and two Navy guys.

Z: You said that the proximity to the Marines wasn't a factor in deciding to move here. Have they since become a major preference for you?

L: Yeah, I'm definitely looking for them now. Whereas before they were gravy, now they're the main entree. For me, these are genuinely masculine guys as opposed to queens strutting their stuff down at some leather bar. I don't have any Marines come in here and ask, "What did you do for your last brunch?" They're very down-home. I enjoy talking with them if I'm sitting here on my porch. I often give them directions if they're looking for housing or a hotel or something. Recently, one Marine saw my Texas flag and told me how he's eighteen years old, and lived in Odessa, and it was his [imitates regional accent:] "First day I been to the beach! I never been to the ocean in my en-tire life!" What I enjoy is their eagerness and earnestness and their sincerity and their enthusiasm. In the midst of a jaded world of jaded, burned-out queens, it's very nice to find someone who, "Golly!," they're so excited. And that they can be "Golly!" so excited over their first blow job or getting fucked or sucking your dick. It's refreshing.

And it's refreshing that there's no agenda of queens. [Lance counts off on his fingers:] "*What* do you do for a living? *What* kind of car do you have? *How* much money do you make? *Where* do you vacation?" [Laughs.]

Z: Are you aware of regional differences in the men who come to you?

L: I really enjoy the Southerners or the Texans or the Midwesterners or the Rocky Mountain guys the best. But, Jeff, the top one [in Lance's log], he's from Southern California. I thought he was from Colorado or something. Eight-inch cock, married, wedding ring, comes over, has one beer, won't sniff poppers. Four orgasms every time. He'll come here, bring his own dirty movies, and he snorts snuff while you're having sex. Have you ever been with anyone who snorts snuff?!

Z: You've written in your log: "Jeff is love, Jeff never faileth."

L: He's just fabulous. He's about six foot tall, short dark hair, blue eyes, no facial hair, a little body hair, rock-hard body—more like a baseball player than a football player or body builder. Every time he comes it gets better.

In March, I had sixty-four orgasms. For a forty-nine-year-old man, I think that's pretty good. But if I did not have sex and sat here just watching, it would be painful. I never turn on videos just for video's sake. I think masturbation is a waste of time.

L: Did you want me to go over my log? This "Jason" is the repeat from Palm Springs, the guy that came and got the five orgasms, then he went out to the booths.

Z: He actually came five times?

L: No, *I* came five times. I don't even think he came until the end. This Antonio—I don't remember. And this Dan, he came over before work. Oh! This guy was hung, wonderful, and young. Then this Ted, he's been by several times. From Arkansas. He was real hung with a huge uncut dick. But then recently he called again, and he found out I was the same person [advertised under a different name], and although he came here two or three times, he hasn't come back. So I mean, some of these people, I don't understand. My old landlord has a big apartment complex down the street. He said he got turned on to Marines when he first moved here and fell in love with one. Then he found out that he was one of three lovers in San Diego county of this Marine. [Laughs.] So there's a whole group of Marines that know they're hot properties, and work it.

Z: There was some mention of "trade" in your log. Was this some guy who demanded money and you thought he was worth it despite your normal policy?

L: When I mean trade, I mean that they don't do anything. Nonreciprocal sex. No, I haven't, fortunately to date, ever paid for it. I don't want to get to that point but maybe I will.

What I'm trying to create here, is that the guys have a place where they can go, and that Daddy will take care of all their expenses, will barbecue, and there will always be your kind of beer or hooch. You go to the beach, you can go chase pussy, you can go chase dick, you can go do whatever you want. I mean, I have one Marine who wants to fuck his broads on the hide-a-bed. I said, "As long as you know that Daddy gets his." I'm trying to create sort of a home away from home. Or just sort of be their buddy.

Z: So you do get to be buddies with some of these guys?

L: [Pause.] Yeah. Not as much as I might like. A lot of gay people are like that for me. I call them my "nephews." I have a whole stable of nephews. Mostly they need advice. I remember when I was back in my twenties. I really appreciated the older gay men that took me under their wing, I remember them. They taught me how to hold my beer, and how to stand at the bar. I think one of the problems now with the gay community is—I don't know, I'm not in the mainstream anymore, but I don't think there's the same mentoring system that I remember.

L: I was making big money and was a powerful lawyer in New York, and I had my own beach house on Fire Island. You'd buy shares in a house. I was the only person who had their own bedroom because I was the house daddy. But after a summer there I thought: this is what gay people make for themselves when they are left alone with all this money? A meat rack, discos, drugs, and lists of twenty criteria of whether you're a worthwhile human being? I was from Texas, and I'd say hello to everyone. "How ya *doin'?!*" After three months of being snubbed, I decided New York and Fire Island were not for me. And my friends told me that for the next two or three summers people would go, "What happened to that friendly guy, your house daddy?" After you left, they asked about you! I guess any minority group has its problems. But I think queens are the worst. What an unhappy place. It was all just style and fashion and accessories and bitchiness and gossip and size queens. *Unfriendly* size queens.

Z: You say that you offer Marines great sex, but I'm wondering if there might not be other things that they look for from you. Might there not be something kind of paternal—

L: Oh yeah. I am definitely working that. I am constantly telling people in their thirties and forties and fifties [bellows in stern, lecturing voice:] "You're not a twinkie anymore! You want to start getting laid? You've got to learn how to be a daddy!" Like the landlord down the street that had the Marine

with the three lovers. I keep telling him, "Rich! You're fifty-three!" He still wants to act like he's twenty and go around on his bike and skateboard with these kids. I said, "No! You have to go to daddyhood!" Yes, right now I am working that with a vengeance. This is the new ad campaign. [Shows me ad.]
Z: Can I quote from this?
L: Yeah. It's in *Handjobs* now, and in *Rural American Men*.

I'm real big on "suck Daddy's big dick." Even when they're almost my age. I mean, when I was in law school everyone teased me because they said my motto was, "Eat my big dick, you worm." [Laughs.] For years, that's been my handle. My friend Andrew Holleran put it in his books. But I think that the point that we're trying to make here is that there's a need of these younger military men for the mentor. A lot of the military people I meet do have problems. Like this sailor that wants to come up and spend the next two years here. He was abused by his father, all his teenage years. He doesn't seem to think it was abuse, but he had a sexual relationship with his father. A lot of them have sex fantasies about their fathers. I'm meeting a lot of people that have no fathers, that come from a single-mother home. Most gay men that I know cannot fill that role. They want to be nurtured, they want to be taken care of, they want to cry, they want to tell their story. They can't tell someone, "Steve, you're drinking too much." Or, "Steve, you can't go gambling like that."

I had a period where I went into the gay community actively. For awhile I was thought of by some people as the Mayor of Montrose, which is like the Castro of Houston. At that time everyone called me Mother. I was a house mother, a den mother, the town mother, the village mother. But then I realized after working with all these gay people that just giving this gooey, unconditional earth mother love did not work. They got to get spanked, regularly!
Z: Speaking of spanking, what do you actually do with the Marines?
L: I don't ever get into anything really heavy. Most of it's just light spanking. I never leave any marks, or burns, or cuts. I do have some neckties that a woman friend gave me for tying people up, but they are silly. I have no equipment. People call and say, "Do you have equipment? Do you have a cock ring?" I say, "I have a dick that stays hard for hours. I don't *need* props." I think all that other stuff is for people who can't keep a hard on. Or have premature ejaculations. I don't need frills. I wear most people out. But there is some spanking, and I do get "Yes, sir. Yes, sir. Yes, sir." I mean, you're gonna come down here and take orders, and you're gonna be sitting in your jock strap, and you're gonna be available. You're gonna get breakfast in bed and it's gonna be Daddy's dick shoved down your throat.
Z: Have you found a special willingness among Marines to play that role?

L: I think Marines are good at following orders. Like that officer that disrobed and came to the door nude and on his knees. And I think there's a need in some of those people of wanting orders and direction and guidance. I don't think anyone joins the military who isn't open to direction. They come here, and the dirty movie's on, and the cold beer is here, and it's your place. I mean, you're in charge of how it's gonna go. I've only had one guy leave. And it was mainly because I think he was really more of a gay mainstream kind of Marine. He came in and said, "Oh, you're not my type." No bisexual or heterosexual or bi-curious guy says, "You're not my type." The thing I like about Marines is that there isn't that sort of criteria. I mean, I feel that they are excited, that they want to have man-sex, and they need to get laid; they called you, they have this tension built up, they're horny, they're ready to do it.

I find military guys very comfortable with their animalness and with their sexuality. And spontaneous about it. One day this jogger came by who was a Marine, early on a Saturday morning. I was cleaning house, and he was looking for "Joe." "I'm supposed to meet Joe here to go jogging, my Marine buddy." He came in. He was a handsome guy, had on his green jogging shorts. I was surprised. That was the first time this ever happened. But I am very proud of how I handled it. I said, "Well, maybe you should call him." So he picks up the phone and he dials some number. No answer. I go, "Well, how about a glass of ice water while you wait." "Yeah." He uses the phone again. Still no Joe. "You need to take a leak?" "Yeah, I need to take a leak." So I go and wait in the bedroom. He comes out with a huge hard-on and we go at it like crazy. Then he says, "Maybe I'll try Joe again." No answer. Then he just jogs off.

L: I was born in Texas. Lived all over the country. My father was a college professor, so we moved around a lot. Went to college at San Jose State, and law school at Hastings. Then I moved to Philadelphia, DC, Chicago, New York, DC, Houston, New Orleans, L.A., Palm Springs, Oceanside.

I started knowing at twelve or thirteen that I was gay, looking at all the encyclopedia pictures of Greeks. Had my first experience when I was fifteen, in a bowling alley. I got picked up by the vice squad when I was sixteen. It was a very traumatic experience, very upsetting to my family. Then I had a long period where I had to pretend I was straight. President of my fraternity, big man on campus, blah, blah, blah. Then my fraternity brothers caught me driving around this park where you'd pick people up. So I got exposed there. Then in law school, in my federal prosecutor career—it was very closeted. I had a lover in Chicago and we didn't live together, he lived in a high rise near my high rise, even though we might have spent five nights a week together. That's sort of when I busted out of the closet door. In '80 I left the feds and moved to Houston. My partner and I opened the first gay B&B in Texas. And then I had a gay newspaper with a friend in Houston, and was with a gay newspaper in New Orleans. That's when I first started running ads.

Z: You were never in the military. Did you ever think about joining?

L: I had a high lottery number. It was during 'Nam. And that wasn't a time you wanted to join. I had no interest. My interest in the military has really come in the last years since Twentynine Palms. I think that the acquired taste is more and more of my disgust with the gay mainstream. That whole subculture, I mean—I think it's even worse in Hillcrest [the gay neighborhood in San Diego]. They're just so cliquish down there, and inbred, and— ugh. [Laughs.] It reminds me of the fifty-five-and-over communities in Palm Springs. I don't think it's healthy to live like that. What I like about living here is there's a little girl in back who has a lemonade stand once a month in front of my house. There are old people, there are young people, there are straight people, there are gay people, there are military, are nonmilitary. It's not a ghetto, it's a true community. People in Oceanside are very friendly. When I first moved here it felt like Texas. "Hi, how are you?" "Good, how are you?" You get to know the people. Joanne and Randy, her dog, came by yesterday and I had steak for Randy. I think people have figured out my story, but nobody seems to be upset about it.

L: The last few years I've turned into a real homebody. I'm reading, I'm playing chess, I'm doing my investments, my correspondence. But sometimes I question: is this healthy? Sixty-two orgasms in March and waiting for the phone to ring.

Z: Healthy how?

L: Well, I get the vicious mail, like "Get a life." I mean, maybe I should be volunteering at a homeless shelter.

Z: But you're offering this mentorship to Marines.

L: If we can explore that a little bit. I really do help a lot of people in exploring their sexuality, exploring their problems with women. I used to have a married guy that came to see me every Christmas Eve. We'd have wild sex, then he'd show me pictures of his kids and he'd go pick 'em up. I see a lot of married men that see this as a sexual release but it's not hiring a prostitute, it's not in a park getting arrested, it's not Pee Wee Herman in a dirty bookstore ruining your life getting arrested. You come here, we close the curtains, I have most people park up on the hill so that it can be discreet.

When I tell some of my friends that I think I help people, they just go, "Yeah. Mmm-hmm." My partner, when I used to tell him stuff like this, would say, "Save it for the tourists." But a lot of these people, I do end up giving them counseling. The mentor/uncle/daddy role. I mean, I think I'm an old soul. I don't know what your belief system is. It's a function I have always had. I think one of my gifts is wisdom, and I think people see that, or sense that, or want that. I believe in reincarnation. I've gone through many of my past lives, and to the surprise of one of my gurus, she said, "You have very few female past lives. You always seem to be more comfortable in being a man." I'm very comfortable being a man. I understand women, and I have a lot of empathy and sympathy and so forth, but like that period where I tried to be the den mother: it didn't work. I didn't get laid. These queens did not need a mother. I indulged them too much. They needed discipline, not nurturing.

L: You are the only person I have ever been this open with about my sexuality. I honestly believe that the people who get the most talk the least.
Z: If I were getting more I wouldn't be writing books.
L: This is why I looked forward to your interview. Sometimes when you have to explain it to someone else, as in teaching, you learn it yourself. I was hoping to learn from this interview some of the questions that I struggle with. I keep asking myself: what is wrong with this picture? I have never been happier, watching all this Marine eye candy, plus other assorted beefcake, go by here every day. Getting laid. I just love the ocean, enjoy the sunsets. I think it's my Protestant work ethic. But I was raised as an Episcopalian, which is "gilt without guilt." So I'm very much an Epicurean; I'm very much my nickname to my nieces, "Uncle Mame." "Life is a banquet, most poor fools are starving to death." Sometimes I question whether it's healthy. But also I know—I just took my mother to Vegas for Mother's Day. And I was so happy to be back here. When I'm coming down the hill to my cottage, I put on Tina Turner's "Paradise Is Here" full blast. [Laughs.]

L: One more thing about Marines. Do not kiss them, do not hug them. When they leave, you *shake hands good-bye.* "Thank you. That was just great. Please come back anytime. One day, one week, one year from now, call me." Slap 'em on the back, and they're out the door. *Do not* slap them on the ass. They may do that at the barracks all they want, but don't do that. And don't *ever* try to kiss them.
Z: Have any ever tried to kiss you?
L: If it happens, it happens, but you never initiate kissing or hugging or any affection above the nipple.
Z: Well, you've already discussed in advance what you're going to do—
L: [Shakes finger at Zeeland.] No affection above the nipple!

Doug:
Good Old Boys

Many military chasers are searching for a masculine camaraderie that has eluded them. The subject of this interview, a forty-nine-year-old Southern Baptist and Democrat, says that he has never been wanting for buddies. A former college football player, Doug is six feet nine inches tall and weighs 285 pounds. He speaks with a rich, deep, and luxuriously slow North Carolina drawl.

Doug: I live just outside of Raleigh. The Raleigh-Durham area has got over a million people in it now. Very urban, high-tech type area. To the east, toward the coast, there is nothing but tobacco farms and hog farms. It's very agricultural. But about an hour from where I live is Fayetteville [North Carolina], where Fort Bragg and Pope Air Force Base are. About two and a half hours from here is Jacksonsville, where Camp Lejeune is, and Camp Geiger. There's also a small town called Havelock, where [Marine Corps Air Station] Cherry Point is. The Marines go to all the beaches up and down the coast. And particularly, back during the seventies, when I was most active, it was Atlantic Beach. And then you've got of course the Norfolk, Newport News [Virginia] area, about a three, three-and-a-half-hour drive.

I'm an extremely large guy. When I was fourteen years old I was about six foot four, probably weighed about 210. Very muscular. Looked a great deal older than I was. I had had gay experiences with cousins and friends and things like that, experimenting. My first real experience with a Marine happened when I ran away from home. One weekend I was supposed to be camping with a friend and I said to hell with it, and took off and thumbed to Atlantic Beach. Well, I was thumbing through Havelock and this guy pulls up in his Mustang convertible and gives me a ride on out to the beach. His name was Ross. Thirty-year-old gunnery sergeant. We went and spent the day on the beach. He invited me to spend the night with him back in his apartment in Havelock, and said he would bring me back to the beach the next day. I told him I was twenty years old, so he had no idea how young I was. I said, "Well, I'll sleep on the couch." He said, "No, no, you'll sleep with me."

We go into a one-bedroom apartment with a regular-sized bed. He was probably about six foot tall and weighed about maybe 175. Not an ounce of fat on him, just an unbelievable body. [Laughs.] We get in the bedroom and he says, "Well, I sleep nude!"

I was so scared. Well, I was scared about what I wanted to do so bad. But he initiated it, and it was the first time I ever had anal sex. We had sex several times that weekend, all kinds. He gave me a ride all the way back to home late Sunday afternoon. He actually was the one who talked me into going back home.

This relationship lasted about two years. I would thumb down there, and we wrote back and forth. When I turned sixteen I went down to spend my birthday with him. We went out, and I said, "I just want you to know, I can legally drive your Mustang now." That's when he found out how old I was. We had had sex probably fifteen to twenty times over the two years, and he never realized that I was a fourteen- or fifteen-year-old kid. He broke it off right then. Never even saw or heard from him again. But it kind of whetted my taste for Marines. I kept going to the beach.

Atlantic Beach at this time was a typical Marine town. I would go down there any time I could during the summer. I always picked up a Marine. I never failed. At least one if not more. All kinds of combinations and everything, even mixed-sex orgies, heterosexual and homosexual, all of it going on at the same time with eight-ten guys and girls. It was just a wild time.

This was in my teenage years. I was still growing. I worked out with weights regular, so I got to be a very large man. I'm now six foot nine and weigh about 285. I got a scholarship to play football at the University of North Carolina. I played there five years. During this time I still was going down to the beach occasionally. But after I got out of school, my first job was working for an insurance company. I traveled all over the state. I would spend at least one week a month in either Jacksonville or Fayetteville. Occasionally, Elizabeth City, which is only thirty to forty-five minutes from the Norfolk area. I'd stay in motels, and any night I wanted to when I was in Jacksonville, I would just go out to a typical Marine bar with pool tables. I never had to really approach anybody. Because when I walked in I was instantly looked at as being a big macho guy. I was never associated with being gay whatsoever. And people would come up to me, talking to me. Particularly little small guys. [Laughs.] I never understood that. But they would come up and we'd get to talkin' and get to drinkin' together, and one thing would lead to another.

Zeeland: Was it discussed what you would do?

D: Not really. It would be, "God, we need to pick up some pussy tonight." "Yeah, I am so horny." What is amazing—I've kind of tried to keep track of it over the years—is that about fifty percent of the Marines would wiggle around so that you could screw 'em. I have often wondered if there is some form of homoeroticism in Marine training that makes them that way. It did not happen that way with soldiers from Fort Bragg, and it didn't happen with the Air Force people. That was mainly mutual jerk-offs, and very rarely they would give you a blow job, but mostly it was just give them a blow job and that was it.

Z: How have you reacted when these men wanted you to be a bottom?

D: Well, I've never turned down a good fuck. [Laughs.] I was either a top or a bottom. It just depended on the mood.

It has now been thirty-five years since my first experience with Ross. I know I have slept with at least a thousand Marines. No question about it. I've slept with maybe five or six hundred Eighty-Second Airborne [soldiers from Fort Bragg]. No more than twenty or thirty Air Force. And probably no more than that number of sailors. Now they have a gay bar in Jacksonville. At this time there was not any gay bars at all, but when you went to Norfolk, the Portsmouth area, there were gay bars close to the naval base. Hell, half to three-fourths of the people in there were sailors, and they were quite open with their homosexuality. But I really didn't get to Norfolk that much. I was basically around the Marine bases.

Now this was pre-AIDS. My God. Court Street—it's only about two and half, three blocks long in Jacksonville. Back during the seventies it was wall-to-wall bars, dirty bookstores with your quarter films in back, just one place after another, full of Oriental prostitutes. It was like the midway of a fair, going down that street. Hundreds of Marines. I never did this, but some of my gay friends would go into these bookstores and back into the viewing area and just sit there and suck dick all night long. I was never into that.

Z: Why didn't that appeal to you?

D: Meeting guys at the bars like I did, even though it may be anonymous sex, I could still . . . there's some relationship there. And I think that comes from Ross, the first one. 'Cause I really loved him. He was the first man I ever fell in love with.

Z: Where there other men over the years that you fell in love with?

D: Yes. There were two. My longest relationship was with a guy named Gary. I was working around Havelock in August. August in eastern North Carolina is unbearably hot and humid. It sucks the water right out of you. In the insurance business, you usually worked during the lunch hour, but you had a couple-three hours off in the afternoon, and then you saw people at night. So I had finished all my luncheon appointments and said, "Fuck it, I'm gonna swing in here and get me a beer." It was just a little bitty strip mall with maybe four or five stores in it, right beside Cherry Point. It was called The Pirate's Den. Got right to the door, and saw the sign "Military Only." Which at that time they had bars that civilians couldn't go in. I swung around and said, "Dammit!" and almost walked all over this guy right behind me. I hadn't seen him. He said, "What the hell's wrong?" I said, "I'm sorry, I just wanted a beer." "Goddamn, come on ahead and go on in." That was Gary. The bartender when he saw me, he said, "You gotta go." Gary said, "Naw, he's with me, let him stay, Joe." We proceeded to sit there and drink until they closed at midnight that night. He went back to the hotel with me and we had wonderful sex, or as good as we could as drunk as we were. This relationship went on, oh goodness, at least ten years. He would let me know when he was back either at Camp Lejeune or at Cherry Point. He left and went to Okinawa, stayed a year there. I forget where all he went. He was a lieutenant. Went on up to the rank of captain. He got married, too. His wife never knew that we were having a sexual relationship. I would go to their home and eat supper. She'd say, "You-all go on and get drunk and I'll see you in a day or two." She just thought we were drinkin' buddies, when the whole time we was back to my motel room, having sex. I often asked him why he got married. He said, well, he did love her, she was a nice woman. And she was. Very nice lady. I think it was more because he wanted a military career. He was definitely in the closet.

He had the prettiest chest of hair you've ever seen in your life. And a wonderful goody trail. He wasn't tall at all. He was probably about five foot six, five foot seven. Rather short guy. Again, no fat on him whatsoever. Very muscular, great ripple abs. And he had the nicest, roundest butt you've ever seen. He and I lifted weights a lot together. We were a kind of Mutt and Jeff pair. Back then I had twenty-one inch biceps. After I turned thirty I quit working out with weights so much. I still work out now. That's something else we would do, too; of course, messin' around with the guys, you'd go to the local gym. A macho game of who could lift the most, and things like that. Much as you see in the gay health clubs now. He was from Columbus, Ohio. And I really regretted that we lost contact with each other. Now, being open like I am, and out, I would love to have a long-term relationship with someone like that. But at that time, him being in the military, we just saw each other a couple-three times a month. It was great while we got together, but then he would be somewhere else. Whenever he got back here it was almost like a honeymoon.

Z: I'm thinking that of these large numbers of men you met, probably only a small percentage considered themselves gay.

D: With most of them, the next morning it was, "God, I was drunk last night." Or "I've never done that before." Well, let me tell you. I've been with guys that have never sucked a dick before, and I've been with guys that have. And you can't tell me you've never done that if you know what you're doin'. It's an art form. And even anal intercourse. When a guy wiggles around and reaches over and gets the K-Y jelly, he knows what he's doin'. But most of 'em were in denial. No question about it.

Another relationship lasted five years. We spent a week together every Fourth of July at Atlantic Beach. I'd always take that week vacation. It would be a big drinkin' thing, and we'd go out every night looking at women, and every night back in the motel room having sex. He never, ever said one word about being gay. And he picked me up, really. Like I said, I'm an extraordinarily large fellow. I walked into one of those hard-rock bars, biker-type bars, down at Atlantic Beach. I kept noticing him lookin' at me like a fish nibblin' the bait. Eventually he came over to me and asked me if I was a wrestler. I told him no, I had played football. Anyway, that's the way it started. But about the first of May he would write me or call me, "Are you gonna be at the beach Fourth of July?"

Z: What was his name?

D: Well, his name was Gary also! [Hearty laughter.] He was a good-lookin' guy. He was blond haired, blue eyed, very smooth muscular chest, and stomach chiseled just right. Just average as far as dick, but a good lover. We just had a ball. We did wild, crazy things. Not just the sex, but we just hung around together for a whole week every Fourth of July.

Z: What other stuff would you do with these guys?

D: We would go fishin'. We'd go just rompin' up and down on the beach, maybe play volleyball. Me bein' so tall, I was a pretty good volleyball player. Of course you'd go out to the restaurants and eat. And you always went to the nightclubs at night. "Look at that pussy." In other words, very masculine, all-guy type situations. At this time I was very closeted. Here's a jock football player, there's not an effeminate bone in me. A very masculine-type person. I admire drag queens in that they have an art form, but that turns me off completely. So we were like a bunch of the guys, good old boys, goin' out partyin', drinkin', lookin' at pussy, and then going back and sleepin' with each other. And I think that's one reason I went to the coast so much. I did not want the people around where I lived to know that I was gay. It was my way of being in the closet.

Z: Were you having sex with women at all?

D: Yes. I was dating heavily with a woman. I'll be honest with you. I wanted to be straight so bad. Went to a psychologist while I was in college, trying my damnedest to be straight, but it just was not right for me. I know that I'm gay. I firmly feel that I was born gay. I have made love to a woman and actually been fantasizing about a Marine. I can't tell you the last time I had heterosexual sex. It's got to be five or six years at least. It just doesn't turn me on. It's just not right for me.

Z: Did you ever have any trouble with these guys?
D: I had a couple scary situations. One, we just pulled off the road and parked and I gave the guy a blow job. And after he got his nut off, he pulled a knife out on me. He wanted me to give him money. Fortunately I always kept a pistol with me. I just made him get out. And we were out in the boondocks. Matter of fact, there's a national forest and we had pulled up a logging path in it. So he had to walk ten or fifteen miles back to town.

Another time, after the guy got the blow job, going back to where he was stayin' at, he started talkin', "You damn faggot. Fuckin' queers, we ought to kill all of you!" So I've had it happen. But with the Marines, not that much. The soldiers, Eighty-Second Airborne, are much colder. You feel more threatened with them. I've had great relationships with some of them, but it's just. . . . So many Marines, we could meet in a bar, shoot pool, whatever, and end up with either me spending the night with him, or him spending the night with me. We'd have sex, anal sex, whatever. And the next morning: "God, I was drunk." "Yeah, I was too, let's forget it." And you'd go on back out and go fishin' or play volleyball or whatever you're doing that day. And the next night: "Dammit, if it was that good, let's try it again." With soldiers or Air Force guys it's not like that. That's one reason I like my Marines. Like I said, it's more of a buddy-buddy male relationship, lookin' after each other. This is my friend, I'm gonna take care of him.

Z: Did you ever think about joining the military yourself?
D: Well, when I came along, it was right in the middle of the Vietnam war. When I got out of college, there was five to seven hundred guys gettin' killed every week. I had my degree for four weeks when I got my notice to report to the military induction center for a physical. I knew there was a height limit of six foot eight. I was six foot nine. I'll tell you, I've always said those induction center men were a bunch of perverts. There must have been five hundred guys going in there that day. The first thing you had to do, everybody stripped to their underwear. I was wearing briefs then. Next thing they did was see how tall you were and how much you weighed. I'm six foot nine. They cannot draft me. I could join, but they can't draft me. So they put me in this room, still in my underwear, would not let me get dressed. About six times that day they pulled me out and kept measuring

me. And all day long they were sending these people into the room—I remember there was some guy like five foot six that weighed 300 pounds. And the drug addicts, and the criminals. We were the rejects, in other words. But they would never let us get dressed! We had to sit there in our underwear all day long. I think they got a kick out of that. Finally, about five o'clock that afternoon they let me go.

If it had been a situation other than the Vietnam war, I would have joined the Marines. I would have loved to have been in the Marines. I would have loved the military organization; the skills it takes to be a Marine. But big as I am, I kind of figured I'd be hard for a Viet Cong to miss.

Z: Some men are turned on by uniforms. Do you have any special—

D: The dress blues. I never knew his real name; this happened in Washington, DC. The guy, he went to the motel room with me, and I was basically on my knees givin' him a blow job while he was there in full dress uniform. One of the most erotic encounters I've ever had. He gave me a blow job too. But I will always remember that, because he was sharp.

[When I met him he was dressed up for] dress parade, changing of colors, something like that. There's a name for it. . . . Anyway, everybody marches across the field in their dress blues. All the ribbons and flags and everything. Very patriotic looking, all that stuff. They got grandstands for family and friends to watch this thing from. Afterwards, I was walkin' out and he was walkin' beside me. I said, "You need a ride back to your barracks?" He said yeah. When he got in the car, I basically just put my hand on his knee. "Would you like to go back to my motel room with me?" That was it.

Z: You didn't know anybody in the ceremony? You just went to admire the Marines?

D: Right. Well, just to admire the Marines. I wasn't there cruising to pick up Marines; I was there to watch the ceremony. It was very moving, very patriotic. I just got lucky. Do you understand that? And it's not like I was going to the beach as a vulture looking for young Marines to have sex with. That's not what I did. I went to have fun with the guys, and invariably we would end up having sex.

Z: In going to these places over the years you must have encountered other civilian men who did fit the vulture type.

D: They were the ones that you normally saw in these bookstores just suckin' dick for hours. At that time Jacksonville was wide open and there must have been four or five quarter film stores. And yes, you would see people that would go in there and just blow one Marine right after the other. And you could be sittin' in a bar, and one of the guys would say, "I'm gonna go next door and get a blow job." Boom, he's gone. Fifteen minutes later he was back. "Yeah, it was all right." Everybody knew what he was doin'! Now when AIDS came along, that stopped. Plus they have done a major revitalization of downtown Jacksonville, so most of the bars and all have moved out on the boulevard. It's no ways near like it was. They've tried to make Jacksonville a decent city.

Z: How have things changed in your thirty-five years of pursuing Marines?
D: AIDS came along and everybody got real scared. It became a lot more difficult to pick up someone. They weren't as ready to run and jump into bed with you. Towards the middle eighties, I don't know if it was because I was getting older—of course they're still eighteen, nineteen, twenty years old—or if it was that they were afraid, but there was a big difference in the [way the military men interacted with the female] prostitutes. I'd hear them say things like, "I'm not gonna go with her. I'm not gonna get AIDS."

As we've got into the nineties, my duties and responsibilities at work have been a whole lot more, so I can't get down to the coast like I need to or want to. But just last summer while I was down at Atlantic Beach in a bar I walked into the bathroom to whiz. This guy walked up beside me. I mean, there's four or five urinals there. He whips out, God, it had to have been a nine-inch uncut cock. Drunk as hell, from Alabama, cute as he could be, little bitty guy. He said, "You sure are big," and of course then he looks down at my cock. I said, "Well, you're big too!" He spent the night with me. I really think he was gay, but he was hiding it from everybody. So even at forty-nine years old, I can pick up a twenty-year-old. [Laughs.] It boosted my feelings. "You haven't lost your touch." But it's definitely nowhere near as wild and wide open as it was in the seventies. Of course in the seventies I was in my twenties.

A lot of guys think I'm an old Marine. Oh, I forgot to tell you. One fourth of July, Gary—the five-year one—down at Atlantic Beach he and three of his buddies and I were out drinkin' and raisin' hell. They were sellin' pitchers of beer for like two dollars that night. We were chuggin' one pitcher right after another. One of the guys that came over had just got a brand-new tattoo on his forearm. It said "USMC," with the flag and everything like that. We got to talkin' about tattoos. And the next thing I knew we had driven from Atlantic Beach to Jacksonville and we were at a tattoo shop across the street from Camp Geiger. We were all gettin' bull-dog tattoos. [Laughs.] They all got "USMC" under theirs. I said, "No, I'm not a Marine, I'm not gonna put that on. 'Cause it would be disrespect-ful." But I have got the most beautiful Marine bulldog tattoo on my right shoulder you've ever seen.

Z: What is it about a military guy, and a Marine in particular, that most excites you?

D: Their masculinity. No question about it. The military training gives them a way of thinking that is very masculine. Most of 'em are in excellent shape; they're not real heavy or out of shape. But the main thing is their behavior. Just the attitude of, "I'm gonna look after my buddy." That's it more than anything else.

It's not just sex.

Howard:
Sneaking on Base

Just before this book went to press, Sunday newspaper readers across Great Britain were shocked by the story of "A VULNERABLE CONVENT GIRL WHO SLEPT WITH MORE THAN 150 SOLDIERS IN A SAD QUEST FOR LOVE!"

> Her blind pursuit of sexual partners has left her with deep feelings of self-disgust and remorse. She thought free sex would give her what she craved. *But only now does she realise how she wasted precious years on men who cared only for themselves and not for her* [emphasis original]. She said, "I don't really blame the soldiers—they are the same the world over. But I really am horrified by what I have done with my life. I had every opportunity but threw them all away in this pathetic search for kicks."[1]

Oddly, some of the details included in the story do not seem entirely remorseful. For example, "Once they had their clothes off it didn't matter how many medals they'd won or how good they were on the assault course. If they had the necessary equipment then I was always guaranteed a good time." Or, "Soldiers think about sex day and night so once we got upstairs he ripped off my knickers and bra and we frantically made love on the living room floor. All those cold showers and five-mile runs gave him an extra-muscled body and I certainly wasn't disappointed. He was such a turn-on that I knew I would never go for a civilian again." And, best of all, "At first Louise invited her lovers back to her flat but then began to launch daring raids on army bases. She said, 'I knew that if I could get over the twelve-foot fence I could land a soldier. At about 1:00 a.m. I'd throw my fake fur coat over the coils of razor wire and get a friend to give me a leg up. Sometimes I'd made a prior arrangement to have a soldier waiting on the other side to catch me. Other times I'd just take a risk and drop to the ground in the darkness. Everyone would be in bed but I knew where the barracks were and I'd sneak into their dormitories and wake them up. The guys were always delighted to see me. I'd get them to dress up in their caps or put their khaki shirts on unbuttoned to the waist so I could bury my face in their chests.'"

The subject of this interview devised a somewhat less dramatic method for sneaking on base. Like Bill, Lance, and Don, Howard first developed a taste for sex with military men after he turned thirty. Initially, his reasons were pragmatic: young sailors seemed an easier mark than young gay civilians. But as time went on, he discovered that what he was searching for wasn't necessarily a trick, or even a husband.

Howard: The most fruitful period for me was right around 1988 through 1990, before Clinton was elected president, and before the issue of gays in the military became prominent in the news. I found that the sailors stationed at [Recruit Training Center San Diego]—the ones who had just gotten out of boot camp and were going through their first schools—felt the most repressed and frustrated, and were also the most adventurous, and anxious to have an option other than what they had to go through every day. That was sort of a golden period. I usually found it very easy to get on the base.

On Friday nights, the nights of the graduations, the main gate would change the color of the passes. They would use four or five colors. I started collecting them. I would pick a time in the evening, oftentimes on Friday when the family were arriving from out of town, and just look at the windshields and see which color they were displaying as they were entering the base. That was the main mode that I used. I also found that some sailors would be nice enough to get me onto the base. I did meet a few that began to trust me, and know that I wouldn't do anything totally foolish to get them in trouble.

There was very little of what I called traditional cruising going on. And I really don't feel like I was doing a whole lot of anything extremely devious or seductive when I was there. Basically things just kind of fell into place. The first really notable experience that I had there was a fellow who I just made eye contact with at the McDonald's on the base. I didn't think my stare was that intense, but obviously he picked up on it. He sort of followed me out the door. And then we talked for a while. He had to meet somebody for chow or whatever, and I just said, "Well, stop by the [enlisted] club later and I'll buy you a drink." And sure enough, he was there.

They had the enlisted club divided into rock and roll, rap, and country-western. I started doing really well at the country-western club. It really didn't take much. The guys didn't seem that perceptive when they were looking at me. It should have been obvious that I was not in the military and was not their age. But some of the things that you think are obvious, they just don't consider because you're on their territory. Usually there would be a series of questions, like, "What ship are you on?" or "How long have you been in the Navy?" or "Are you retired?" I tried to be as honest as possible. It usually didn't take long for them to get to the question, "Do you live around here?" I would say, "I only live five or ten minutes from base. You're welcome to come over and watch a movie, or have a couple of beers." To them, that was paradise. Basically it almost seemed like just knowing any civilian, period, would give you some kind of star quality. Because I was one of the only ones daring enough to find ways to go to their clubs. For the most part I found it almost effortless to do this. Usually I wouldn't miss more than one weekend a month.

I'm not the kind of person that would feel that if I had an enjoyable time with these people and made a friend, and there was no sexual contact, that the evening would be wasted. I think I am fairly unusual in that sense. Because I do know some other military chasers in San Diego who really feel that the evening would be totally wasted if they ended up having somebody over and nothing [sexual] happened. I don't feel that I am as dependent on sex as some people are, and I like some of the physical contact I made with these guys when they would let me massage them and still no sex resulted, because I just felt that it was not going in that direction. Either the conversation led me to believe that, or the way they were reacting, even though they were enjoying themselves. Some of them used to just seem to enjoy me admiring their bodies and flexing their muscles and doing stuff like that. They could tell that I was sort of in awe of how muscular and toned their bodies were. And if it looked like it might be sort of risky to pop a question to them, or feel that the eventual result of this would be sexual, I basically held back, and hoped that in the future I might run into this person again, and maybe they'd trust me a little bit more, or they'd be more ready for it. And there were some cases where the first time didn't work out, but they were willing to come over a second time and then something did happen. So there were some situations where my patience, and the fact that I didn't really feel that a sexual adventure was all I wanted from them, did pay off for me.

Zeeland: How did you get around to having sex? Did you verbally suggest it? Or was it something that happened without words?

H: I have a timid side. Usually I would ask them sort of backhandedly if they were "open-minded." Because I was almost afraid that for the majority of them, to classify themselves as gay was like to be branded, and there was nothing worse in the world to some of them than being a fag. But in a few cases, where I felt that their awareness level was a little bit higher, and I started noticing something about their tastes in music, or things about their background that had led me to believe that they were a little bit more worldly, then I would be a little bit more direct. But in more cases than not, I was doing very little seducing. A lot of them grew impatient and made the first move.

Z: What did you want to do sexually with these guys, and what did they want to do sexually?

H: I believe that the classic stereotypes usually hold true that sailors want to get a blow job and Marines want to get fucked. But I did find that sailors were a more diverse lot than I had thought. Some of them also wanted to do what their Marine counterparts wanted, and some of them wanted to be more experimental sexually. I really have found that the most risky sexual type of behavior is the one that I perform the least. I have never had anybody ever fuck me. And I've only been a top when somebody had a strong desire for it. If it was almost of a juvenile or first-time nature, where there was a lot of experimenting, and it never reached a high-pitched level of a major sexual conquest, that was okay by me. Some of the most enjoyable experiences I've ever had were some of the ones that didn't end up to be a major sexual encounter.

In many cases these guys had interests that would be similar to mine. I could engage in conversations with them that probably people in the gay community wouldn't feel as at ease about. At the time, I was a buyer for a large record store, and I was really up on music. Even some of the hard rock and heavy metal that was not my music of choice, I knew enough about it to carry on a conversation with these "dudes." A lot of times I would have posters of Iron Maiden or Def Leppard at my disposal, or maybe even an extra promotional cassette. This was another thing that was an aid to me, that although I was at a job where I was underpaid and wasn't really going anywhere careerwise, I had something that they really looked up to. But even something as simple as the fact that I happen to be a baseball fan. It was a big help if I knew a little bit about the teams from their area. These people were thinking about life back home. All I had to do was just say something like, "Oh, I knew a person from a town that was thirty miles from where you live," and that would be enough to get them excited. Even though I'd never been there myself.

Z: Did you have a preference between gay and straight sailors?

H: I'd say it was more just a different way of dealing with them. If they were gay, things would flow more naturally, and I could be myself, as opposed to putting on a display and then worrying about a guilt trip afterward, which did happen in quite a few instances. Basically I would adjust my approach depending on my instinct as to what this person was like, and how willing they were to feel comfortable in a situation with somebody like me that in reality, in most cases, they really did have very little in common with. I mean, in terms of everything from my age to my background to lack of military experience. I was just trying to get a feel of where their heads were at and how much experience they had with people that were gay, and if they did make a prejudiced remark, whether they were just doing it because of the amount of pressure they were under, or whether that's the way that they really felt. I felt that I was the one that had to be flexible. Because in most cases I was older, and more educated. I was late myself in having my first gay experience, so I didn't want to be too judgmental with somebody who came from a background that was repressed or had not been exposed to it, and who felt a lot of guilt, and in some cases might even quote the Bible.

I never told them, "You know, this isn't working out. I better take you back now." Because I felt that that would be a very insulting thing to do, and would really shatter any good feelings or trust. Plus which I might run into these people again when I went back.

I guess you could sort of call it a performance, or faking it. But I didn't feel like ethically I was doing anything that was of a real lowlife nature. I felt I was just testing the waters. Sometimes, if a question became uncomfortable, such as my experience with women, or being married, I would have to be a little bit evasive or deceptive. Because it's almost like a survival technique, just the way that they view you. A lot of them wanted you to be cool, and not too effeminate. And I certainly wouldn't ever do anything to them that would have them totally turn on me, thinking I was evil. However, just a simple sexual act, you never know what the result is going to be. And in several cases, they were guilty or uncomfortable the next time they saw me. And they did avoid me. But in other cases they just came up and said, "Hi, how's it going?" And then some of course I never saw again.

Z: Did any of them ever turn on you?

H: Yeah. I did have a very scary experience which slowed me down considerably. It was at a point where I was feeling fairly invincible in that I had never had anybody do anything worse in my presence than maybe drink too much and puke, or start talking in a violent nature. But never verbally threatening me. But after all those years of thinking that I was wise enough not to let that ever happen to me, I did end up in the emergency room.

This happened almost five years ago. It was an evening where everything seemed to be going in the direction of a sexual experience. I mean, I had the foldout bed there, I was giving him a massage, he seemed to be getting aroused. And then what I thought was a natural thing to do—I assumed he wanted a blow job—all of a sudden he started choking me. Everything happened so fast that I realized that he probably hit me in the face, but I was trying so hard to make noise, and prevent him from going any further, that I don't actually ever remember him striking me. I don't know if I was just a little bit overanxious that night, and perhaps the fact that he was a lot shorter than me, although certainly more muscular, but I felt no threat. Also, I met him right at the Naval hospital and he was a corpsman.[2]

I was fearful of pressing charges. I reported it to the person that handled the hate crimes here for the police department, but I really had a hard time in my own mind even classifying it as a hate crime. It happened in my apartment. And, you know, when the cops came, and they were taking me into the ambulance, the sailor actually—some of the neighbors were looking over to hear what the commotion was all about. He actually pointed at me and yelled, "He raped me!" That was pretty shocking to me. I felt like I was doing what I had always done, for years and years and years. It was a very scary moment. In my entire life I had never been attacked or mugged. It was such a shattering experience to me.

I never saw this person again, but for a while I thought he would somehow track me down. It took me a long time to have somebody over after that. I was slowing down to a certain extent anyway, and realizing that it was no longer as easy as it had been in the past for a variety of reasons. But over a year went by until I invited another sailor into my house, who seemed like he was very nonthreatening and was in uniform.

Z: How did your attraction to Navy guys originate?
H: In the late seventies, most of the sailors that I saw in San Diego were very dumpy and unattractive. I worked in the Ocean Beach area, where a lot of them would be heading to the beach. I would observe them, and compare them to some of the collegiate types and surfers, and I just never found sailors back then to be as attractive. And then suddenly there was this dramatic turnaround. I know it couldn't just be me. There was a tremendous turnaround in the caliber of guys that were joining the various branches of the service, at least in this town. I think that something happened in the eighties that was probably given a boost by the movie *Top Gun*, and some of the advertising campaigns that the military had. But for whatever reason, some of

the cream of the crop started showing up in San Diego. Some of the best-looking hunks I'd ever seen were joining the Navy.

I started noticing the military guys wandering around what would later become the historical Gaslamp Quarter downtown, but in the early eighties was a place that had a much seedier reputation. And I was astounded by how many of them were attractive, and how many of them were adventurous, and how effortless it became to find one that was basically looking to meet somebody, and be shown around. And then it became heightened later on, when I started finding ways to get closer to the bases where they were stationed, and eventually get on the bases themselves.

Z: What was your type before then?

H: Still fairly young, lean, attractive, all-American types. Most of the guys I liked had a certain wholesomeness about them. Very few of them would have a tough, aggressive nature to them; they wouldn't really have a swagger, or rebellious mannerisms. Then when I started meeting military, I was still finding a lot of the wholesomeness, but I was also finding some of the ones that were a little bit more macho. My taste started diversifying, and I started becoming more accepting of guys who didn't fit this goody-two-shoes American ideal like the guys that I used to be attracted to in college, and the guys that were from solid middle-class families. These military guys who came from all parts of the country were exposing me to another part of Americana that I had never really had much contact with, because the only two places that I had ever lived were New York City, until I was thirteen, and then San Diego ever since then.

I come from a working-class Jewish family. A very loving, caring family. I'm a first-generation American. My parents weren't educated. I was part of the baby boom generation, but I had to work my way through college, and wasn't able to go away to school.

I found it fascinating that so many of the all-American military guys that I was meeting came from the Midwestern states and the Bible belt. I started finding Southerners more charming, whereas in the past, I was always led to believe that they were bigoted rednecks. It made me come to terms with some of my own prejudices [toward] some of the people who I felt were of a lower class, almost "white trash." But I also learned how commonplace physical and sexual abuse is. These guys started confiding in me. Things like being molested as kids, or having really bad parents that are uncaring. And you just really feel—you feel a lot of compassion for people that didn't have a family like mine. And I started, you know, finding out how sweet some of these kids were, even with the backgrounds not typifying what I thought of as the American ideal. But there were certain things that once they got to know me, some of them would tell me about, that they would not feel comfortable telling guys their own age, and their own standing in the military. It made me think that I had a lot to learn about this country.

Z: Did it start at some point to become a near-exclusive preference, or were you also meeting civilians and looking at civilians?

H: I'd say that, for a while there, it reached a very near exclusive point. Only because I was so amazed at how easy it was to meet them close to and on their own territory, that I thought to myself: to meet the same quality person in terms of attractiveness in the civilian world, with all the competition in the gay environment, would be a waste of my time, when I could venture out off the beaten track, and find something that's close to my ideal, and in some cases was my ideal. So why would I even bother? Oftentimes I would only go to the gay bars for a change of pace, or because one or two continuous gay friends in the community would ask me to join them. But usually during the time that I was scoring at the military clubs, when I went to a gay bar, I went there with the mind-set that although I might have a good time, the chances of me being picked up, or me picking up somebody, were going to be minimal. Whereas when I went to the military base I felt like I had a much better chance of having that evening turn out to be quite memorable.

H: I went to NTC [Naval Training Center San Diego] fairly regularly for a period of about four years, including when they were already doing some downsizing and some of the schools were closing there. And from those visits to the NTC base, I probably had about thirty-five or forty different guys come over to my apartment, and only about half, or even less, turned into a sexual experience. So possibly only about fifteen from NTC. During that same time I would occasionally find my way over to 32nd Street, and try and get onto the base there. I had two or three successful encounters at 32nd Street.

A few of the sailors called me back. And a few of them, if I ran into them and they had nothing else going on, they would ask me what I was doing. Obviously the ones that are the most gratifying were the ones that did get comfortable enough to call. For the majority that usually wasn't the case, but there were some repeat visitors. Then there were some where I just felt a special charge, because they just got so close to me. And I had to do my best to hold back. But I loved just the intimacy and the camaraderie, and the fact that they would treat me as one of their counterparts, and call me "dude" and whatever, just like I was another one of the guys. To me that had its own set of fantasy-related images.

Z: You had that sense of being buddies with them?

H: Yes, I did. Oftentimes we would do something like go to a movie, or go out to dinner. And there were a couple cases where guys became close friends with me, and they felt very comfortable in my company. I never used the "G" word, but they basically knew that I was interested in them. One would hug me in front of his girlfriend, and do things like—One time I invited him to a party that a friend of mine had, and although it was in Hillcrest, it was predominately a straight party. And he was so thankful that I took him away from his horrible life on the ship, which he basically loathed, that after a few beers, right there in the middle of the street, he hugged me over and over and over again, while cars were driving by and honking. And these people didn't even know that there was nothing sexual going on between us.

There was another case, one of the earliest friends that I had—basically, I felt he was gay but didn't yet know it. However one time I do remember him bringing his backpack into my bedroom, and actually changing his clothes in front of me. He was wearing this very skimpy underwear with just about everything showing, and he didn't feel at all uneasy about the fact that I was looking right at him the whole time he was changing. And he did sometimes get very close to me. He was sort of shy, and sometimes he would get overly thankful that he was my friend, but I just felt like he just wasn't ready.

And there were some guys that were definitely having problems adjusting to military life, and I was their only civilian contact. In some cases there was a sexual encounter, and in some there wasn't, but they basically needed somebody to talk to, that they could tell things to of a very personal nature, that the guys in their company or on their ship could not be told about. They just needed somebody a little older to confide in.

Z: Was that burdensome to you, sometimes?

H: No, it was never burdensome to me. However, I was so used to being dependent and attached to some of them, that when some of them became too attached to me I did not know how to handle it. Because I knew about having family in San Diego; I knew about my job and my responsibilities. I needed a certain amount of time to myself. And I know that some feelings were hurt.

There was a guy who I had a brief relationship with, and maybe four or five sexual encounters, about a decade ago. I had known that he had left San Diego, but I didn't know where he went. Now, because I've lived in the same place for eleven or twelve years and my phone number hasn't changed, somebody wouldn't have a very hard time finding me. I got a phone call [on my answering machine] last year, and the person identified himself, and said something like, "You probably don't remember me, but I was in the Navy around 1986, and we were friends, and I just want to make sure you're the same Howard." He didn't say where he was calling from, who he was, or what phone number I could reach him at. I haven't heard from him since. It was gratifying to know that he was thinking about me. But he just wasn't willing to go to the next step and tell me where I could get ahold of him if I wanted to. So it was sort of a flashback to those times of just how unpredictable and bizarre some of these guys were.

There were some ongoing soap operas that occurred, such as one sailor who had moved up to San Francisco, moved into a gay area of town with his girlfriend, invited me up a couple of times, and did have an interest in me, but, because of his background, and guilt, and certain feelings that he had about his masculinity, could never reconcile it, and just blew up into a rage about an incident where his—this woman that he was living with—I really wouldn't necessarily even classify her as a girlfriend—walked in while we were intimate.

Z: Intimate how?

H: Actually we were just sort of—We weren't in a sexual act. He was massaging me, and I was massaging him. And we were almost looking like two guys that were sort of wrestling on the ground, and she happened to walk in. He totally blamed the entire incident on me, and was not willing to concede some of the feelings that he had for me. It strained our friendship. I still do call him about once a year, just to let him know that I still think about him, but obviously we don't see eye to eye. Even now that he's over thirty, and he's been divorced from the military for going on ten years, he has not come to terms with his feelings for other men.

H: Once I had a masculine guy come over that I met at the country bar at NTC. He asked if I had any women's clothes. He wanted to wear women's clothes during the sexual act. And he also went into the bathroom and asked if he could borrow a razor to shave off some hair from his chest and close to his butt. I told him that I usually didn't keep women's clothes around, but we did the best we could under the circumstances. That was his fantasy. He wanted to be the woman for the night.

Z: So you were you able to improvise.

H: Well, I think I did find something, somewhere in the closet that looked like it possibly could come close to looking like a blouse or something. I don't really see how I could have improvised when it came to underwear.

Z: But I mean, you were prepared to negotiate. You didn't throw him out the door.

H: Oh, no. Because of his good looks and masculinity I found it kind of charming. But then when I ran into him about a month later he really gave me a guilt-trip dirty look. I found a way to confront him, and not let him get away from me, and just explained to him that whatever happened,

happened, and you have to realize that you may hate yourself for letting your true feelings and desires show, but I didn't do anything to you personally that should lead you to give me a nasty vicious look. I was nice and hospitable, but he couldn't deal with the fact that he was having some very perverse feelings.

Z: Speaking of clothing, do you have a special attraction to uniforms at all?

H: No, actually I don't. What I do sometimes find attractive is when they wear the sweat pants and the jogging shorts with the Navy and Marine insignias on them. I like those quite a bit.

H: There have only been a few encounters worth mentioning that have happened since 1990. For the most part it's dwindled down now to where, although I don't think of the situation as hopeless, unless I find some new options I'm not expecting to ever see a period like I had when I was going to NTC. However, whenever I hear about something new happening, like for example [Naval Air Station] Miramar becoming a Marine base, and having a whole new group of guys there, I start thinking that well, who knows, maybe I'll find some way to go into another area surrounding another base and find something that I'll be shocked that I didn't know about sooner. Maybe I should force myself to stay out a little bit later, and try going to Tijuana, or someplace like that. But I'm no longer willing to make the pursuit an end in itself, and turn it into an all-nighter until I find what I'm looking for, like, you know, some other people that I know. I do feel, though, that if I was about ten years younger, it would be a little bit easier for me.

Recently I broke a long dry spell. A couple of months ago, I went to Flicks. I ran into a guy who had just gotten out of the Marine Corps. He and two straight Marines were traveling cross country, and they knew all about each other, and they were all experiencing America, I guess. He just was going out for the night, and I happened to strike up a conversation with him. We went home, he spent the night. That was one of the only experiences that I've had recently. And it happened in a gay bar. So it is possible.

Z: How old was this guy?

H: About twenty-three.

Z: What attracted him to you?

H: Just the fact that I was probably the first person to go up and in a friendly way ask him how he was doing, and he was new in town, and it was just a classic case of being at the right place at the right time. I'm realistic enough to know that not that many young sailors and Marines are attracted to somebody twice their age.

Z: Have any of these guys asked you for money?

H: No. However, there were a couple that I loaned money to—small amounts—that I should have known better, because what they were calling a loan was more of a gift. But I don't ever remember willingly thinking of any of my sexual encounters with military guys as picking up hustlers. There were some cases where I would take them out to dinner. Or if there was alcohol to be consumed, and they didn't have much money on them, certainly I would make sure that I would have a few beers in the refrigerator. But generally I would never let myself fall into that trap. I actually have fallen into that trap more with civilians.

Z: Earlier you referred to your competitors . . .

H: Although I don't consider myself a competitive person in other aspects of life, I do see these other military chasers as competition, to be quite frank with you. And although I've come to understandings with some of them, in almost every case in the past when I was more active, I found that if an opportunity presented itself, their needs were such that they would jump right in there and do whatever they could to try and take a person away from you who you were just starting to get to know. I felt that they should respect my own peculiar way of going about things, and if I was taking a long time to get to know somebody, that they should stand back and not get in the way. On the other hand there were probably some times when I was guilty of the same thing. I couldn't consider myself completely innocent during my heyday, either.

Z: One guy tried to get you thrown off of NTC?

H: Well, basically, the person would always be laughing behind my back when he saw me, because I was an intruder into this little private world he had. I'm assuming the person we're talking about was in the Navy at one time, although I heard he got kicked out. And he was always giving me dirty looks, and threatening to get me kicked off the base. But I realized that just about all the people involved at the places he hung out knew what he was up to, and I really started feeling more and more comfortable there, that I had very little to worry about.

I did have a couple of uncomfortable experiences, where a few sailors asked me some very pointed questions, and I did have one of these security guys actually think that I was in the NIS. When you look out of place, and you don't blend into the scene, then you have to be aware that some people are going to think that you have shady or devious intentions. But for the most part, out of the hundreds of times that I've frequented these places, I had very little problem.

Z: Did you ever think about joining the military?

H: No. At the time when I would have been most likely to join, the Vietnam War was going on, and I was happy to be going to college. Later on, when I started finding myself attracted to military, I was already approaching the age when I would soon be too old to join. So no, I really felt happy just being fortunate enough to have settled in a town that had the largest military population.[3] Incidentally, the main reason for my family coming here was that my older sister married a Navy lieutenant. He was stationed here. I come from a very tight-knit family. And we followed my sister out here.

Z: Did you ever feel any sexual attraction to your brother-in-law?

H: No. But I did look up to him. I had this desire to travel, and he was going all around the world. When I was a little kid he was sending me things from Australia and Japan. And when I was very young, I did believe that joining the Navy made you a man.

Z: In pursuing sailors, have you ever hoped to find a husband?

H: I think right now, unless I dramatically alter my lifestyle and become much more focused and organized and settled, it would be very difficult for me to enter into a long-term relationship. But I still hope for some adventures. I don't believe that one-nighters are something that I should be doing on a continuous basis anymore. Maybe I've lowered my expectations and standards, but I feel that if I had two or three really great experiences a year, I would be more than satisfied. And right now, I think that if I could have one sailor that would feel close to me, and think of me as a buddy, I would be really stoked.

Anonymous:
Why?

The writer of this lubricious e-mail spiritedly touches on most of the major themes that unite contributors to this book: the passion for an organic, embodied, archetypal, "authentic" masculinity; for immersion in *numbers* of servicemen; and for a "pure" homosocial camaraderie—but one that allows for sex between men.

Hey man don't know if you would have time to answer this but I would really appreciate it if you could. First of all, thanks. Until today I thought I was some kind of perv. You made me feel kinda similar to others and that was a relief.

I was getting my hair cut and there was a magazine I was reading while waiting. Was kinda weird but was better then the girlie fashion ones. It had an article in it about [gay "spree killer" Andrew Cunanan[1]], and I was skimming it cause the woman cutting my hair was coming around a lot. When I got to the part about all the guys who horse around with each other in San Diego I ended up throwing a rod right there. Good thing for those plastic cape things when they cut your hair! It all started making sense. So I was trying to write down your name (the author, if this is really you reading this, I hope it is) hoping I could find you on the net. When I got to the end there was a Web site. Far out! I got home and have been on this damn eye burning lap top for about three hours reading everything a couple times associated with your site. It's about 3 a.m. and I gotta get up in a couple hours. Shit.

From your San Diego stuff it made sense. First I thought, and still want to ask you how all those Navy guys can risk going to places like that. Won't they be seen? Then I remembered going down to Oceanside to visit my grandpa as a soph in college. I don't remember the details, tried to forget, but it was the first time I did it with a guy, well the second I guess but first guy except for my best friend. And it continued for a couple days.

I kinda remember meeting a couple jarheads in the big gym down there. I remember staying over night at some military dude's apartment and getting in major shit with my grandpa. I remember being told to come over after these two guys in the gym saw me showering, and I remember about three military (Navy I think) guys being brought into the bedroom I was in. I have no idea where they came from. One at a time over a couple hours. Those couple of days were crazy. I remember the guys in the room saying "this is the kid we told you about from Golds" and then they would just come in and hold up their legs. I freak thinking about it, but I remember it was so kinda bad it was cool. It grossed me out, but the fact these brick shit houses were spreading for me was I think the turn on. I also met a guy on the [nude] beach called Blacks.

Fuck, now that I'm accessing that part of the brain, I remember him picking me up after we were grabbing each other in the water. He was a monster. I also remember doing him in the rear on the beach in front of a chick and two other military guys. He loved it having those people watch. I think I was numb or still freaking out. It was without a rubber and to this day I'm still totally freaked about the whole AIDS thing because of that.

Well stuff like that went on. And after reading your site it all made sense. I mean I started remembering the guys I met when I was [working near a submarine base]. I partied with them and hauled them up to [a remote area]. There we all went skinny dipping, but they crapped out for the rest of the hike. Actually they were pathetically out of shape for sub guys I thought. Shit and I remember my best friend in high school who went to Lackland AFB. First dick I ever grabbed even before mine. Even the Royal British Marine I hung out with here last month. Nothing happened but just liked hanging with him for a couple days. It was really kinda (don't laugh or think stuff) special.

Fuck the memories go on. Well this is the deal. I hope you didn't delete me already. I now live [overseas]. About a week ago, another Navy ship was in. The fleet seems to be here like once a month. The streets were taken over by thousands of jarheads. So why was I hard every time I walked down the main tourist stretch to my gym? Fuck. I thought I was a total mental case after that. I mean I got about halfway home and finally after seeing all these perfect guys with their idiot mentalities I had to run into a hotel lobby bathroom. I was in there about an hour totally fantasizing about magically renting a hotel room and luring them all up to make them do each other in front of me. I know, psycho me.

Well I read your Web [site] and I guess I'm not alone. My name is, well later on. Please keep this stuff between us dude okay. It didn't hit me till I read your story about the Marine guy who just liked being around guys. More comfortable and stuff. Fuckin' A. Thank you! But what the hell does it say about me? Scary stuff! I won't even tell you about my job now, you'll say it all makes too much sense.

I was starting to trip myself out. I mean I like chicks. I was engaged and with her for eleven years. Sex and everything. But she got tired of me wanting to be with my buds all the time hunting, climbing, etc. She called it "going out to leak testosterone." She said she couldn't compete with my "male bonding" all the time. What scared me is it didn't even phase me. Kinda dug it, the freedom. Fuck, if I had to do it over I would be on some ship or base right now. Just dig having other dudes around all the time. Is that bad?

Well sorry, didn't know I could even type this much, shit. Thanks for being a bud and reading . . . not trying to make you a shrink. Just really dug reading the stories about the guys and what they think too. I feel really, I dunno, just better. Will sneak your book here if they even sell it over this way. Does this mean I'm writing a celebrity? Do you even read this or some staff lady? Yikes!

If still reading, I'll lay the rest of the cards on the table. I hope this doesn't offend. Close your eyes staff lady! I worked [in a job that allowed access to an Army base]. I hit the [PX] food court thing and when I used the cans, it was like the one you described in your story. Only more so. If interested I could tell you about the muscle magazine type guys there. (I work out a lot too.) So things would happen in there. And I don't know why black Army guys make me harder than my chick. But it started to be a habit. I would come up with any excuse to get on base. From there the gyms, pools, saunas, bathrooms. Fuck I was like an addict. I never did more than beat off with them, cause they would usually split faster than me when we blew. But it was the best. I even found a dirty bookstore off base where all the guys go (in uniform even on lunch) and there are no doors to all the video booths. It's like it's totally cool to just whack it in front of other guys. Wow. It seems so cool. I know, I guess I am weird.

Well, my last request is this. I'm 28 now, very built (snuck a cycle of steroids into the country) and because of that I am having roid rages. (Will fuck my clothes hamper if it wasn't made of broken bamboo. Ouch!) And more ships will be in I think. How the hell do you hook up with a dude who has been at sea and you know is horny? Out of the thousand plus these aircraft carriers hold, there must be at least one. I got a girlfriend here now, but the sex is lousy. You can't exactly throw her around. (Too small.)

I don't know if you would even want to help me with something like that, but one side of me just digs hanging with my old friends as BUDS only. I really miss them. But honestly, since I don't know you, I'll admit I want to gang bang like the things you wrote about so bad too. Will never admit it to myself, but other dudes (straight, like me) really fuckin' send me. Like it's more fun since you're not supposed to. And it's just too weird that

the only dudes I've fooled around with are in the military. Wasn't intention-
al at first. Just coincidence I guess, but does your book explain why now
those are the only dudes I would ever mess with? God I'm fucked up!

Tried a gay bar once. For about ten minutes. Got thrown out. Someone
grabbed my ass and I hit him before I knew what I was doing. The bouncer
threw me out. Fuck he was totally cool looking and acting. Guys see me in
the shower and make comments about it a lot, but I'm too scared to do
anything at my gym. I guess I thought I was a freak until I read your stories.
I beat off about six times to your site. My dick is sore and my brain is
freaking. And I checked and no bars like that here. So any advice on where
they might go? Do you know any guys in the Navy? Is there a way to meet
this group that was kinda alluded to in all these writings of yours? I'm very
in shape, good looking, and VERY STRAIGHT, and always have lots of
friends from the gym, teams at school etc. Fuck, please don't repeat any of
this. Please.

Well I better go. Will use beer as an excuse for spending so much time
with someone I don't even know. But feel like I'm actually talking to
someone about this for the first time. Thanks for listening if you did.

Tom:
The Brotherhood of Marines

Hi my name is [deleted]. I had viewed your website and am e-mailing you to request assistance. I am twenty-five years old and am in the process of trying to enlist in the Marine Corps. I have identfied with the "community" for the past seven years but have chosen abstinence recently because I know that my prior affections are considered conduct unbecoming. I am trying to attain a bond with someone who may be able to hone me so as to make my behaviors and manners more convincing to the Corps. I am not concerned about giving off "vibes" as I come off as "normal" as the average man, merely I wish to convey to whomever I may appear in front of that I already have several of the traits required to fulfill my duties as a Marine. Any assistance you can offer I do greatly appreciate.

Semper Fi
[Name withheld]

I am a civilian. I have always wanted to mess with military dudes, but time and circumstance has prohibited it. It is now time. How can I go out to Camp Pendleton and hook up with hot dudes in San Diego area or other miliatry bases?? I need a bottom Marine with a bubble ass and long thick dick . . . But, mostly I need a masculine man to be my buddy and take me around to party and just practice intense male bonding, a cirlce jerk with other marines or military dudes would be the greatest . . . while we explore each others masculinity/bubble asses and the like. Send pictures, infor. to"

[Name withheld]

Sometimes I feel like a fraud. People write to me in the belief that I'm some sort of Super Military Chaser. They ask me where to cruise sailors on their next vacation. How to seduce a straight ex-

Marine at their workplace. A wheelchair-bound man implored me to send some military boys his way:

> Please don't give up on me like the others have done. Gay men are too quick to say no; too slow to say yes. I should know having the door slammed in my face too many times; being punished and dis-possessed myself. Please write me, Steve. Love is all we have in this too-intolerant world. Fear destroys. I await your reply.
>
> Semper Fi
[Name withheld]
>
> P.S. I'd appreciate those names and addresses!

One writer even suggested:

> In a sense you are a DI training hordes of proto-chasers and GI chasees in the techniques required to find each other. Hope you enjoy the role of building the bridges and social forms for a new path that could, in time, become as well-established as leather and drag. Your Web site could easily become a match-making and pick-up point. Do you want that role?

But so far I haven't received any mail from military men interested in meeting military fantasizers. I think about what Martin said about gay uniform fetishists: that servicemen tend to view them as unwanted fan clubs. And I think of what Andrei said: "People should meet each other on their own, it's better that way."

My ex-Marine ex has urged me to come clean: as military chasers go, I'm not that good. Yes, I've devoted most of my adult life to the pursuit of soldiers, sailors, Marines (and one airman who eventually confessed that he wanted to be reincarnated as Karen Carpenter). I've destroyed one GI's marriage. I've infiltrated four on-base jobs to be closer to military men. I've asked that my cremated remains be poured into the piss trough of a Marine Corps enlisted club. And I've written these books.

But the truly obsessed don't have time to write books. They're constantly on the move, prowling bases, video arcades, rest rooms, tattoo parlors, bars, bus stops, and the Internet. In San Diego there's this guy who lives in a van. Wherever military boys are, he can be found, at any hour of the day or night, sneaking into businesses that have barred him for years, risking arrest, beatings, and worse. I often wondered how he managed to make a living. Finally I found out. He sells cactuses on consignment. But when I asked him why he likes Marines his answer was fairly simple: "They're masculine. They're in shape. They're easy prey."

For a long time, when civilian men approached me with their military chaser stories, I brushed them off. Part of it is that I am suspicious of strangers. Sometimes, part of it was gay ageism. But part of it was fear: What uncomfortable truths might their stories reveal about me?

Like Bill, I find servicemen the most beautiful men in the world. Admiring them can be a noble thing. But I don't want to become—or help anyone else become—another Vulture Dick.

After the publication of my last book, I embarked on a secret mission. Leaving the plenitude of San Diego sailors and Marines far behind, I lit out for hypercivilian Seattle. I wanted to find out if—cut off from my familiar stimuli—I could eroticize civilian men.

I tried, I really did. After months of going without seeing short hair, pants that fit, and clean-shaven faces unpocked by metal, I managed to coax along something resembling a crush for a drummer in a post-grunge band who moonlighted at my corner pizzeria. But it was like trying to get sick off a flu vaccine.

Then, shopping at Tower Records one day I happened to glance at a young man who did not even look necessarily military, just some short boy in ball cap and jeans. Words cannot convey the vertiginous heart-pounding arousal that enveloped me as I tagged after him about the store and out into the parking lot—where he met up with three obvious Army buddies.

It appears that I'm a lifer.

But military trade is an endangered species.

The toughest question any interviewer has yet asked me is this: Don't I feel bad about making a public commodity out of private moments that men have enjoyed in secret? My answer is only in part a rationalization. By the time *Barrack Buddies* was published, the military sexual underground of Frankfurt, Germany had gone the way of the Berlin Wall. By the time *Sailors* came out, Navy initiation rituals that used to involve two days of cross-dressing, spanking, and simulated oral and anal sex had been reduced to twenty minutes of jumping jacks. Just last month the enlisted club I wrote about in *The Masculine*

Marine was torn down on personal order of the Commandant of the Marine Corps (he is said to have compared it to Sodom and Gomorrah). It seems that most of the things I write about are disappearing or already gone. Again and again in this book military chasers speak of "the good old days." Though a few contributors are still in their heyday, there can be no doubt that heightened anxieties accompanying increased awareness of military gays have contributed to a diminishing willingness of straight military men to play the roles traditionally ascribed to "trade."

Discharges are up, and fluidity is down.

At the same time, "Don't Ask, Don't Tell" *has* probably led to at least a slight increase in the number of military men willing to self-identify as gay, particularly in noncombat job specialties. These days, even Mr. Cactus-on-Consignment has been poking his nose into gay bars—and confesses to sometimes being reduced to sex with civilians, whom he likens to tofu burgers.

The following interview could just as well have fit into *The Masculine Marine*, but it makes a poignant and highly appropriate close to this volume. Tom is a tall, muscular, red-headed, twenty-six-year-old. As an infantry Marine, he found the intense buddy love that most of my other gay Marine interviewees reported eluded them. After six years of service, he left the Marine Corps because he felt "sexually frustrated." But now that he is free to have all the gay sex he wants, Tom haunts the America Online USMCM4M chat room, hoping to connect with the love between men he knew back when he was "repressed."

Tom: Growing up in Alabama I was total white trash. Both of my parents worked in a factory. We were flat-out poor. Growing up in that area, you're either going to go into the military, or you're going to work in the factory. It's just a really, really desolate area. My senior class had twelve people.

I never knew any gay people. There was one guy in Alabama I had sex with, but he was married with kids.

When I was stationed in Quantico, Virginia, I was nineteen and I was just like, "I got to find gay people."

I used to go to this punk rock club in DC. They had copies of the local gay paper there, the *Washington Blade*. I picked up one, then I picked up a few more. And I answered a personal ad. This guy lived in North Carolina. He was like forty-one, or forty-two. And he was looking for military guys to have as pen pals. So I started writing to him, and he came up with the idea:

"We're gonna run a personal ad for you in every major gay paper we can think of. 'Active-duty Marine, nineteen, seeks active-duty Marine.' " To me this just sounded like a very bad idea, because I couldn't figure out how I could do it without getting busted. But he came up with the idea that all the responses would be routed through his home address in North Carolina. He would take the letters, put them in manila envelopes, and send them to me.

This ad ran all over the country, even in *The Advocate*. And I was getting —oh my God. I got thousands of responses. I had all these doctors and lawyers sending me pictures of their homes and their Mercedes. I just freaked out because I didn't realize—I knew there was a segment of the gay population into military, but I didn't realize how seriously some people took it. They had never even seen what I look like, yet they were just, "Come live with me right now!" Every day I was getting these huge manila envelopes just packed full of responses from everybody imaginable.

In more cases than not, they would [include] pictures of their dick or something. That was awkward, especially when I was on ship. To this day, [Tom's civilian "sidekick"] still doesn't understand that. He still sends gay porn, gay magazines, and gay pictures [to military guys]. I've tried to tell him. He's like, "Well, they can just hide it." I said, "You can't hide anything on ship." And because you're going to places like Thailand, where drugs are really prevalent, you are constantly having every item in your possession searched, without warning. People will swoop down into your berthing area. They go through your wallet. They go through everything. That's just something that civilians don't take into consideration. In the military you don't have the same privacy that civilians have.

I remember one day on ship I got a package. People crowded around because my good buddy who started the ad—he had dated a Marine sergeant, so he knew to be careful. And he always sent like *Newsweek* and *Time*, stuff like that. So whenever I got a package people assumed it was from him, and they wanted to grab a magazine. This package came from someone else who decided to put gay porn in there. I kind of halfway opened it. I looked in there and I seen the cover. I was like, "Shit." I threw it in the rack. People were pawing for it. "Is that *Sports Illustrated*? Is that *Playboy*?" I was like, "No, no, no. It's personal letters." And they're like, "That's a magazine!" And I had another package to open which did have magazines in it. That was the only thing that distracted them from grabbing that.

Tom told me a story about another gay Marine who was not so lucky. The guy received a package when he was on deployment in Somalia. All the other Marines crowded around, saying, "Mom sent cookies; we want some!" With his buddies watching, the Marine unpacked a large dildo and a note that read "Since you aren't gettin' any . . ."

T: Getting thousands of letters from complete strangers really, really freaked me out. I didn't enclose a picture in my ad. I couldn't believe that they were sending all this stuff to me and they didn't even know what I looked like. I wouldn't respond, and they would keep writing, and keep writing, and keep writing. You'd think after awhile they would get the point. But they were like pit bulls, they weren't gonna let go. I got sent a watch that was really, really expensive. I don't remember how much I got when I pawned it, but it was a lot. This guy had never wrote before, had no idea what I looked like, and he sent me a gold watch. That totally blew me away. It was really flattering, but it was really dumb at the same time. There are some sad lonely people out there.

I only heard from a few other active-duty Marines. One of them turned out to be on Camp Pendleton. He was on the same camp I was, yet we were so scared to meet face to face. We were just writing letters back and forth until we gained each other's trust. Finally, we met. Every weekend I went out to the YMCA in Oceanside and played basketball. I told him to meet me on the basketball court. So he shows up there, and it was like the biggest day of my life. I had never known another gay person, or had a gay friend. And this one being a Marine and all—it was something I looked forward to forever.

He was a sergeant, an MP. Really good-looking. He had a friend with him; he was another active-duty Marine. He was married but he was gay. I was just like really, really excited, just thrilled to death. They're like, "You wanna go out tonight?" "Yeah." So I went back to the barracks and took a shower and we went down to Hillcrest.

Within thirty minutes of being around them I had never felt so dejected in my life. The one that was married was doing incredible amounts of crystal. And the MP—he got into the club and he just totally changed. He became this flaming arrogant queen who was too good for anybody. All they cared about was drugs and sex. That's all they talked about all night. I was just totally let down. I never went out with them again.

But after I came out to all my straight friends, I kind of got to play around with them a little bit. [Laughs.] I had told seven, total. One of them, Andy Warden, he's another big redheaded guy from the country. He was one of my really good buddies. He was a golden glove boxer in college, and I wanted to learn how to box. So every now and then we would go down to the gym and punch on the bag and whatever. Even after knowin' I was gay, it didn't change anything with him. He was still really, really close to me. Some of the other guys I told, we kind of grew apart. They were still friendly and all, but. Andy was one of the few guys where nothing changed. It didn't matter to him.

One night we were at the e-club drinkin'. And he started asking questions about being gay. As soon as we started talking, I could just see somethin' was gonna happen. Because he knew way too much. I mean, he was sayin', "So, you're probably attracted to really masculine guys." I'm like, "Yeah." And he named some of the other guys in the unit. "Yeah!" All the other guys I'd been lusting after for years, he knew. It was weird. So we were talking about that for awhile. Then he started asking me, "So what do you do in bed?" and stuff. It just became more and more blatant. He started really taking it to the gutter, asking me, "What does your come taste like?"

We were getting drunker and drunker. The e-club was closing so we had to leave. We were walking back to the barracks. He said, "Well, I'm too wired to go to sleep." I'm like, "Yeah, I am too." He wanted to go to my room to watch television. My roommate wasn't there.

I started getting nervous. I tried to change the subject to things other than sex. But after we talked about some other things, he just blurted out, "You know, I can't think of anything else but playing around with you." That's what he said. I looked at him like "What?" "That's all I can think about now, is what it would be like. I wanna do it."

I was laying in my bed. He was settin' in a chair about twenty feet from the bed. I'm like, "Are you sure?" "Yeah." Then there was like—We were both just really, really nervous and nobody knew what to do next. I was thinking, okay, is he gonna come over and get in the bed? Or am I supposed to go over there? After like twenty seconds we both started laughing. I finally said, "Okay, look. Here's what we do. I'll go get in the shower. You go to your room and you get in the shower. If you decide when you're done showering that you still want to do it, come back up to the room. I'll be in bed with the lights off. Just come get in the bed. If you don't want to do it, I'll see you in the morning and we'll pretend like this never even came up." He's like, "Okay, good idea." So he goes back to his room. I jump in the shower. [Laughs.] Two minutes pass and I hear the door opening. I thought, "God. I guess he wants to do it." I came out, turned off the light and jumped into bed.

It was the weirdest thing, because I know for a fact that he's predominately straight. But he must have wanted to try this for years because he just went at it. I mean, you'd think with a straight guy there would be certain things he wouldn't go for. But he covered all the bases. He was just really, really into it. We done our thing and then I got up and went into the shower, and he comes and climbs in with me. Thirty seconds later, we're going at it again. Get done with the shower, I got in my bed, and he laid in my roommate's bed. Two hours later he was back over in my bed again. I was like, "Jesus." We were both really inexperienced. But we made up for it in enthusiasm.

Zeeland: He kissed?

Tom: Yeah! That's what I mean. He was extremely passionate about the whole thing. I've been with gay guys who didn't do some of the things he did.

The next morning we got up and didn't talk about it. We went to the chow hall and ate breakfast. We were walking back, and he goes, "You know, I really enjoyed last night, but I don't want to do it anymore." Which shocked me. But he was saying that he didn't want that to become part of his life. He didn't want to be gay. He'd better walk away from it now and go back to women.

I was kind of crushed, because that night, after we were done, I was just on cloud nine. I thought, hey, I've got a boyfriend now. And he was so macho, so strong, and had a body from hell. We had a lot of common interests. I was elated until he told me that. So once again I was crushed.

The next guy I fooled around with was another straight guy. There was nothing really exciting about that. It was basically just a grope-and-feel kind of thing. He didn't really respond. It happened walking back from a bar in Hong Kong. We were walking down some alley by the ship. He kind of fell. Because he thought he was close to a wall and he tried to lean up against it. I put my arm around him. I was trying to kind of like hold him up. We were both standing there taking a piss. He was shaking it off, and I think he caught me looking at it. "What, you want to do it for me?" I kind of knew that as drunk as we were, if I just reached down there real quick and said, "Yeah," and touched his dick, he wouldn't think anything of it. I groped him a little bit. He groped me back. That was about it.

And there was one more guy, Matthews. The minute this guy stepped foot on base, I was just in love with him. He was this nineteen-year-old blond, blue-eyed guy from Georgia. The day he showed up, there was like twenty other young Marines being taken to their unit. I thought, "God, I hope he comes to Alpha company." And he did. And me and this other guy, we kind of adopted him because he was new to the unit. We took him under our wing, and kept him away from a lot of the bullshit that happens to new guys. And my excuse was, "He's from Georgia, and I'm from around that area." Because normally, the so-called salty guys who've been in for a while have their little cliques, and the younger guys have their cliques, and they don't really intermingle that much off duty. Anyway, we became really, really close. I'd known him for probably a little over a year when I told him.

He was actually the first person in my life that I ever told I was gay. This was during the height of the debate over gays in the military. And all anybody ever talked about on base was fag-bashing. Hearing that every day, coupled with not knowing any other gay Marines, and the only person I was communicating with that was gay was the guy who had placed the ads, and he was in North Carolina—I was just freaking out. I just had to get it off my chest.

One night we got off work. I said, "Do you want to go to the e-club tonight and drink?" And it was something we did all the time, so he said, "Yeah, I'll go." So we got to the e-club, and I had to get really drunk before I could get up the courage to tell him.

I was getting really, really sloshed, and the whole night Matthews was playing pool. He was looking at me. I could tell he was concerned. He could see that something was wrong with me. So he quit playing pool and he came over and sat down at the table. He started complaining about how he wasn't getting laid. And once he started talking, I said, "Matthews, I have something I gotta tell you. I'm gay." He looks at me and goes, "Well, I don't mind, but *I'm* not gonna do anything with you." He thought the reason I said that was because I wanted to play around with him. He had been talking about how horny he was. It was just bad timing. I was like, fuck. That wasn't the response I was looking for the first time I came out. I said, "No, no, that's not why I'm telling you."

We left the e-club and went back to the barracks. We were up on the second floor, leaning out over the railing, and I was just crying. In a way, it felt really, really good, but at the same time I was just freaked out because— he was reinforcing me that it wasn't going to change our friendship, but something was telling me that it was.

For a week or two after that we were really uncomfortable around each other. But it was more me than him. I guess I just didn't trust him enough. Him being from Georgia, he had never known any gay people either. Little things were different. Before, whenever we'd go to the e-club, he'd come up to my room and we'd change clothes right there. Now, whenever he was going to change from uniform to civilian clothes he went into the bathroom rather than do it in front of me. And I was just kind of let down by all that. But after a few months, everything went back to normal. We both got back on track. It was like it had never happened. I think in the long run it just made us closer, because he was like, "God, I can't believe that I'm the first person you told. It's flattering."

A couple years passed. I was getting ready to get out. Actually, a year or so after I told him I started noticing things. Whenever he would get drunk (which wasn't that often—he would drink with me, but normally he'd cut himself off and I'd keep going) he would say little things that should have let me know. He would ask me, did I ever find him attractive. And I would say no. Which was a total lie. I was still madly in love with him. But I was afraid if I told him I found him attractive it would scare him off. And then, a couple times—I remember one time we were in his room. I was telling him how frustrating it was to be around so many guys that I found to be so cute, and having to take showers and be on a ship with them. It was something I kidded about all the time. He was like, "Well, thank God you never tried to rip my shorts off." I was laughing, and he was like, "But then again, it might turn me on."

We were sitting in the room one night watching football. This was another time when I was drunk and he wasn't drinking at all. We were talking about the game and stuff, and all of a sudden he goes, "You know what I wanted to do about thirty minutes ago?" "No, what?" "I almost came over there and started blowing you." I about fainted. It just came out of the blue. I was like, "Okay. . . ." I didn't know whether to laugh, or what. I was totally freaked out. He was getting all fidgety and nervous, which told me right off the bat he wasn't kidding. He's like, "But I didn't know how you would react, so I didn't want to do it." I'm like, "Honestly, I don't know how to react." And he's like, "Yeah, I mean, I've been curious about trying it since the last year or so." I'm like, "Why? Is that from being around me?" He's like, "Yup. Just that and natural curiosity." I didn't know what to say. He started telling me there was a guy on ship that he had a crush on, and that it was really difficult for him.

Like an idiot, I didn't try anything. I could have. But I was so drunk and freaked out by the whole thing. This was the guy that I had feelings for forever, and he's like, right there in front of my face. But I just didn't know how to deal with the situation. Finally, he got too freaked out, and he's like, "I'm going to my room." The next day I wanted to talk about it some more, but he did not want to talk about it at all. Finally, he goes, "Look, if it ever happens, this is how it's going to happen. We're gonna come back from the club drunk one night, and if it happens it happens. But that's the only way." [Laughs.] Well, he wouldn't go to the club with me anymore after he told me that. So nothing ever happened.

T: What I learned was that the tougher the unit, the more homoerotic the units were. I guess because them being in infantry or recon, that was enough to reinforce their masculinity. So they could . . . do things and not question themselves, or have other people question them.

I started out at Quantico, Virginia. That place was really bland and boring. The whole two years I was there, nothing very homoerotic ever happened. When I went to an infantry unit on Camp Pendleton, I just couldn't believe some of the things the guys did there.

I went from Quantico to Horno. That was like the first time I had been around real infantry Marines. And it was just a big shock how everybody there—I mean, it's kind of weird, 'cause it was extremely homophobic, yet extremely homoerotic. And I think the reason it was so homophobic was because it was homoerotic. [Laughs.] You know what I mean?

Like the circle jerks. That just blew me away. Because in Quantico, people who had came there from fleet grunt units were always making jokes about that. We'd be out in the field, and they'd be saying, "Yeah, my fire team, out in the field we used to have circle jerks all the time." And we all laughed about it. The guys who had never been to the fleet, we'd go, "Oh, that's sick. You bunch of fags." But yeah, out in the fleet, that's like totally, totally common. Even back in Horno, people would crowd around the television in the barracks, four or five guys watchin' a straight porno. To start off with, you know, a couple of people would say, "God, this makes me want to jerk off." And finally somebody would say, "Aw, to hell with it," and they would start jerkin' off. But during the actual thing, there was no conversation. Afterwards, there'd be a few joking comments, but.

Nobody saw that as being the least bit homoerotic. And at the time, I didn't either. It wasn't that big a deal. It was so commonplace. In the squad bay, or in the barracks room, whatever the case, everybody had lots of space between them and their buddy. Each guy would have his own chair. They were just kind of scattered out. Most guys would have, you know, the poncho liner over their lap. A few guys didn't. But I think even if you did want to look over at the other guy's dick, you probably couldn't see it because all the lights were off except for the television.

On the ship it was a lot more blatant, because the physical space was confined, everybody was more . . . exposed, I guess. [Laughs.] That for me was a little bit more of a big deal. Because on the ship we would crowd in the corner—There would be a television in one corner, and there would be like six or seven guys in really close proximity, watching it. And they would start jerkin' off there. And that's kind of like a bigger thing, because you're just so squashed in together. But what me and my buddies did, we just laid in our racks, and you know the racks are like three or four high on a ship. Usually we'd close the curtain. We'd have our head leaning out the rack watching it and jerkin' off. Passin' the lube back and forth.

There was this one guy named Mark. He was another big, redheaded country guy. It's like there's clones of us. [Laughs.] He was bigger than me, six foot two, from upstate New York. Really big guy. Everybody called him my bigger brother. We were like really close friends. He was really open-minded, considering he comes from such a small town.

The last few days before we got on the ship, everybody was making jokes about who was going to be the "bitch" for the platoon and all that. And whenever stuff like this would come up, Mark, that was the guy's name, would always make comments like, "Honest to God, I would totally let a guy suck my dick. It wouldn't bother me at all." And a few other guys would actually agree with him. Everybody else just kind of laughed, or didn't pay any attention to it. But once we got on ship, I was kind of remembering those things they were saying. You know, we're laying there jerking off, and I couldn't help but think about it. So I just started looking over at him. And after a few weeks, he had to know. Everybody else's eyes were glued to the television. I was just watching him. And I know for a fact he was getting a thrill out of it, because after a while it got to the point where he would make sure he was at an angle to where I could see everything.

This happened at night. The next day, as we were working together, it was never talked about. We never even made a joke about that. And he was not the least bit uncomfortable around me. But as we we're gettin' off the ship, and everybody's like kind of saying goodbye—because at this point we didn't know whether we were going to be in the same platoon anymore or not—he came up to me and he hugged me and kissed me on the neck. And he said, "I'm gonna miss puttin' on my little show for you."

T: I know a lot of the lil' homoerotic stuff I encountered daily bores most gay dudes. If it doesn't involve sucking and fucking, most guys don't want to hear it. But to me, those little details tell the big story. They explain the strange balance of homoeroticism and homophobia in the military.

I told you the first two years I was in Quantico, Virginia, and that nothing significant happened there. Well, nothing major did, but I can remember a few little things.

This guy's last name was Breyer. I don't remember his first name, and I barely knew him, but we were in the same platoon. Morning formations—we'd all go up there at 6:45. We'd all be milling around waiting for everybody to show up and get organized. And several times during the morning formations I would hear him saying stuff like—Well, he had a buddy who got out. I never knew this guy, because he got out before I got there. But he used to say, "Since so-and-so left, nobody jerks off with me anymore." I guess his thing was that, in the morning, right after they ate breakfast, him and this guy would go back to the room and jerk off before they came to formation.

I don't know if that was necessarily gay or whatever, but it just seemed strange. A lot of times, Friday and Saturday nights, when we were all setting around drinking, he would bring it up. Whenever he'd bring it up, a lot of guys would get uncomfortable and leave. Because it was something that he just talked about entirely too much.

T: My best friend the last few years I was in was a guy named Austin. The whole time I was in, he didn't know I was gay. He knows now, and we're still really good friends. Well, me and him were really really super-close buddies. I remember when we came back off float and we first started living together, we were having a lot of classes and stuff. I got in the habit of—I don't know how I started doing this, but—we'd go into the classroom, and a lot of times we'd just sit on the floor. Pretty soon we had this routine of where he would sit down, cross his legs like Indian style, and I would lay on the floor in front of him, and I'd have my head in his lap. And people at first used to go, "Oh, look at the two fags." You know, little comments, not necessarily vicious, just kidding comments. But as time progressed I noticed that more and more of the other guys started doing the same thing. And then one of the lieutenants noticed it and he had us put a stop to it. We were having one of the classes, and there was like six or seven people laying around like that, and he's like, "I'm gettin' really tired of seeing this. Clinton didn't lift the ban. Quit layin' all over each other."

T: At Horno I was in first platoon. We had this really, really short guy, who was like five foot one. His last name was Jones. And then second platoon had this really short guy, who was like five foot three. His last name was Pinky. And I've always had a thing for little short guys. A total midget fetish. I call 'em pocket puppies. And it seemed like my Marine buddies had the same affection toward short guys, because these guys were like the pets of the platoon. Everybody loved 'em, everybody constantly petted 'em, and was real protective of 'em. They were just overly sweet to 'em. Like, havin' 'em set on their laps, and tellin' their buddies, "Isn't he cute?"

One thing that was kind of dehumanizing was that we would always make 'em wrestle each other. It was like, "Our short guy is tougher than your short guy." And we used to have them in the squad bay. They'd be wrestling around and stuff. And then one night, some guy—we were all drunk of course, and these two little guys are wrestling. They'd been going at it forever, and they were tired. We wouldn't let 'em stop. And some guy started yelling, "Jones!," because he had Pinky pinned, "Rip his shorts off! Rip his shorts off!" I was thinkin', "Yeah, yeah, yeah!" Because both these guys were like totally adorable. So they went at each other, tryin' to strip each other completely naked. One of 'em did end up naked before it was all over. He broke free and ran to the bathroom. But everybody got a big thrill out of it.

That was something I noticed the whole time I was in the Marine Corps. Little short guys were always—everybody loved 'em, everybody wanted to be around 'em. I don't know what it was. I understand why I felt that way, but I never figured out why everybody else did.

T: Whenever new guys came to my unit at Horno—I think it's in any infantry unit. There's always some kind of initiation ritual. It's actually like a month or two of mild hazing. Nothing really severe, but you get taunted and fucked with and tested. Everybody's just trying to see what kind of character you have.

Pulaski was infamous for fucking with young boots when they came to the unit. I mean, he was just ruthless. He came from Force Recon. He was like the big warrior of the platoon. He had a sadistic side to him, more so than the rest of us. Even some of the crueler guys, when it came to initiation rituals, they wanted to keep Pulaski out of it. They tried to plan it when he wasn't around because he had to take everything to an extreme.

We had these new guys come in. Me, Pulaski, and two other guys were sitting around in this guy's room watching basketball playoffs and drinking beer. Everybody was pretty close to drunk. And Frederickson, who had only been there four days, walked by the room. Pulaski called him in there. He wanted to get the new young guys drunk. Frederickson was this little guy, probably about five feet four. He looked out of place in the Marine uniform. He looked like a little kid. I knew he was gonna catch hell. Pulaski started trying to make him drink huge quantities of beer.

Forrest was another guy that was friends with me and Pulaski. He was in the room. And somehow or other, I can't remember how it all started, but everybody started playing games of—taking a mouthful of beer and spitting it across the room into somebody else's mouth. And everybody the whole time was totally messing with Frederickson. Just giving him hell. And at some point we ripped off his shirt. All he had on was his PT shorts. And Forrest wrestled him down and started licking his face. I don't know why he started doing that, but Frederickson started freaking out, and was like totally spazzin', screaming, "I'm not a queer! I'm not a queer! I'm not a queer!" [Laughs.] I don't know why it freaked him out like it did, but he literally panicked. And once he panicked we all honed in on that, we all jumped down there and started doing the same thing. Everybody was licking him all over and stuff. Finally he broke free.

Pulaski was known for having these huge testicles. It was totally unnatural. Anybody that would see him in the shower, they couldn't help but make comments. Any opportunity he had to take them out and show them off, especially when he was drunk, he would do it. So whenever he got drunk, somehow or other he would find a reason to pull out his testicles. Everybody would make comments about them or whatever. He got them out, and he was stretching the sac out, and another guy that was in the room, poured some beer into—Pulaski had made like a bowl. Pulaski was saying to Frederickson, "I'm gonna make you drink this beer out of my ball sac." Frederickson's like, "No, no! Fuck no!" "You're gonna do it!" And Forrest is like, "I'll do it." Before anybody could blink or even register what he said, he did it. [Laughs.] So Frederickson wasn't the guy who done; it was Forrest. And remember, Forrest is the guy that originally held Frederickson down and started the whole licking thing.

Nobody really freaked out. Everybody in the room was like, "Oh God, that's so gross!" But that was it. The next morning it was kind of like spread around the whole company what Forrest had done. And they actually didn't give him a hard time. It was almost like he was cooler in everybody's eyes for having done something that was over the top.

Forrest was married. I never thought of him as being gay.

T: Sometimes on the ship you see two guys layin' in a rack together side by side because they want to read the same magazine.

After you've been out there for a few months, and you've been devoid of any physical contact with your wife or girlfriend or whatever, I think Marines just get starved to be touched by almost anybody. I mean, everybody on ship, but especially the Marine infantry, and especially when they're in the berthing area, and there's no Navy guys or anything, it's just the guys that you trained with—the family and no outsiders—then they get really, really affectionate toward each other.

I know why gay guys—Well, I don't know why gay guys want [military guys]. But I know the difference is that if you're touchy-feely or affectionate with a gay guy, one of 'em probably wants it to lead to sex.

But after I came out to my friends, most of that went out the window. Except with me and Matthews. Matthews was the only one that I remained affectionate like that with. Like I could go into his room in the morning before he got up and plop down on his bed. But with the other six guys, I lost all physical affection between them.

T: The guys in your book *The Masculine Marine* that were saying there's a lack of camaraderie in the Marine Corps aren't in infantry or recon units. I think almost anybody in infantry or recon units has to notice that there's a really strong brotherhood there. Everybody has a buddy. I went through four or five buddies because I was in for so long, but at any point in your career in an infantry unit you have one best buddy that you do everything with. It's almost like there's couples. Everybody has that special buddy that is always there with them, at work and off work, and usually they arrange it so they're roommates. Some of them are a lot closer than others. [Laughs.]

Everybody used to always say that me and Austin were boyfriends. They didn't use that term, but that was what they meant. Because we went *everywhere* together. And I had other buddies that I was that close to, too. But people get sent to different units, so it's like, every year you get divorced and you marry somebody else.

I remember there was this couple Masters and Michaels. Masters was from San Francisco. He was really open-minded about gay people. He told me that. And any Marine that's from San Francisco, everybody's going to rag on them about that. Well, Masters and Michaels were inseparable, just like me and Austin. And on the ship, everybody would kid them and say, "We know you two are having sex." It was just an ongoing joke. Because they were a lot closer than even I was with my buddies. Even I found it strange how close they were 'cause they were really inseparable. Whether or not they were ever doing anything, I don't know.

But even these other guys, the more typical buddies, I would definitely say that they really love each other. In Quantico, which wasn't as tight as the infantry units, this one guy got killed in a car wreck. We had a little memorial service. Everybody was treating his buddy like he was a widow. Everybody was walking by him and hugging him. And he was crying. It was really sad, but it was really touching. I had only been in a year when that happened, and I just thought that was the most awesome thing on the planet. Because at that time I had wanted the Marine Corps to be just that tight-knit. And everything I've seen during my career reinforced that. The camaraderie is definitely there. In infantry units. I don't know about what we call "pogue" units, you know, secretary, clerks.

I enjoyed my buddy relationships more than any boyfriend I've ever had. I would take that love over any so-called love I've ever encountered in a gay relationship. And that's one reason why I personally think—and I get a lot of flak for this—that the "Don't Ask, Don't Tell" policy is the only workable solution. Because my theory is, if you allow openly gay people in infantry and recon units, it's going to wreak havoc. I say that because almost every gay man I've talked to about the Marine Corps—the only interest they have whatsoever in the Marine Corps is sex. And they don't appreciate the sacrifices that Marines incur.

Especially "Marine groupies," guys that chase Marines. They like to think of themselves as being one of the guys when they're around Marines. They think they know what Marines go through, and they feel their pain, and they think they're somehow connected to them. But they don't have—and I don't think any civilian has any idea of the physical or mental stress. The physical part of it is grueling. The humping, the running, and all that. Some of these gay guys—Gym culture is really big in the gay community. You see a lot of gay guys who have really impressive physiques. And they think because they have that—They were really fond of telling me that they could kick my ass during the daily grind that Marines go through out in the field and all just because they're buffed up and pretty. But I don't think they realize that the typical, scrawny 140-pound Marine, when it comes right down to it, is going to run them in the dirt. Because of the fieldwork. That's what I mean by the physical side of it. And the mental side is, they don't understand what it's like to—all of a sudden: boom!—you're gone for six months, away from the people that you love, your boyfriend, girlfriend, whatever. That's why it rubs me the wrong way whenever I'm at a bar with four or five Marines, and then some civilian guy is there, and he has this attitude that he's one of the guys.

The only thing gay people appreciate about the Marine Corps is the possibility of sex between Marines. And knowing the gay people I have met, I've just felt, with their mentality, if they were put in an infantry unit—I don't think it would work. There's a few gay people who can make it in an infantry unit, and do well at it. I know from being there that it's really, really tough. The only reason that I was able to survive in a Marine infantry unit for six years was because I grew up so repressed in Alabama. Because I was accustomed to shutting down my sexual feelings, I was able to do it. But I don't think that the average out gay man can.

But Tom did do his part to fight the gay ban.

T: Back when the national debate over gays in the military was raging on—oh God. There was so much homophobia going on then. It was insane. That's all you heard, twenty-four hours a day. And I remember, every company has like this little billboard of where people post current events or whatever. Oh, every morning there would be fresh homophobic propaganda in there. "Homosexuals are on the front line of corrupting American society." It was constantly plastered with that type stuff. Well, I was in People for the American Way and ACLU, so I used to get stuff like that and stick it up there at night and see how long it lasted. [Laughs.] And of course by 9:00 a.m. it was ripped up and in the trash.
Z: How did you happen to join those organizations?
T: Well, right as the "Don't Ask, Don't Tell" thing started up I just thought, if I get busted, I'm gonna want some representation.

I'm sure you've noticed the tattoo on my right arm, the big tattoo? It's a cover-up job, because underneath that I had an "ACLU" tattoo. That caused quite an uproar. Well, actually most of the Marines were too ignorant to even know what the ACLU was. They always asked, "Oh, is that the college you went to?"

As soon as I got out I had it covered up. It served its purpose.

Tom had one last story for me.

T: There was another guy on ship who I just had a major crush on, Robert White. He was beautiful. And he was a big, big homophobe. One day he was over in the area where me, Jason, Mark Shields—the guy I used to watch jerk off—Phillip Estevez and some other guy—he was over in the area we slept in. He was sayin' some viciously homophobic things. I kind of like started defendin' homos, and then Estevez said, "Well, I got a gay uncle." And then Shields said, "Well, I've got gay friends." And after we all kind of started talkin' with him, that was like all it took, was maybe ten minutes. And then later on he was one of the guys I told. He went from being a huge homophobe to—well, he was still kind of uncomfortable with it, but he accepted it. Before I told him, we used to give each other massages all the time. There was this guy on the ship who somewhere along the line had been involved in sports medicine. So he was kind of like the masseur or whatever on ship. He was proud of his ability to give massages. We'd all be sitting around watching television or whatever, and he'd come around and start massaging our shoulders. He just loved to do that. He started teaching me how to do it. [Laughs.] I'd tell him, "Well, do it to me and then I'm gonna do the same thing to you." And he would tell me as I was doing it, "Oh yeah, that's perfect. Keep doing that." [Laughs.] It was a huge thrill, because he was gorgeous and had a nice body. And then he started teachin' White, the homophobe guy. Me and White started workin' out together, and after we got done, we'd give each other massages. Shoulder massages, back massages. Whenever we'd work out on our legs we'd do leg massages. I mean, that was totally homoerotic. Because we'd come back from the gym down in the bottom of the ship. We'd take a shower, we'd go back to our rack with nothin' but our towel on. He would lay on the rack, I'd rub his back, his legs. I'd get in the rack and he'd do the same thing to me. Here he was givin' a guy a full body massage just wearin' nothin' but a towel, yet he was a huge homophobe.

After I told him that I was gay, this massage thing, it stopped altogether. He was still buddies with me. But he didn't want to touch me anymore.

"The problem with straight men," observes author Mark Simpson, "is that they're repressed. The problem with gay men is that they're not."

Reference Notes

Acknowledgments

1. Michael Lowenthal, Ed., *Flesh and the Word 4: Gay Erotic Confessionals* (New York: Plume, 1997), pp. xiii, xv.

Introduction: The Bitterest Envy

1. According to George Chauncey, Jr., "The term trade originally referred to the customer of a fairy prostitute, a meaning analogous to and derived from its usage in the slang of female prostitutes; by the 1910s, it referred to any 'straight' man who responded to a gay man's advances. . . . Trade was also increasingly used in the middle third of the century to refer to straight-identified men who worked as prostitutes serving gay-identified men, reversing the dynamic of economic exchange and desire implied by the original meaning. Thus the term trade sometimes referred specifically to 'straight' male prostitutes, but it also continued to be used to refer to 'straight' men who had sex with queers or fairies for pleasure rather than money. . . . So long as the men abided by the conventions of masculinity, they ran little risk of undermining their status as 'normal' men." *Gay New York: Gender, Urban Culture, and the Making of the Gay Male World 1890-1940* (New York: Basic Books, 1994), p. 70.

2. Chauncey, p. 22.

3. Gabriel Rotello, *Sexual Ecology* (New York: Dutton, 1997), p. 41; Michaelangelo Signorile, *Life Outside: The Signorile Report on Gay Men: Sex, Drugs, Muscles, and the Passages of Life* (New York: HarperCollins, 1997). As part of the inspiration for his book condemning "body fascism" and the "cult of masculinity" among contemporary gay men, Signorile confesses to unprotected sex with an "absolutely perfect" Navy petty officer, p. xxxi.

4. In his manifesto *Toward the New Degeneracy* (New York: Edgewise, 1997), Bruce Benderson confirms that trade is very much alive in the U.S. civilian underclass, too. "The street macho can be intensely homophobic and homosexual at the same time. The mixture of libido and flamboyant ego that spills out of the underclass male, as well as his familiarity with the skills of prostitution, make him available to both sexes in many instances." A hustler Benderson knew "was intensely attracted to women and had a wife but was probably capable of a whole pattern of relationships

with men on a deeply felt level. . . . If he'd been 'outed'—if he'd been forced to articulate all the libido he'd accumulated around the ritualistic episodes of cock-sucking
into something rational and community-minded—he probably would have lost his
complicated erotic relationships with the women and men in his life. There are sexual
impulses which are too fragmented to base an entire sociological identity upon. To
brand them simply as 'closeted' is intolerant and presumptuous"; p. 49.

    5. See Gilbert Herdt, *Guardians of the Flutes: Idioms of Masculinity* (New York:
McGraw-Hill, 1981).

    6. Quentin Crisp, *The Naked Civil Servant* (London: Fontana, 1977), p. 96.

    7. An ex-Marine of my acquaintance who works as a doorman at a gay billiards
club in San Diego told me about a couple who frequent the bar: a pre-op transsexual
and her twenty-two-year-old active duty Marine boyfriend. (All her boyfriends are
Marines, he reports.) Informed that the doorman was a former Marine, this boyfriend
snarled "Who, that fag?" To which his girlfriend replied, "Watch out who you're
calling a fag. You suck my dick every night." The doorman concluded: "I guess he's
not ready to come out yet." But how many "gay" men date transsexuals?

    8. Over the years I have encountered many outrageously effeminate military
chasers, but such men did not answer my call to contribute to this book.

    9. Interview with K., Washington, DC, January 19, 1998.

    10. Or is it, as my friend Bart once suggested to me, merely hypocritical?

    11. It goes without saying that real-life military specimens cannot always live
up to the exacting demands of the gay imaginary. After years of absorbing iconic
images of sailors through advertising, Tom of Finland drawings, and films such as
Kenneth Anger's *Fireworks*, Rainer Werner Fassbinder's *Querelle*, and even
South Pacific, military fantasizer Brad met up with a Navy man via a gay underwear fetish computer board. This flesh-and-blood embodiment of Brad's sailor
dreams turned out to be a portly and balding middle-aged man who "looked like
an accountant" and "gave me the worst blow job of my life." Personal correspondence, March 4, 1998.

    12. James Gardiner, *A Class Apart: The Private Pictures of Montague Glover*
(London: Serpent's Tail, 1992), p. 58.

    13. Allan Bérubé, *Coming Out Under Fire: The History of Gay Men and
Women in World War Two* (New York: Free Press, 1990), pp. 110-111. Interestingly,
during World War II as now, the "most available" (sailors) and the "least available" (Marines) are more widely desired—or at least more often discussed—than
men occupying the middle ground.

    14. Myth-propagating gay porn may even provide readymade excuses for some
modern-day sailors to "experiment," and for some Marines to avoid the appearance
of actively experimenting.

    15. As the newest and most corporate-civilian of the U.S. service branches, the
Air Force allows the least room for fantasy. Availability figures into the ranking, here,
too. Few chasers eroticize military men without being exposed to them, either in the
flesh or through sexually charged images in popular culture. To be sure, gays typically view flight suit-clad Air Force pilots as just as alluring as sailors or Marines. But
pilots are officers, and as such are less likely to be found broke and staggering the

streets of military towns. And Hollywood cast Tom Cruise as a *Top Gun* Navy pilot. (For an analysis of homoeroticism in *Top Gun*, see Mark Simpson, "Top Man: Tom Cruise and the Narcissistic Male Hero," in *Male Impersonators: Men Performing Masculinity* [New York: Routledge, 1994], pp. 229-252.) Despite the rich possibilities hinted at by the recruiting slogan "Aim High," I have yet to hear from one military chaser who favors airmen over men of the other three U.S. service branches. (Or other four service branches. But in peacetime, the United States Coast Guard is administered by the Department of Transportation.)

16. Crisp, *The Naked Civil Servant,* p. 96.

17. Gardiner notes: "Any military uniform gives the wearer an air of potent and virile masculinity, and consequently it has a strong homo-erotic appeal. Soldiers have taken advantage of this appeal for at least the past two hundred years, and have sold their bodies for sex in order to supplement their poor pay. Xavier Mayne (in *The Intersexes,* Florence, 1910) suggests that pay was so poor in earlier periods that prostitution became a necessity. . . . By the nineteenth century the tradition of the soldier prostitute had become widespread, and all [British] garrison towns and ports had pubs and well-known 'trolling' areas where soldiers and their prospective clients could meet. . . . Soldiers were sometimes involved in organised forms of prostitution. There was at least one known procuress operating from a confectioners shop near the barracks in Regent's Park, and soldiers were found to have been working along with Post Office messenger boys in the homosexual brothel in Cleveland Street which became notorious when exposed in 1889. When one of the defendants in this case, Jack Saul, himself an ex-soldier, published his (undoubtedly ghost-written) memoirs in 1881 under the title *The Sins of the Cities of the Plain, or the Recollections of a Mary-Ann* . . . he stated: 'This is the experience of all the men of my regiment, and I know it is the same in the First, The Blues, and every regiment of the Foot Guards.' The tradition of male prostitution in the Armed Forces, and particularly the London based Guards Regiments, lasted until relatively recently"; Gardiner, *A Class Apart,* pp. 50-52.

Adds J. R. Ackerley: "The Household Cavalry are a fine body of men, much admired for their magnificent physique and the splendour of their accoutrements, but it will hardly be claimed for them that they are—or at any rate were—refined in their tastes and habits. Conscription and improved rates of pay may have brought some alteration to the scene, but in my father's young days and on into my own, sex and beer and the constant problem of how to obtain these two luxuries in anything like satisfactory measure on almost invisible means . . . represented the main leisure preoccupation of many guardsmen and troopers. Nor is this surprising. Healthy and vigorous young men, often, like my father, the merest boys, suddenly transplanted from a comparatively humdrum provincial or country life into a London barrackroom, exercised and trained all day to the bursting point of physical fitness, and let loose in the evening, with little money and large appetites . . . in uniforms of the most conspicuous and sometimes provocative design—it is hardly surprising that their education in the seductions and pleasures of the world should take rapid strides." J. R. Ackerley, *My Father and Myself* (New York: Harcourt Brace Jovanovich, 1969), p. 23.

Ackerley also quotes from the essay "I Joined the Army," by Frank Griffin, included in *The Sins of the Cities of the Plain, or the Recollections of a Mary-Ann*: "When a young fellow joins, some one of us breaks him in and teaches him the trick; but there is very little need of that, for it seems to come naturally to almost every young man. . . . We then have no difficulty in passing him on to some gentleman, who always pays us liberally for getting a fresh young thing for him. Although of course we all do it for the money, we also do it because we really like it, and if gentlemen gave us no money, I think we should do it all the same"; p. 200.

According to the *Encyclopedia of Homosexuality*, "In the American navy (until pay was substantially raised with the end of the draft in the early 1970s) . . . male prostitution in port was quite common among enlisted sailors, sometimes for nominal sums as an excuse for a desired sexual contact. . . . Not infrequently, the poverty-stricken sailor would first earn some money offering himself for fellatio with a homosexual male, then take the money so earned and spend it on a female prostitute"; Stephen Donaldson, "Seafaring," in *The Encyclopedia of Homosexuality*, ed. Wayne Dynes (New York: Garland, 1990), p. 1174. See also Rolf Hardesty's essay "Hollywood Marines" in this book.

18. Jean Genet, *Querelle* (New York: Grove, 1974), p. 140. Note Sublieutenant Seblon's deification of "The Sailor." In the early 1950s, Samuel Steward (a.k.a. porn writer Phil Andros) dropped out of academia to open a tattoo shop that was "a natural magnet for the very young boot sailors stationed at nearby Great Lakes Naval Training Center." He once received an anonymous letter: "Dear Phil, I stood and watched you for a long time the other night. You had a lot of sailors in the shop. I think that you must have the most romantic occupation in the world. I have always liked sailors. You come closer to them than anybody. Does it not give you a feeling of domination over them to tattoo them? Do you not feel that the Sailor thereafter carried around with Him, to the end of His days, your mark upon Him? And does not the act of tattooing become the testing of Him? If He flinches, are you not His Master? Is He not the slave, bearing your mark? Or from another angle, does not the sailor thereafter carry with Him your own creation beneath His skin? Do you not symbolically go with Him to the far places? [. . .] Do you not with Him hear mermaids singing? Can you not know a little, then, of a way of life which is denied to most of us? Do you not (a small part of you in Him, in His skin) actually accompany the Sailor on His far wanderings? Are you not part of Him, flesh of His flesh? When, panting and naked, He braces Himself on His strong bronzed young thighs to guide Himself between her legs, do you not ride high on His shoulder in the design you applied there? Or are you not crushed between His brave and swelling pectorals and her flattened breast? Or ride the bucking-horse from the peak-point of His pelvic bone. You are with the Sailor forevermore. . . . And did He not receive you with His blood? Are you not—and your skill—coupled with Him in a mystic vow of comradeship?" Samuel M. Steward, *Bad Boys and Tough Tattoos: A Social History of the Tattoo with Gangs, Sailors, and Street-Corner Punks, 1950-1965* (Binghamton, NY: The Haworth Press, 1990), p. 42.

19. The reasons why gay civilians are attracted to military men are often not unrelated to the reasons why men actually join the military. More than a few military chasers are persons who have been prevented by circumstance from enlisting. (Others are themselves active-duty servicemen or veterans.)

20. Personal communication from a gay academic, December 25, 1996.

21. "Some danger-loving gays may 'actually get off on the risk of physical abuse from the Marines. If a gay hits on a straight Marine, the consequences can be very unpleasant, or very pleasant, depending on what you're into.'" Duncan Spencer, "Leatherboys and Leathernecks," *Capital Style*, March 1998, p. 45. This quote was falsely attributed to me.

22. Steven Zeeland, *The Masculine Marine: Homoeroticism in the U.S. Marine Corps* (Binghamton, NY: The Haworth Press, 1996), pp. 176-177.

23. In 1919 Newport, Rhode Island, "One man from the [USS] *Baltimore* became so drunk that 'cocksuckers . . . put him in the street and rolled him of all the money he had.'" Lawrence R. Murphy, *Perverts by Official Order: The Campaign Against Homosexuals by the United States Navy* (Binghamton, NY: The Haworth Press, 1988), p. 12.

24. Steven Zeeland, *Sailors and Sexual Identity: Crossing the Line Between "Straight" and "Gay" in the U.S. Navy* (Binghamton, NY: The Haworth Press, 1995), p. 73.

25. "Not well known is that the fact that a great deal of the motivation for those generally heterosexual sailors who become repeatedly involved with gay men as trade is not sexual or financial at all. The young common sailor, generally at the bottom of the shipboard hierarchy and often dismissed with contempt by civilians at large, finds himself treated like royalty, his male ego enhanced, his gripes given sympathetic attention. Instead of taking orders all the time, he finds himself in a position to give them. Instead of the usual sterile environment of cramped shipboard quarters, he gets to relax in a home environment where he can kick back, watch television, and have his every need attended to"; Donaldson, p. 1175.

26. Mark Simpson, personal correspondence, November 10, 1995.

27. Signorile, p. 298. See also Daniel Harris, *The Rise and Fall of Gay Culture* (New York: Hyperion, 1997). Harris reprimands "men who grovel before heterosexual society by referring to themselves as 'straight-acting' or 'straight-appearing,' terms that reveal a degree of self-hatred unique among even the most conformist of ethnic groups, who would never stoop to such slavish behavior, fawning over the virility of their white masters"; p. 59.

28. George Chauncey, Jr., "Christian Brotherhood or Sexual Perversion?" in *Hidden From History*, ed. Martin Duberman, Martha Vicinus, and George Chauncey, Jr. (New York: Dutton, 1989), pp. 295-317.

29. Murphy, p. 7.

30. Chauncey, "Christian Brotherhood or Sexual Perversion?," p. 301.

31. Murphy, p. 11.

32. Chauncey, "Christian Brotherhood or Sexual Perversion?," p. 297.

33. Murphy, p. 31.

34. Ibid., p. 35.

35. Chauncey, "Christian Brotherhood or Sexual Perversion?," p. 305.

36. Ibid., p. 299.

37. Chauncey, *Gay New York,* p. 70.

38. Chauncey, *Gay New York,* p. 66. The investigator Chauncey quotes "was unhappy about the commotion so many unruly sailors caused . . . and disapproved of their actions. In no way, however, did he indicate that he thought the sailors looking for sex with the fairies were themselves fairies or otherwise different from most sailors. The investigator himself observed 'two sailors . . . in the company of three men who were acting in an effeminate manner.' He labeled the effeminate men 'fairies' even though it was the sailors who were 'making overtures to these men to go to their apartments [and the men] declined to go.'"

39. Chauncey, pp. 315-316.

40. Harris, pp. 151-154.

41. In his book *Hard To Imagine: Gay Male Eroticism in Photography and Film From Their Beginnings to Stonewall* (New York: Columbia University, 1996), Thomas Waugh offers an alternate take on the gay porn "conversion narrative." He calls it "utopian"; p. 263.

42. Personal correspondence, September 10, 1997.

43. Signorile, p. 301.

44. There may be some generational shift between pre-Stonewall homosexuals, best represented here by David and Rolf, who eroticize servicemen as a straight Other, and post-liberation gays, who eroticize sameness and group belonging. But there is also considerable overlap.

45. Rena Bulkin, *Frommer's '97 Washington, D.C.* (New York: Macmillan, 1997), p. 9.

46. I am indebted to historian Allan Bérubé for sharing with me his observations on the current sex panic.

47. In his 1966 book on the famous homosexual panic of Boise, Idaho, John Gerassi points out that homosexuality was common among the trappers and lumbermen who settled Idaho. But perhaps most surprising to contemporary readers who have come of age since Stonewall is Gerassi's observation that mutual masturbation sessions were "a ritual not only at Boise High but common to every high school, prep school, and boarding school in the country, not to mention colleges." John Gerassi, *The Boys of Boise: Furor, Vice, and Folly in an American City* (New York: Macmillan, 1966), pp. 33, 133. Thirty years later, a front-page article in *The New York Times* announced that American high school students no longer shower together in gym class or after football practice. The reporter speculated that the new fear of same-sex public nudity might be due to increased modesty; to feelings of inadequacy generated by idealized images of the male body in advertising; and to discussion of homosexuality, making students more fearful of being gazed upon desirously. A letter to the editor decried the homophobia of this last speculation. But no one pointed out that male teenagers have long been fearful that sexual desire might erupt in their own bodies. Increased discussion of gay identity would seem to inevitably strengthen the perception that a spontaneous hard-on must inevitably point to coming out, making teenagers ever more uncomfortably self-conscious of

the locker room as classic gay porn backdrop. Dirk Johnson, "Students Still Sweat, They Just Don't Shower," *The New York Times*, April 22, 1996, p. A-1.

48. Michaelangelo Signorile, *Outing Yourself* (New York: Random House, 1995), quoted in Frank Browning, *Queer Geography: Journeys Toward a Sexual Self* (New York: Crown, 1996), p. 153.

Rolf: Hollywood Marines

1. I would continue to work in and around the entertainment industry through the 1960s and 1970s, serving on-camera as interviewer (initially, of celebrated authors with books to peddle), as panelist, and as occasional announcer. Off-camera, I worked as a market researcher and as a speech-writer for CEOs. Later, I emceed the arena shows given as part of the tours at a large studio.

2. Thanks to many a kiss-and-tell biography published since 1970, we now know that, from the start, Hollywood had played host to a thriving tribe of homosexuals. But the vitality of that tribe had waxed and waned with the changing times. In the 1920s, for instance, same-sex liaisons had paced the decade's roaring spirit of "anything goes." But, in the 1930s, the new Hayes Office and the anti-hedonistic mood of the Depression had driven celebrity same-sexing behind locked doors (where George Cukor and Cole Porter presided over the town's two most elegant "closet salons"). Then, after Pearl Harbor, Hollywood's homosexuals had reemerged, working overtime to make America's fighting men feel welcome. In the 1950s, the studio system had begun to stumble, dogged by the new medium of television. But the problems of mega-studios meant opportunities for smaller production companies and for independent agents. One of those, with the given name of Henry, specialized in a new breed of young leading men, chosen entirely for their looks, not for their acting ability. Henry insisted on renaming his young charges according to a strict formula: The first name had to be monosyllabic and attention-grabbing; the second, multisyllabic and white-bread. Hence: Tab Hunter, Rock Hudson, Troy Donahue, and the rest of Henry's trademarked roster. Rumor had it that Henry had one other prerogative: To get his agency's full attention, a young prospect was urged to permit certain liberties to the fleshy, middle-aged Henry—liberties that reportedly involved a king-sized rubber sheet and a bottle of mineral oil. (Henry's agency would stumble badly in 1967 with a radical change in the taste of teenage moviegoers signaled by *The Graduate*. Almost overnight, studios turned away from Henry's pretty boys and toward real actors who could project believability and a strongly individual character.) Once Henry had satisfied his "curiosity," his young men were free to find other social outlets. Those whose same-sexing proved more than just opportunistic often showed up for chic gatherings in a canyon-side mansion above Beverly Hills. This belonged to a titled Dutch spice importer and his companion, the heir to a bottled-cola fortune (who had approached me at the end of some event I was emceeing in my white tie and tails). The first hour of a typical party in that elegant house included a few females: aged stars such as Gloria Swanson, ageless character actresses such as Agnes Moorhead, plus a few of filmdom's lipstick lesbians. But, when the women

withdrew, the serious pairings could begin. In 1968, having moved into that Edwardian three-story, I tried to ape the style and ambiance of the canyon-side parties, with fair success.

3. Those were 1968 prices. By 1975, with the end of America's involvement in Vietnam and of the draft, the decreased supply of troops and the increased demand for their services would drive those prices way up.

4. By the mid-1970s, with fewer prospects wandering San Diego's streets and with more clients clamoring for service, Abner would hand lists of numbers to young men he'd not yet prequalified.

5. For a detailed history of the military involvement in all-male porn, from the late 1940s through the 1980s, see my two-part article, "Reviewing the Troops," in the February and March 1990 issues of *Manshots* magazine.

Wormy: Hell Bent for Leathernecks

1. See Samuel M. Steward, *Bad Boys and Tough Tattoos: A Social History of the Tattoo with Gangs, Sailors, and Street-Corner Punks, 1950-1965* (Binghamton, NY: The Haworth Press, 1990), pp. 40-41.

Gayle: Double Penetration

1. Charles Henderson, *Marine Sniper: 93 Confirmed Kills* (New York: Berkley, 1986).

Andrei: A Family Tradition
and Denis: Raised on Soldiers' Milk

1. The closest thing North Americans have to a *bahnia* is a sauna, though that doesn't convey the heavily social aspect and the paralyzing heat of the Russian variant. In a large, spacious bathhouse, sex-segregated groups wash themselves on stone benches, in between trips to both a dry sauna and a wet one (called a *parilka*), where the scorching temperatures lead people to beat themselves and their friends with birch branches before running out coughing. A plunge into an ice-cold pool follows. The ritual is completed back in the changing rooms, where friends laze around for hours, eating and drinking. This process is repeated up to ten times.

2. Russia still has a compulsory, twenty-four-month military service for all men over eighteen. Boris Yeltsin has repeatedly promised to turn his army into a professional one by 2000, but there are no signs that this will come to pass. You avoid serving if you are already enrolled in a military academy, a five-year, specialized post-secondary school. Graduates are considered officers and may choose to pursue a military career afterwards (naval cadets are required to give at least five years of service to the navy after graduation, but other sectors of the military do not always require such commitment). It's the uniformed cadets of such academies who are so vis-

ible on the streets of St. Petersburg; there are twenty-two academies in the city, covering all departments of the military, from naval and space technology, to police and border-guard specialties. Compulsory military service is also avoided if you can prove to be medically unfit (or if you can afford to pay to be proven so), or if you somehow manage to slip through the cracks of bureaucracy and avoid getting found by the police until you're twenty-seven years old (highly unlikely and risky). You can also delay your service by continuing studies at an accredited university (but must complete your twenty-four months before the age of twenty-seven), or reduce it by studying at a special military university, essentially a civilian institute which incorporates some military training into the scholastic program. Sons of highly placed military personnel have also been known to manage cushy or truncated services.

3. References to either sex with uniformed personnel, paid sex with them, or at least an attraction to them are to be found in the works of John Rechy, James Baldwin, Gore Vidal, W. H. Auden (a poem about sex with a sailor), Christopher Isherwood, E. M. Forster, J. R. Ackerley, Donald Vining, and Jean Genet.

4. Rick Sky, *The Show Must Go On: The Life of Freddie Mercury* (New York: Carol, 1994).

5. Sexually, Andrei prefers to be the passive, anally receptive partner. However, his methods of arriving at that position—from picking them up to telling them what to do in bed—are nothing less than active.

6. As soon as I found out about Andrei's cramped living conditions, my first thought was: "What does Grandma think?" Andrei prefers to think that his grandmother merely guesses at what's going on, but it was clear to me that she knows exactly what he's doing. She saw the revolving door routine with her daughter, and now she's seeing it with her grandson. When I met her, and asked whether she thinks Andrei has a lot of friends, she said, "Oh, so many! He's very popular!" Before he left the house, he warned that he might be coming back late with a friend, or two. "I wouldn't expect anything else," she said, "just bring home something to eat or some vodka this time—your friends always eat so much!"

7. Steve Kokker would like to thank Andrei and Denis for their time and instruction, Mark Simpson and Tom Sluberski for their skills of introducing people, and James Roach for his valued ideas on straight-man theories.

Maynard: Servicing Sailors

1. In 1992, Rear Admiral David R. Oliver Jr. reportedly told a conference of shipyard workers that the Navy "may close all its Bay Area installations in part to avoid the region's 'concentration of homosexuals and their influence on military personnel.'" Marcy Rein, "Buy Me a Drink, Sailor?" *The Bay Guardian*, August 26, 1992, p. 23.

2. Gay veterans activist David Clemens explains: "The military has a long history of allowing some servicemembers who engage in gay sex to remain on active duty. See Allan Bérubé, *Coming Out Under Fire: The History of Gay Men and Women in World War Two* (New York: Free Press, 1990), pp. 160-162, 243, 261, 275, 326. During the Vietnam era, the exception to the discharge policy for

those committing homosexual acts was sarcastically dubbed the 'Queen for a Day Rule.' See Randy Shilts, *Conduct Unbecoming: Gays and Lesbians in the U.S. Military* (New York: St. Martin's, 1993), p. 199. The 1993 'Don't Ask, Don't Tell' legislation put the loophole into federal law for the first time. To claim exemption from discharge, the 'Queen for a Day' is required to prove all elements of a five-prong test [10 U.S. Code 654]:

1. that the homosexual acts are a departure from the member's usual and customary behavior, and;
2. the acts are unlikely to recur, and;
3. the acts were not accomplished by the use of force, coercion, or intimidation, and;
4. that the member's continued presence in the Service is consistent with the interest of the Armed Forces in proper discipline, good order, and morale, and;
5. that the member does not have a propensity or intent to engage in homosexual acts.

"In addition, a servicemember cannot use the loophole (and will not receive an Honorable Discharge) if he attempted, solicited, or committed a homosexual act in any of the following circumstances [Department of Defense Directive 1332.14 (21 Dec 93) 'Enlisted Administrative Separations']:

a. By using force, coercion, or intimidation;
b. With a person under 16 years of age;
c. With a subordinate in circumstances that violate customary military superior-subordinate relationships;
d. Openly in public view;
e. For compensation;
f. Aboard a military vessel or aircraft; or
g. In another location subject to military control under aggravating circumstances noted in the finding that have an adverse impact on discipline, good order, or morale comparable to the impact of such activity aboard a vessel or aircraft.

"According to Servicemembers Legal Defense Network [SLDN], it is now rare for a servicemember to prevail in a 'Queen for a Day' defense under the 1993 statute. However, some servicemembers have been successful under this exception, most by presenting evidence of a heterosexual life to the discharge board. The kinds of evidence these servicemembers have used includes (1) testimony about heterosexual relationships in their lives, (2) unusual circumstances at the time of the gay acts (i.e., the death of a spouse or parent, a divorce or trauma from an abusive relationship), (3) witnesses who say they have never seen any indication of homosexual behavior, and (4) expert witnesses such as psychologists or sexologists. See the SLDN 'Survival Guide,' 1996, http://www.sldn.org."

For an analysis of ways in which military policies prohibiting homosexuality make homosexuality more "speakable," see "Contagious Word: Paranoia and 'Homosexuality' in the Military" in Judith Butler's *Excitable Speech: A Politics of the Performative* (New York: Routledge, 1997), pp. 103-126.

3. *Betty and Pansy's Severe Queer Review of San Francisco* (San Francisco: Bedpan, 1992).

4. Thomas Avena and Adam Klein, *Jerome: After the Pageant* (San Francisco: Bastard, 1996).

5. *The Complete Reprint of Physique Pictorial* (Cologne: Taschen, 1997).

6. Note the contradiction between Maynard's salmon metaphor and Tennessee Williams' (Introduction, p. 8). For another exploration of the confusion between "the prey and the preyed upon, the fucker and the fucked," see Mark Simpson, "Tijuana Brass," in *It's a Queer World: Deviant Adventures in Pop Culture* (Binghamton, NY: The Haworth Press, 1999).

Rick: Aries Marine Bull-Pussy

1. Michael Grumley, *Hard Corps: Studies in Leather and Sadmomasochism* (New York: Dutton, 1977).

Don: Interview with a Pornographer

1. For further comments on military men in gay video pornography, see the "Marines Like to Be Looked At" chapter of Steven Zeeland, *The Masculine Marine* (Binghamton, NY: The Haworth Press, 1996), pp. 101-114.

2. A catalog of Don's videos is available from TBS, 3802 Rosecrans, Suite 351, San Diego, CA 92110, USA.

Howard: Sneaking on Base

1. Louise Oswald, "How a Lonely Convent Girl Slept with 150 Squaddies in Sad Search for Love," *Sunday People*, April 5, 1998, pp. 5, 8.

2. Navy hospital corpsmen are among the U.S. servicemen most often stereotyped as likely to be gay.

3. The Norfolk, Virginia area has a larger Navy population than San Diego does.

Anonymous: Why?

1. Steven Zeeland, "Killer Queen: Chasing Sailors with Andrew Cunanan—Suspected Queer Serial Killer and Versace Murder Suspect," *The Stranger*, July 24, 1997, pp. 10-17. "Anonymous" read the reprint of my article in *The Face*, September, 1997, pp. 138-142. Cunanan frequented San Diego gay bars popular with sailors and Marines, and sometimes posed as an Israeli intelligence officer. His father was a retired Navy officer, and his alleged first victim was ex-Navy lieutenant Jeffrey Trail. It's common for civilian gay men in the San Diego bar scene to impersonate military personnel. What set Cunanan apart was that he did not have sex with the servicemen he courted.

Order Your Own Copy of
This Important Book for Your Personal Library!

MILITARY TRADE

_____ in hardbound at $49.95 (ISBN: 0-7890-0402-X)

_____ in softbound at $19.95 (ISBN: 1-56023-924-7)

COST OF BOOKS_____	☐ **BILL ME LATER:** ($5 service charge will be added)
	(Bill-me option is good on US/Canada/Mexico orders only;
OUTSIDE USA/CANADA/	not good to jobbers, wholesalers, or subscription agencies.)
MEXICO: ADD 20%_____	
	☐ Check here if billing address is different from
POSTAGE & HANDLING_____	shipping address and attach purchase order and
(US: $3.00 for first book & $1.25	billing address information.
for each additional book)	
Outside US: $4.75 for first book	
& $1.75 for each additional book)	Signature _____
SUBTOTAL_____	☐ **PAYMENT ENCLOSED: $** _____
IN CANADA: ADD 7% GST_____	☐ **PLEASE CHARGE TO MY CREDIT CARD.**
STATE TAX_____	☐ Visa ☐ MasterCard ☐ AmEx ☐ Discover
(NY, OH & MN residents, please	
add appropriate local sales tax)	Account # _____
FINAL TOTAL_____	Exp. Date _____
(If paying in Canadian funds,	
convert using the current	Signature _____
exchange rate. UNESCO	
coupons welcome.)	

Prices in US dollars and subject to change without notice.

NAME _____

INSTITUTION _____

ADDRESS _____

CITY _____

STATE/ZIP _____

COUNTRY _____ COUNTY (NY residents only) _____

TEL _____ FAX _____

E-MAIL_____

May we use your e-mail address for confirmations and other types of information? ☐ Yes ☐ No

Order From Your Local Bookstore or Directly From
The Haworth Press, Inc.
10 Alice Street, Binghamton, New York 13904-1580 • USA
TELEPHONE: 1-800-HAWORTH (1-800-429-6784) / Outside US/Canada: (607) 722-5857
FAX: 1-800-895-0582 / Outside US/Canada: (607) 772-6362
E-mail: getinfo@haworthpressinc.com
PLEASE PHOTOCOPY THIS FORM FOR YOUR PERSONAL USE.

BOF96